Economic Spillovers, Structural Reforms and Policy Coordination in the Euro Area

Contributions to Economics

www.springer.com/series/1262

Further volumes of this series can be found at our homepage.

Günter S. Heiduk/Kar-yiu Wong (Eds.)
WTO and World Trade
2005. ISBN 978-3-7908-1579-5

Emilio Colombo/Luca Stanca
Financial Market Imperfections and Corporate Decisions
2006. ISBN 978-3-7908-1581-8

Birgit Mattil
Pension Systems
2006. ISBN 978-3-7908-1675-4

Francesco C. Billari/Thomas Fent/Alexia Prskawetz/Jürgen Scheffran (Eds.)
Agent-Based Computational Modelling
2006. ISBN 978-3-7908-1640-2

Kerstin Press
A Life Cycle for Clusters?
2006. ISBN 978-3-7908-1710-2

Russel Cooper/Gary Madden/Ashley Lloyd/Michael Schipp (Eds.)
The Economics of Online Markets and ICT Networks
2006. ISBN 978-3-7908-1706-5

Renato Giannetti/Michelangelo Vasta (Eds.)
Evolution of Italian Enterprises in the 20th Century
2006. ISBN 978-3-7908-1711-9

Ralph Setzer
The Politics of Exchange Rates in Developing Countries
2006. ISBN 978-3-7908-1715-7

Dora Borbély
Trade Specialization in the Enlarged European Union
2006. ISBN 978-3-7908-1704-1

Iris A. Hauswirth
Effective and Efficient Organisations?
2006. ISBN 978-3-7908-1730-0

Marco Neuhaus
The Impact of FDI on Economic Growth
2006. ISBN 978-3-7908-1734-8

Nicola Jentzsch
The Economics and Regulation of Financial Privacy
2006. ISBN 978-3-7908-1737-9

Klaus Winkler
Negotiations with Asymmetrical Distribution of Power
2006. ISBN 978-3-7908-1743-0

Sasha Tsenkova, Zorica Nedović-Budić (Eds.)
The Urban Mosaic of Post-Socialist Europe
2006. ISBN 978-3-7908-1726-3

Brigitte Preissl/Jürgen Müller (Eds.)
Governance of Communication Networks
2006. ISBN 978-3-7908-1745-4

Lei Delsen/Derek Bosworth/Hermann Groß/Rafael Muñoz de Bustillo y Llorente (Eds.)
Operating Hours and Working Times
2006. ISBN 978-3-7908-1759-1

Pablo Coto-Millán; Vicente Inglada (Eds.)
Essays on Transport Economics
2006. ISBN 978-3-7908-1764-5

Christian H. Fahrholz
New Political Economy of Exchange Rate Policies and the Enlargement of the Eurozone
2006. ISBN 978-3-7908-1761-4

Sandra Gruescu
Population Ageing and Economic Growth
2007. ISBN 978-3-7908-1905-2

Patrick S. Renz
Project Governance
2007. ISBN 978-3-7908-1926-7

Christian Schabbel
The Value Chain of Foreign Aid
2007. ISBN 978-3-7908-1931-1

Martina Eckardt
Insurance Intermediation
2007. ISBN 978-3-7908-1939-7

George M. Korres (Ed.)
Regionalisation, Growth, and Economic Integration
2007. ISBN 978-3-7908-1924-3

Kerstin Groß
Equity Ownership and Performance
2007. ISBN 978-3-7908-1933-5

Ulrike Neyer
The Design of the Eurosystem's Monetary Policy Instruments
2007. ISBN 978-3-7908-1977-9

Christian Roland
Banking Sector Liberalization in India
2008. ISBN 978-3-7908-1981-6

Bas van Aarle · Klaus Weyerstrass
Editors

Economic Spillovers, Structural Reforms and Policy Coordination in the Euro Area

Physica-Verlag
A Springer Company

Dr. Bas van Aarle
University of Maastricht
Tongersestraat 53
6211 LM Maastricht
The Netherlands
b.vanaarle@algec.unimaas.nl

Dr. Klaus Weyerstrass
Institute for Advanced Studies (IHS)
Stumpergasse 56
1060 Vienna
Austria
weyerstr@ihs.ac.at

ISBN 978-3-7908-2535-0 e-ISBN 978-3-7908-1970-0

DOI 10.1007/978-3-7908-1970-0

Contributions to Economics ISSN 1431-1933

Cover-design: WMX Design GmbH, Heidelberg

Printed on acid-free paper

9 8 7 6 5 4 3 2 1

springer.com

Preface

Starting point of most of the chapters in this book has been a research project ("Economic Spillovers and Policy Coordination in the Euro Area" (tender ECFIN/C/2004/01)) that was prepared by the Institute for Advanced Studies Carinthia (IHS Kärnten) for the European Commission, Directorate General Economic and Financial Affairs.

The main objective of this project was to provide estimates of the magnitude of economic spillover and the impact of economic policy coordination on economic performance in the euro area. The evidence on the economic spillover and impact of policy coordination in the euro area that was found during this project, has been consecutively worked out in the chapters of this book. In this way, the book aims at contributing to the ongoing debate on the need for greater flexibility in EMU's budgetary rules and on strategies for structural reform in capital, labour and product markets in the EU.

We are very grateful to Dermot Hodson for his guidance of this project from the side of the European Commission and to all authors for sharing their interests in these topics. We thank Niels Peter Thomas, editor of the Springer series *Contributions to Economics* for his stimulating and careful guidance during the preparation of the manuscript. Gabriele Keidel of Springer carefully proofread the entire text.

June 2007, *Bas van Aarle and Klaus Weyerstrass.*

Contents

Preface v

Contributors xi

1 Economic spillovers, structural reforms and policy coordination in the Euro Area: An overview 1

Klaus Weyerstrass, Koen Schoors and Bas van Aarle

1.1 Introduction 1
1.2 A working definition of spillovers 3
1.3 Overview of the literature 6
1.4 Overview of the main results 13
1.5 Policy implications and avenues for further research 17
References 22

2 Budgetary spillovers and short-term interest rates 27

Bas van Aarle

2.1 Introduction 27
2.2 Methodology and literature 28
2.3 Fiscal spillovers at the aggregate Euro Area level 30
2.4 Fiscal spillovers in the Euro Area at the country level 36
2.5 Conclusion 49
Appendix: Characteristics of the dataset 50
References 52

3 Budgetary spillovers and long-term interest rates 55

Peter Claeys

3.1 Introduction 55
3.2 Deficits and interest rates: is there any robust evidence? .. 57
3.2.1 Static versus dynamic models 57

3.2.2 Capital flows and crowding out in open economies.. 61
3.2.3 Monetary integration and crowding out 62
3.3 A stock-flow fiscal VAR for open economies.................. 63
3.4 Crowding-out effects of fiscal policies............................ 73
3.5 Spillovers of fiscal policies... 74
3.5.1 Relative fiscal shocks and relative crowding out...... 75
3.5.2 Crowding out in small open economies 80
3.5.3 Robustness checks.. 93
3.6 Conclusion 94
Appendix A: Domestic economy: SVAR models with exogenous debt ratio 97
Appendix B: SVAR models with yield 98
References... 101

4 Budgetary stabilisation and the level of public debt 107

Niko Gobbin

4.1 Introduction.. 107
4.2 A look at fiscal theory and empirics 108
4.3 Threshold regression models 112
4.4 Data description and regression set-up 115
4.5 Results... 117
4.6 Conclusion 122
Appendix A: Data sources and definitions 122
Appendix B: ADF unit root tests 124
Appendix C... 124
Appendix D: Years above the threshold................................. 125
References.. 126

5 Spillovers from economic reform... 129

Klaus Weyerstrass and Johannes Jaenicke

5.1 Introduction.. 129
5.2 Determination of mark-up ratios.................................... 130
5.3 Mark-up and macroeconomic performance.................... 137
5.3.1 Total factor productivity growth 137
5.3.2 Employment 140
5.3.3 Unemployment rate 142
5.3.4 Labour productivity growth..................................... 143
5.4 The influence of regulation on the mark-up 145

5.5 Conclusion 150
Appendix: Data sources and definitions 152
References 153

6 Macroeconomic and welfare effects of structural and budgetary policies: spillovers in the MSG3 model 155

Reinhard Neck and Gottfried Haber

6.1 Introduction 155
6.2 Effects of structural policies 156
6.3 Budgetary consolidation policies 162
6.4 Structural reform and budgetary consolidation 176
6.5 Sensitivity analysis: monetary versus inflation targeting 185
6.6 Welfare Effects 191
Appendix: The MSG3 Macroeconomic Global Model 198
References 201

7 Have Europe's labour markets become more flexible? An exercise in measuring the relative flexibility of wages across countries and time 203

Andrew Hughes Hallett, Christian Richter and Xiaoshan Chen

7.1 Introduction 203
7.2 Methodology: The analytic background and estimation technique 205
7.3 The empirical evidence on wage flexibility 207
7.4 Statistical results 208
7.5 The benchmark and indicators of wage flexibility 211
7.6 The US wages spectrum 214
7.7 Country by country results 215
7.8 Conclusion 223
Appendix: Time frequency techniques and the estimation of time-varying spectra or cross-spectra 224
References 229

Index 233

Contributors

Xiaoshan Chen
Department of Economics
Loughborough University
Loughborough, LE11 3TU
United Kingdom

Peter Claeys
Facultat de Ciències
Econòmiques i Empresarials
Universitat de Barcelona
E-08034 Barcelona, Spain

Niko Gobbin
Department of Economics
Faculty of Economics and B. A.
Ghent University
Hoveniersberg 24
B-9000 Ghent, Belgium

Gottfried Haber
Department of Economics
Klagenfurt University
Universitaetsstrasse 65-67
A-9020 Klagenfurt, Austria

Andrew Hughes Hallett
School of Public Policy
George Mason University
Fairfax, VA 22030, USA

Johannes Jaenicke
Faculty of Economics
University of Erfurt
Nordhäuser Str. 63
D-99089 Erfurt, Germany

Reinhard Neck
Department of Economics
Klagenfurt University
Universitaetsstrasse 65-67
A-9020 Klagenfurt, Austria

Christian Richter
Department of Economics
Loughborough University
Loughborough, LE11 3TU
United Kingdom

Koen Schoors
Department of Economics
Faculty of Economics and B.A.
Ghent University
Hoveniersberg 24
B-9000 Ghent, Belgium

Bas van Aarle
Faculty of Economics and B.A.
University of Maastricht
Tongersestraat 53
NL-6211 LD Maastricht, Netherlands

Klaus Weyerstrass
Institute for Advanced Studies
Stumpergasse 56,
A-1060 Vienna, Austria

1 Economic spillovers, structural reforms and policy coordination in the Euro Area: An overview

Klaus Weyerstrass, Koen Schoors and Bas van Aarle

1.1 Introduction

Macroeconomic policymaking in the European Union's Economic and Monetary Union (EMU) is characterised by an asymmetric division of competences: While monetary policy is conducted centrally by the European System of Central Banks and the European Central Bank (ECB) in particular, structural and fiscal policies remain under the responsibility of the individual Member States, but they are subject to intensive consultation and multilateral surveillance. Article 99 of the EC Treaty calls on Member States to regard their economic policies as a matter of common concern and to coordinate them in the Council, with a view to achieving, inter alia, higher non-inflationary growth and a better standard of living.

This commitment to economic policy coordination is given effect in a number of ways. The Broad Economic Policy Guidelines guide the economic policies of Member States and the Community, encourage structural reforms in product and factor markets and promote fiscal discipline. The Excessive Deficit Procedure prohibits budget deficits in excess of 3% of GDP. The Stability and Growth Pact encourages Member States to run budgetary positions close to balance or in surplus over the medium term. The Lisbon Strategy promotes structural reforms in labour, product and capital markets with a view to achieving higher growth and more jobs.

EMU increases the degree of economic interdependence between Euro Area Member States. Sharing a common currency and a single monetary policy implies a higher probability that economic policies and developments in one Member State will spill over to the rest of the Euro Area. There is a broad consensus among economists that this increased interdependence justifies a strong degree of economic policy coordination between Euro Area Member States.

This book analyses economic interdependence in the Euro Area and provides estimates of the sign and size of economic spillovers and the impact of economic policy coordination concerning structural and budgetary policies on economic performance in the Euro Area. A better understanding of economic spillovers will contribute to strengthen economic governance in the EU. More specifically, evidence on the comparative importance of different types of economic spillovers will contribute to the ongoing debate on the need for greater flexibility in the EMU's budgetary rules and on strategies for structural reforms on capital, labour and product markets.

An important question that will be analysed, is whether there exists a coordination dividend, i.e. gains from implementing structural and budgetary policies in a coordinated way. Throughout this book, the term "coordination" should be understood in a rather narrow sense in that it refers to a situation in which autonomous Member States pursue commonly agreed goals. The farther reaching concept of the optimisation of a common objective function by a single economic authority is not the object of this study.

The academic literature offers mixed results with regard to the precise nature of economic spillovers under EMU, the benefits of structural reforms and the gains from economic policy coordination. Following insights initiated by Rogoff (1985), cooperation between different economic policy-makers, e.g. between governments and the ECB and in particular between governments only (excluding the ECB from their agreement) can be counterproductive compared to a situation without coordination, due to the adverse reactions of players that do not coordinate their policies. In general, the benefits from coordination will depend on a large number of factors and the specific situation. Given also the complexity of the interactions between policymakers in the EMU, no general answer is to be expected from a theoretical analysis alone.

There is in fact much dissent in the policy literature about these questions. For example, Allsopp et al. (1999) stress the importance of fiscal policy coordination in the case of fiscal consolidation in order to reduce output losses. However, De Grauwe (1999) is rather critical of this recommendation, stressing instead the importance of monetary policy applied in conjunction with fiscal policies. Some recent contributions on policy coordination within the EMU can be found in Hughes Hallett et al. (2001), for example. Coordination may in particular be justified in the presence of significant spillovers. Bayoumi et al. (2004) estimates that structural policies on the goods and labour markets in the Euro Area would not only increase production in the Euro Area. Due to international spillovers, other countries and regions like the US would also gain.

1.2 A working definition of spillovers

In a monetary union, budgetary laxity in individual Member States may affect other members that follow prudent policies, due to the presence of spillovers from fiscal policies. Especially if the no bail-out clause stating that no Member State can be forced to step in for another state's liabilities is not totally credible, there are risks that individual fiscal irresponsibility impairs economic performance in the other Member States. In this case, profligate fiscal policies in some countries might harm other less profligate members via higher borrowing costs, especially if markets believe that members would have to stand in for peers that became insolvent. If this is the case, the profligate members could 'free-ride' on the backs of the others. These negative consequences of irresponsible fiscal policies could be avoided by coordinated budgetary discipline.

Regarding structural policies, negative spillovers may arise if reforms are undertaken only in one individual country or a very limited number of Member States. Such an isolated action would be likely to improve the respective country's competitiveness at the expense of other Member States. In this case, non-cooperative structural reforms competition is likely to arise; clearly an analogy with the non-cooperative tax competition and social dumping strategies and the associated 'race to the bottom' mentioned in the public finance literature could be made. In contrast to such a structural reform competition stands a coordinated, harmonised implementation of structural reforms which internalises the spillovers and fiscal consequences of structural reform efforts in the Euro Area. Thus, not only concerning budgetary policies, but also regarding the implementation of structural reforms, coordination can be expected to pay off.

In general, different types of spillovers are relevant in the Euro Area context: (i) *External vs. internal spillovers:* External spillovers originate from interactions between the Euro Area and the rest of the world. In particular, developments in the US economy and world trade e.g. influence the Euro Area economy significantly, especially via trade linkages and the euro/US dollar exchange rate. Prices of oil and other raw materials are determined in international markets largely beyond the control of the Euro Area but having potentially strong spillover effects on its economies. Internal spillovers originate from the economic linkages between the Euro Area countries as briefly outlined above. (ii) *Shock vs. policy induced spillovers*: This is particularly relevant from the perspective of policy action. Policy induced spillovers imply a direct influence of policy measures undertaken at the individual country level on other individual countries. Coordination mitigates negative consequences from policy errors and internalises the consequences of spillovers from non-coordinated policies. Policy coordination may also be beneficial to address spillovers produced by macroeconomic shocks hitting either all Euro Area countries symmetrically (like oil price shocks) or individual countries (like German unification). (iii) *Direct vs. indirect spillovers*: In the context of the Euro Area, direct and indirect spillovers of the different countries are present. Direct international spillovers operate mainly through trade linkages. In addition, indirect spillovers working through the common interest rate and the euro exchange rate are also important. As an example, an overly expansionary fiscal policy by one country may result in higher interest rates, influencing all other Euro Area Member States. Furthermore, fiscal policy measures may induce exchange rate reactions affecting all members of a monetary union. (iv) *Positive vs. negative spillovers*: In the case of positive spillovers, individual policies reinforce each other. In the case of negative spillovers, policy measures are mutually inconsistent and in conflict to each other. Obviously, this difference has implications for the design of coordination. In the presence of negative spillovers, there is a stronger need for monitoring, corrective mechanisms, and sanctions in case of non-compliance. While there is often a clear theoretical notion why a certain spillover is likely to be positive or negative, empirical estimations may not always confirm theoretical priors. The interactions of spillovers, non-linearities and the complexity of dynamics may lead to indeterminate outcomes concerning sign, size and timing of spillovers.

The following spillover channels from fiscal policies and structural reforms in the Euro Area are relevant: (i) *Output/trade channel*: Fiscal and structural policies, because of their effects on domestic output, will significantly influence the demand for imports in an integrated space such as the Euro Area. This will influence the net exports in the rest of the Euro Area. These spillovers propagated via the "trade channel" are a classic example of positive spillovers. (ii) *Price channel*: Fiscal and structural policies, because of their effects on domestic inflation, will influence inflation in other countries due to "pass-through" via import prices. In addition, such price changes induced by policies are likely to lead to relative price changes resulting in spillovers via the "competitiveness channel". In the Euro Area, nominal exchange rates have been irrevocably fixed, but *via* differences in the price levels, the real exchange rate does matter. (iii) *Interest rate and exchange rate channels*: In the Euro Area, fiscal and structural policies can induce changes in the short-term interest rates and exchange rate of the euro, implying interest rate and exchange rate spillovers via the "interest rate channel" and the "exchange rate channel". These last two types of spillovers in the Euro Area are related to the standard "beggar-thy-neighbours" arguments for policy coordination enabling the internalisation / attenuation of the negative spillovers from fiscal policies resulting from these channels. It is also important to realise here that Euro Area countries are likely to differ in the spillovers they experience from changes in the common short-term interest rate and the euro exchange rate. (iv) *Government debt channel*: In the Euro Area, government debt will affect long-term interest rates. Spillovers will occur if financial markets do not price the risk of government debt of individual countries appropriately due to, e.g., the possibility that the no bail-out clause is not perfectly credible. In that case, excessive fiscal debt in individual countries leads to higher real interest rates in all Euro Area countries. (v) *Structural reform channel*: Structural reforms on the output and input markets shall enhance competition, resulting in higher productivity growth, increased employment and reduced unemployment. This induces spillover effects, e.g. growth enhancing supply-side measures undertaken by individual countries increase imports from the other Euro Area members, thereby positively influencing the other countries' public finances.

Economic spillovers can contribute to the presence of common elements in national business cycles. With the start of EMU, the discussion about the existence of parallels in the European economies' business cycles has gained importance. On the one hand, a common monetary policy may foster macroeconomic convergence by providing a common short-term interest rate and exchange rate. On the other hand, it may also increase divergence since it is very likely to be more inadequate for countries that have a lower degree of similarity in macroeconomic shocks and business cycle synchronicity compared with the Euro Area average. Whether there exists a "European business cycle" therefore plays a crucial role for success or failure of the union. While there appears to be a consensus in the literature that the European economies indeed share some common elements in their aggregate cyclical behaviour (Artis et al., 1998), opinions diverge concerning the question whether or not this common component has gained importance for the national economies. Most econometric studies however suggest increasing similarities between the national business cycles with ongoing European integration.

The outline above of the spillovers from fiscal and structural policies in the Euro Area brings us also to the main subjects studied in this book. This book estimates and analyses: (i) the link between fiscal and monetary policies in the Euro Area; (ii) the link between public debt and long-term interest rates in the Euro Area; (iii) the link between budgetary stabilisation and the level of public debt in the Euro Area; (iv) the spillovers from structural reforms in the Euro Area, (v) the scope for the coordination of fiscal policies and of structural reforms in the Euro Area, and (vi) wage flexibility in the Euro Area.

1.3 Overview of the literature

There is a substantial amount of literature directly or indirectly dealing with the channels and effects of the spillovers listed above. This section provides an overview of the existing literature relevant for the study of macroeconomic spillovers in the Euro Area and which served as a starting point of the studies in this volume.

(i) The link between fiscal and monetary policies: short-term macroeconomic spillovers

A number of studies use VAR, i.e. vector autoregressive models to analyse macroeconomic spillovers. Ahmed et al. (1993) study macroeconomic spillovers between the US and the rest of the OECD using a two-country structural VAR (SVAR) model. Canova and Dellas (1993) analyse bilateral trade interdependence and common disturbances in a group of 10 industrial countries. Kim (1999) undertakes a comparative study of the G-7 countries modelling them as interdependent in fluctuations in world commodity prices and exchange rates. Kim and Roubini (2000) identify the effects of US monetary policy on the non-US G-7 nations. They find that two offsetting effects are at work: (i) an exchange rate depreciation is expansionary via the trade channel, (ii) a rise in the Federal Funds rate (and, in response, a domestic interest rate increase) decreases interest-sensitive spending worldwide, and a subsequent fall in US output decreases the demand for exports of other countries.

Giordani (2004) builds a SVAR model to analyse the impact of US macroeconomic shocks on Canadian output, inflation, interest rate and exchange rate using both Impulse Response Functions (IRF) and Variance Decompositions (VD). Moreover, he compares the IRF of the SVAR model with the IRF of a theoretical model that incorporates the interactions between the Canadian and US economies in a New-Keynesian (NK) framework. It is shown that the IRF of the SVAR model and the NK model resemble each other relatively closely.

Beetsma and Giuliodori (2004) use a SVAR model to study the cross-border spillovers of fiscal shocks via the trade channel. Fiscal expansions in Germany, France and Italy are shown to increase their imports from other European countries significantly. This supports the potential scope for the coordination of fiscal policies in the Euro Area.

Generally, these studies find that (shocks to) foreign variables, through various spillovers, have a non-trivial impact on domestic variables. A similar conclusion results when analysing variance decompositions: typically, foreign shocks can explain a certain fraction of the variance of domestic variables. The importance of cross-border spillovers is typically highest for variables such as exchange rates, current account balances, prices and interest rates and lower for real variables such as output and fiscal balances. To estimate the spillovers from the rest of the world (ROW) on domestic variables in a VAR framework, these papers implement a small open-economy assumption. A VAR model of a small open domestic economy and that of a large foreign economy/ROW are analysed simultaneously. This is achieved by imposing a block exogeneity restriction: domestic variables are postulated to enter the external block equations neither contemporaneously nor with lags. Put differently, external variables are a linear combination of external shocks only, whereas domestic variables are generated both by domestic and external disturbances. If this restriction is accepted, one can decompose the sources of variations of the variables by their origin - domestic or foreign. The fraction of the variation due to innovations in foreign variables provides a measure of the extent of international spillovers.

Spillovers from fiscal policy are not confined to the trade channel. In particular, a fiscal expansion or contraction in one or more Euro Area countries may affect both short- and long-term interest rates, an effect that is transmitted to other countries via the common monetary policy in the Euro Area or via the integrated capital markets. A VAR model can be used to estimate the spillovers from fiscal policy on monetary policy (and vice versa) in the Euro Area. EMU has raised a lot of interest in the issue of monetary and fiscal policy interactions both from a theoretical and empirical perspective. In theoretical analyses, the emphasis has been on strategic elements (see e.g. Buti et al., 2001, for an overview). Empirical analysis has focused on the related question on the complementarity and substitutability of monetary and fiscal policies (see in particular Mélitz, 2000). In the first case, a restrictive monetary policy is accompanied by a restrictive fiscal policy and vice versa. In the second case, a restrictive monetary policy is accompanied by an expansionary fiscal policy response and vice versa.

Muscatelli et al. (2002) use a SVAR model of the output gap, inflation, a measure of the fiscal stance and the short-term interest rate to analyse the interactions of monetary and fiscal policies in G-7 economies. It is found that monetary and fiscal policies are increasingly used as strategic complements and that the responsiveness of fiscal policy to the business cycle has decreased since the 1980s. Bruneau and De Bandt (2003) estimate SVAR models with monetary and fiscal policies in case of the Euro Area, France and Germany. Dalsgaard and Des Serres (2000) estimate SVAR models with monetary and fiscal policies for eight Euro Area Member States. Garcia and Verdelhan (1999) estimate an SVAR with monetary and fiscal policies for the aggregate Euro Area.

VAR models can be used to look at aspects of policy interdependency, such as the link between government spending and revenues. An important question in the literature concerns the existence of causal links between government spending and taxation. This issue of causality and exogeneity can be phrased as the "tax and spend" vs. the "spend and tax" view. According to the former, changes in tax revenues cause changes in government spending, whereas the latter supposes that changes in government spending induce adjustments in tax revenues in order to match the changes in financing needs. Blanchard and Perotti (2002) and Fatas and Mihov (2000) investigate the effects of both types of causality by imposing the appropriate identifying restrictions on revenue and spending shocks in both regimes in their fiscal SVAR model. Koren and Stiassny (1998), Garcia and Henin (2000) and De Arcangelis and Lamartina (2004) also address the possible links between taxes and spending using an SVAR model.

(ii) The link between public debt and long-term interest rates

An important dimension of spillovers in a monetary union concerns the link between public debt and interest rates: since no no bail-out clause ever is totally credible, there are risks that individual fiscal irresponsibility leads to higher interest rates throughout the monetary union. Moreover, at higher debt levels such a process is getting more and more self-reinforcing. Indeed this danger would be a vital reason to amend the SGP with stricter procedures regarding the debt level rather than focussing too much on deficits.

Recently, there have been a number of contributions in the literature on monetary and fiscal policy interactions analysing the interdependence between monetary and fiscal policy in the perspective of intertemporal solvency. In this so-called "Fiscal Theory of the Price Level" (FTPL), the fiscal policy decisions may affect the equilibrium price level/inflation rate in the so-called "non-Ricardian" regime where the fiscal authority disregards the intertemporal solvency constraint. In that case, the price level and monetary policy have to adjust to ensure government solvency. Cochrane (2001), Daniel (2001), and Dupor (2000) address in more detail the theory of the FTPL, also considering open economy aspects. Bayoumi and Masson (1998) study the implication of the FTPL in an EMU perspective.

At the empirical level, Sala (2004) works out identifying restrictions of the FTPL and analyses them for the US. Testing of the FTPL focuses in particular on the feedbacks between fiscal deficit and government debt. Semmler and Zhang (2004), for instance, find evidence of non-Ricardian regimes in Germany and France for the period 1970:I-1998:IV as deficits did not react to debt levels in line with Ricardian predictions. In addition, they test the interdependence between the deficit and short-term interest rates.

Claeys (2004) constructs a structural vector error correction model (SVECM) to analyse the interactions of monetary and fiscal policies. Fiscal shocks are identified as short-term deviations from the intertemporal government budget constraint. Normally, the effects of these departures from solvency are to increase interest rates, but this effect disappears largely in a monetary union. While the framework is fully consistent with the FTPL, it cannot test this theory directly as the effect of inflation is not included.

An interesting way to analyse the spillovers from government debt in a monetary union or a fiscal federation is found in Landon and Smith (2000). The authors analyse the impact of debt accumulation by the central and sub-central governments on the creditworthiness of other federal members and find significant spillovers. Although their analysis is applied to the case of Canada so that we cannot directly relate their results to the Euro Area, there seems to be a number of interesting parallels with the Euro Area case, an aspect which is also acknowledged by the authors. Ardagna et al. (2005) extend this analysis to the issue of national versus global spillovers.

(iii) The links between budgetary stabilisation and the level of public debt

The Euro Area countries vary considerably in the amount of government debt. It can be argued that one cannot ignore this condition when analysing the effects of fiscal policy and deriving implications concerning spillovers and policy coordination. The idea that the initial level of debt could play an important role is put forward in the above mentioned FTPL literature and also in the literature on so-called 'non-Keynesian' effects of fiscal policy. This literature argues that due to expectation effects, wealth effects and supply side effects, the standard Keynesian effects of fiscal adjustments may not hold under all conditions. In particular, the initial level of debt is likely to be crucial: if government debt is high, the private sector will expect that a fiscal expansion will cause much higher taxation fairly soon and reduce its consumption and investment, possibly by such an extent that the initial expansionary effect of the fiscal stimulus is actually followed by a recession. Similarly, the announcement and implementation of fiscal retrenchment can positively affect private spending in a situation of high government debt.

Several studies -see e.g. van Aarle and Garretsen (2003)- analyse the importance of the initial level of debt for the effects of fiscal policies by distinguishing different high and low debt regimes and testing how these regimes affect outcomes of fiscal policy.

Given the previous analyses, the question can be posed how the spillovers from public debt and the spillovers from fiscal deficit compare. Clearly, they share a common element since the stock of debt is necessarily the sum of the fiscal deficit flows in the past. The spillovers from debt work mainly through its effect on the credibility of monetary policy, and hence through interest rates (via the effect on future inflation that monetary policy has to bring about, and via the possible bail out effects in the monetary union). Deficits may also affect cyclical conditions in the short run; they can also be interpreted as resulting from strategic games of governments vis-à-vis the central bank (this even more so in a monetary union). Of course, the short-term deficits aggravate the longer term debt spillovers. Empirically, the distinction between both effects can be hard to make, unless stricter identifying restrictions are imposed.

(iv) Spillovers from structural reforms

The removal of structural rigidities in the capital, goods, and labour markets would positively affect the growth potential of the Euro Area economy. By establishing an effective internal market, by boosting research and innovation, and by improving education, structural reforms aim at creating productivity and employment.

Deregulations on the goods, labour, and capital markets aim at increasing competition and achieving productivity gains, resulting in lower product prices and thus reducing inflationary pressure and stimulating final demand. Sauner-Leroy (2003) concludes that until 1993, i.e. in the run-up to the introduction of the Single Market Programme, profit (i.e. price-cost) margins fell, but recovered subsequently thanks to the realisation of efficiency gains, resulting in falling unit costs while output prices remained stable.

Structural reforms reduce the mark-up of prices over marginal cost by increasing potential and actual competition. As the example of the telecommunication sector has shown, the liberalisation of formerly regulated markets tends to reduce prices and to increase productivity. The main reason behind this success is the fact that the economies of scale have disappeared as the result of emerging new technologies (Coppens and Vivet, 2004). Since entry barriers are reduced, the number of firms increases, entailing a positive impact on job creation.

Employment is also supported by the fact that lower profit margins are accompanied by lower real wage claims and thus by reduced structural unemployment. More competition in product markets tends to lead to lower wage mark-ups. Thus, both mark-ups are generally positively related (Jean and Nicoletti, 2002). Deregulation of the labour market works in a similar fashion. Increased labour mobility and wage flexibility induces wage moderation by limiting the scope for exploiting economic rents.

According to modern growth theories, structural policies and institutional settings have an impact on the path of long-term economic growth. To some extent, regulation is necessary to ensure the functioning of market economies, for example in the areas of competition, natural monopolies, consumer protection, property rights and environmental protection. Institutions can increase efficiency by correcting market failure. On the other hand, over-regulation might worsen the resource allocation and reduce the incentives for innovation, thereby exerting adverse effects on the growth potential.

Structural reforms affect economic activity through numerous channels (Ahn, 2002; Griffith and Harrison, 2004; European Commission, 2004). Direct and indirect effects can be distinguished. As structural reforms reduce production costs (mainly administrative costs) and remove barriers to enter new markets, productivity is increased directly. In addition, indirect effects occur through three channels: firstly, a higher degree of market contestability reduces the market power of incumbents. As a result, the mark-up of prices over marginal cost decreases. Factor inputs are used more efficiently, and the allocation of goods and services is improved. In addition, less productive firms are forced to leave the market, thus aggregate productivity rises (allocative efficiency). Secondly, companies are encouraged to reorganise work, reduce slack and increase work effort. The under-utilisation of production factors is diminished (productive efficiency). Thirdly, incentives to research and innovate in order to move to the modern technology frontier are improved (dynamic efficiency). On the one hand, dynamic efficiency gains enhance the economy's long-term growth rate while advancements in allocative and productive efficiency raise the levels of productivity and output but not their growth rates. On the other hand, dynamic efficiency advances may take more time to accrue than allocative and productive efficiency gains from structural reforms.

Estimating the impacts of product market reforms undertaken in the European Union over the 1980s and 1990s, Griffith and Harrison (2004) conclude that product market reforms reducing barriers to the entry of new firms, removing price controls and diminishing the government engagement in production, reduce economic rents as measured by the mark-up of value-added over the sum of labour and capital costs. The decline in economic rents in turn benefits employment and investment. A positive impact of regulatory reforms, in particular those removing barriers to entry and thus reducing the mark-up, on investment is also found by Alesina et al. (2003). Gjersem (2004) argues that the full scope for efficiency improvements has not yet been fully exploited in the European Union, despite the product market reforms that have been implemented over the past years.

As in the case of fiscal policies, cross-country spillovers may also arise from structural reforms. Reforms on factor and goods markets implemented in individual countries can be expected to benefit also the other Euro Area countries. In addition, the ECB is supported in conducting its stability oriented monetary policy. The positive effects of structural reforms are internationally transmitted through various channels (Bayoumi et al., 2004). Firstly, the countries are linked by international trade. Competition enhancing reforms in one country will result in increasing domestic output, employment, consumption and investment. Part of the additional demand falls on imports, thus directly enhancing foreign output. In the exporting country, the additional output will lead to increasing tax revenues and an improving government budget. This positive trade effect is partly compensated as within a monetary union, lower inflation in a country implementing structural reforms improves directly the respective country's international competitiveness. Cross-country spillovers arising from product market reforms can be expected to outweigh international spillovers brought about by labour market reforms. This can be attributed to the fact that labour market reforms benefit in particular employment and thus private consumption, while competition enhancing product market reforms promote investment which has a higher import content than consumption.

In addition to trade linkages, structural reforms can be expected to result in wage moderation and thus lower inflation and in a decline of the sacrifice ratio, i.e. the cumulative output gap required to permanently cut the inflation rate by one percentage point. This supports the ECB in ensuring price stability. Low inflation achieved by structural reforms allows a less restrictive monetary policy stance. As inflation expectations also decline, long-term interest rates are lower, thus supporting fixed capital formation across the entire Euro Area. Stimulated growth in the other Euro Area Member States brought about by structural reforms in individual countries also support fiscal policies. By the working of automatic stabilisers, revenues are higher and expenditures are lower, hence facilitating fiscal consolidation.

Using a variant of GEM, the IMF's new large-scale micro-founded multi-country general-equilibrium model with nominal rigidities, a recent study (Bayoumi et al., 2004) estimates that structural reforms on the goods and labour markets in the Euro Area increasing competition and reducing the price and wage mark-ups to US levels would increase production in the Euro Area by 12.4 percent. Due to international spillovers, other countries and regions would also benefit: US output, e.g., would rise by 1 percent. Cross-country spillovers depend crucially on the reaction of the exchange rate. The increase in competition results in a real depreciation of the euro as the relative supply of Euro Area goods rises. In addition to the effects on output, the reduction in mark-ups associated with product and labour market reforms positively influences the ability of monetary policy to stabilise output and inflation.

While a coordinated implementation of structural reforms would be beneficial for all Euro Area countries, a lack of coordination might be harmful. Structural reforms on the product and factor markets improve a country's international competitiveness. Thus, if only some individual countries pursued such policies, they would improve their positions partly at the expense of other Member States, whose structural disadvantages would be increased further.

1.4 Overview of the main results

Chapter 2 by Bas van Aarle studies the short-run spillovers of fiscal policy in the Euro Area. To this purpose, VAR models are estimated. First, the Euro Area countries are considered as an aggregate entity. In a next step, VARs are estimated for the individual Euro Area countries to gain more insight into spillovers at the disaggregated level. In a monetary union, fiscal policy actions implemented in individual countries affect all other Member States via the common monetary policy and thus the common short-term interest rate. Fiscal expansions undertaken in individual countries may induce inflationary pressure in the respective country which, by definition, affects the area-wide inflation rate. This may force the common central bank to raise its policy rates which also leads to an increase in short-term market interest rates. The analysis of short-run budgetary spillovers in the aggregate Euro Area suggests that a reduction in the budget deficit results in a small but positive effect on output. This result suggests the prevalence of positive non-Keynesian effects of fiscal consolidation. Crowding-in effects and positive supply-side effects from fiscal consolidations are the most intuitive explanations for this finding. A fiscal consolidation in the Euro Area only weakly affects short-term interest rates and inflation. The disaggregated analysis reveals that in most cases there are significant positive direct output and inflation spillover effects from the rest of the Euro Area. Moreover, Member States display substantial differences in the spillovers from fiscal consolidations in the Euro Area. These differences can be explained by differences in trade links, differences in the size and structure of the economies, and differences in initial fiscal conditions.

In *Chapter 3,* Peter Claeys focuses on the crowding out effects of deficits and their accumulation in public debt. The analysis is based on an empirical model of fiscal policy and interest rates, together with a small economic system. A first methodological contribution is to include public debt – in addition to deficits – to analyse crowding-out. The second contribution is to analyse spillovers by extending the model to open economies. The main result is that spillovers mask the effects of fiscal policy on long-term interest rates. With the exception of some highly indebted countries, there are hardly significant interest rate responses to changes in domestic fiscal policies as such. Changes in the fiscal stance do not affect so much relative country spreads, but rather spillover to aggregate Euro Area interest rates. We net out the spillover effects of public deficit and debt accumulation on a country's interest rate by benchmarking the model on aggregate Euro Area conditions. We find that for given Euro Area interest rates, changes in fiscal policy affect the country spread, but do not lead to significant responses in relative interest rates following country-specific fiscal shocks. The consequence is that any individual country would not even benefit partially from consolidation of its own public finances. A coordinated action for bringing down debt ratios across the EMU would pay off with overall substantially lower long-term interest rates. Nonetheless, there is some indirect evidence that this spillover is not related to EMU but mainly derives from financial markets, casting some further doubts on market discipline. We deduce this from the responses of interest rates for the Euro Area as a bloc being only slightly stronger than for the individual Member States.

As a complement to the analyses of Chapter 2 and 3, Niko Gobbin looks in *Chapter 4* for potential non-linearities in the real effects of fiscal policy actions on economic activity. In particular, the question is addressed whether the spillovers from public debt depend on the size of the debt level. Empirical support is found for the hypothesis that the effects of fiscal policy actions in the EU-15 depend on the initial level of government debt. Specifically, a highly significant and precisely estimated threshold value of 10% for net debt and 62% for gross debt is identified. The level of government debt mainly affects the impact of changes in disposable income and changes in government consumption and subsidies on private consumption. The overall impact of changes in taxes and social security expenditures is unambiguously smaller above the threshold debt level, while the impact of changes in government consumption and subsidies does not depend on the debt level. The results also show that crossing the critical debt level does not mean moving from a Keynesian state of the world to a non-Keynesian one. Although this chapter analyses spillovers within rather than between countries, the results are valuable to evaluate policy coordination. If the transmission of fiscal policy actions depends on the debt level, a common EU-wide fiscal policy will have asymmetric effects on individual Member States. The Maastricht deficit criterion might for example be harder to achieve in a country with a higher debt level because the positive feed-back effects of fiscal consolidation on private consumption are mitigated. This provides an additional rationale for the debt convergence criterion.

Chapter 5 by Klaus Weyerstrass and Johannes Jaenicke analyses the benefits of structural reforms on factor and product markets in the Euro Area. The reduction of structural rigidities on the capital, goods, and labour markets should reduce mark-up ratios, enhance the growth potential and boost competition in the Euro Area economy. This enhanced competition will reduce the mark-up of prices over marginal cost, leading to higher total factor productivity (TFP) growth, increased employment and lower unemployment. The empirical investigations focus on the effects of the deregulation of the goods and factor markets on total factor productivity growth by affecting the mark-up, i.e. the deviation of prices from marginal costs. Structural reforms that achieve greater competition in product, labour and capital markets are found to generate positive macroeconomic effects in the forms of higher productivity and employment as well as lower unemployment. Econometric estimates suggest that a reduction of the relative mark-up in the Euro Area by around 10 percent – about the current difference with the US level – would raise average total factor productivity growth in the Euro Area by around 0.6 percentage points.

Chapter 6 by Reinhard Neck and Gottfried Haber analyses and evaluates the macroeconomic and welfare effects of structural policies and of budgetary consolidation in the Euro Area. Structural reforms implemented in individual countries affect all other Member States of the monetary union directly due to the trade linkages as well as indirectly via the common monetary policy and integrated capital markets. Higher growth in the country implementing structural reforms also boosts growth in the other Euro Area countries by increased imports. By the working of automatic stabilisers, faster growth results in increasing government revenues and decreasing government expenditures. Thus, discretionary budget consolidation is facilitated. Such budget consolidation measures in turn lead to decreasing interest rates reinforcing the positive effects both for the country which has originally implemented supply-side reforms and for all other countries of the monetary union. In addition to the trade channel, structural reforms aiming at intensifying competition result in lower interest rates as more competition reduces the inflationary pressure. These cross-country links between the effects of structural reforms and fiscal policies are studied by means of model simulations.

The MSG3 Model, a structural multi-country model, is used to perform simulations in order to derive numerical values of macroeconomic spillovers for key macroeconomic policy target variables like GDP, price level/inflation, (un)employment, etc. under different policy shocks both for individual countries and for the entire Euro Area. The study finds non-trivial gains from economic policy coordination in the Euro Area. Firstly, coordinated budgetary consolidation can help to crowd-in private investment through lower long-term interest rates. Secondly, coordinated structural reforms generate higher GDP, lower interest rates and reduced budget deficits and government debt levels. Thirdly, a combination of coordinated budgetary consolidation and structural reforms by Euro Area Member States can help to bring about a permanent improvement in the economic and employment performance. These findings show that the most effective way of achieving permanently higher output and lower public debt without undesirable side-effects is via a Euro Area-wide coordinated design of both structural reforms and budgetary consolidation policies

In *Chapter 7,* Hughes Hallett, Christian Richer and Xiaoshan Cheng concentrate on one of the main channels though which structural reforms affect economic outcomes, namely increased wage flexibility. Despite the concern about wage flexibility in the policy debate, there are no firm estimates in the literature, no accepted methodology for making such estimates, and little more than anecdotal evidence of the "greater than", "less than" kind. The authors therefore investigate the degree of wage flexibility in a sample of European countries, in particular at the business cycle frequency. They examine whether flexibility differs across countries, whether it is really higher in countries outside the Euro and whether it has been increasing over time, especially after the increased market pressures with the coming of the Euro, or whether joining the Euro Area has instead reduced the incentive and perceived need for the kind of reforms that would produce greater labour market flexibility. It is found that, contrary to popular wisdom, the US markets do not have greater flexibility in a general sense. But it does have less wage persistence and greater flexibility at the business cycle frequency, and short-run flexibility may have been increasing relative to the long-run persistence in wages. Euro Area wages, by contrast, are more persistent, and show short-term spurts of higher flexibility which are not sustained. Moreover, since 1998, wage flexibility in Europe has slumped in what looks like "reform fatigue" once countries were safely inside the Euro Area. This goes a long way in explaining why labour market reforms are often discussed and advocated in Europe, but so seldom undertaken. The fate of Harz IV in Germany, the new labour laws in France, and pension reform in Italy are three obvious examples of that pattern of behaviour.

1.5 Policy implications and avenues for further research

While the studies in this volume find crowding-out and spillover effects of fiscal policies on interest rates, some issues deserve further research. Among those aspects that could be examined more closely, one important topic is the source of the spillovers in the EMU. If spillovers are mainly related to capital market integration, fiscal policies probably have global rather than regional effects. An extension of the results to incorporate the fiscal stance in other OECD countries, especially the United States and Japan, could shed light on this question. Monetary union is a complete overhaul of both the monetary and the fiscal policy regime. The foundations for governments' financing decisions have changed completely, and they are regulated by a combination of deficit rules and the no-bail-out clause. The estimates presented in the various chapters of this book are probably a conservative lower limit on the importance of spillovers. In order to explicitly take EMU conditions into account, an empirical benchmark would need to be constructed that mimics the effect of monetary union. Uniform monetary policy settings can be simulated as in Beetsma and Giuliodori (2004).

Another issue to be studied further concerns the possible instability of the results regarding the effects of fiscal policies, as diverging effects might arise from strong fiscal consolidations, changes in the composition of the budget, political turmoil, etc. Testing explicitly for the significance of structural breaks could help to locate the origins of such shifts. In particular, it would be useful to ascertain whether stronger spillover effects in the EU started with the Single Market Programme in 1992 or have changed their character since 1999. Statistical tests could be applied to search endogenously for break dates in the empirical model.

Finally, the total costs of the short-run impact of net lending shocks have to be compared against those of the long-run rise in interest rates. As a related issue, the eventual crowding-in of private investment needs some quantification to provide a view of the benefits of fiscal discipline. Fiscal policy is not the main driver of long-term interest rates. In addition, not all fiscal expansions consist of unproductive expenditures, and government bond finance competes with private issuances for funding. The role of productive government expenditures should be considered.

Structural reforms on the product and factor markets should strengthen competition in the Euro Area. In a more competitive environment, the scope for exploiting economic rents would be reduced. As a result, mark-ups would decline, i.e. prices would come closer to marginal cost. According to our estimates, even though the fostering of competition with the Single Market Programme has reduced mark-up ratios in the Euro Area, they are still substantially higher than in the US; mark-ups in the Euro Area are also larger than in the UK. In future research on mark-ups in the Euro Area, the results presented in Chapter 5 of this volume could be complemented by sectoral analyses, as in Przybyla and Roma (2005).

Significant deviations of prices from production costs distort the efficient allocation of resources. Prices are higher and output is lower than under more intensive competition. These inefficiencies negatively affect technical progress and the growth potential of the economy. Endogenous growth models conclude that fostering competition may reduce rents to be accrued without engaging in innovation by more than post-innovation rents. Thus, reforms that reduce mark-ups would induce firms to engage in innovation activities. As a result, total factor productivity (TFP) would be supported. Panel estimations in Chapter 5 indicate that a reduction of the mark-up in the Euro Area by 10 percent (which is around the difference to the US level) would raise average TFP growth by around 0.57 percentage points. Besides total factor productivity, employment and the growth rate of labour productivity would also be supported. Lack of competition, in particular on the labour market, may induce trade unions to claim parts of the economic rent. Structural reforms reduce the mark-up of prices over marginal cost by increasing potential and actual competition in both product and labour markets.

The institutional framework is an important determinant of the degree of competition. The latter in turn determines the scope for setting prices significantly above marginal cost. In the labour market for example, the presence of regulations allows employers' and employees' associations to share economic rents. Labour market regulations protecting workers or providing generous benefits to the unemployed tend to increase the reservation wage, thus leading to higher wage demands. Companies will react by decreasing their workforce. Both longer unemployment benefit durations and a higher benefit replacement rate would positively influence the mark-up. In contrast, a higher degree of wage bargaining coordination would allow taking economy-wide developments in the wage negotiations into account. Thus, a higher degree of coordination would reduce the wage pressure and thus the mark-up.

An important aim of the investigation of structural reforms in the Euro Area in the present volume is to derive welfare implications and policy implications concerning spillovers from structural policies and from the interactions between structural and fiscal policies. As some of the panel estimations in this volume exhibit unsatisfactory statistical properties, further research on the effects and institutional determinants of the mark-up ratios, however, is certainly needed.

The macroeconomic and welfare effects of both structural reforms and budgetary consolidations have been determined by means of simulations with the MSG3 Model, a dynamic, intertemporal, general-equilibrium model of a multi-region world economy. Structural policies have been implemented by assuming that total factor productivity will gradually increase over a period of five years to a level 0.57 percent higher for the Euro Area as a whole. For individual countries, the TFP shift varies between 0.54 and 0.75 percent. If TFP increases in one country only, real GDP of the country directly affected rises over six years and then stays at the higher level forever. The current account improves permanently, the public-sector deficit remains below baseline values, causing public debt to fall indefinitely. Employment rises slightly (with a minimal permanent effect), inflation falls temporarily. Euro Area countries not directly affected exhibit only temporary positive spillover effects to GDP, small permanent negative ones to the current account and positive ones to public deficit and debt. Interest rates rise in the short run and fall below baseline in the long run. A productivity shock to the entire Euro Area brings about positive effects for all Member States. Interestingly, also the effects on Germany and Italy are stronger than in the case where only one of these countries is affected. Hence, there are positive spillover effects from a coordinated structural policy in the Euro Area.

Besides implementing structural reforms, different strategies of consolidating the general government budget have been analysed by means of model simulations. The results of these simulations can be briefly summarised as follows: After a decrease of public investment, long-term interest rates overshoot and stay above baseline values, with negative effects on capital and wealth. This leads to public debt overshooting in later periods of the simulation; hence the original improvement of the public sector's debtor position is reversed in the long run for the countries/regions that reduce public investment. From this, we can conclude that both the short-run and the long-run effects clearly speak against using public investment as a means of consolidating the budget of the public sector. Thus, in the following, decreases of public consumption and increases of lump-sum taxes (or, equivalently, decreases of lump-sum transfers) are considered. In addition to implementing only one of these measures at a time, as a third option a combination of reducing public consumption and (to a lower extent) net taxes has been analysed.

In the country/region directly affected by the budgetary consolidation policies, all simulations are characterised by a Keynesian reaction of lower than baseline real GDP and employment in the short run and a non-Keynesian reaction of higher than baseline real GDP and employment in the medium term. The former effect is the familiar result of a reduction of (public or private) demand. The non-Keynesian effect, which in most cases exceeds the short-run Keynesian effect, is mainly due to the reduction of the public deficit and hence public debt, resulting in lower rates of interest and higher private wealth; it is also partly due to the increase in competitiveness as shown by the improved current account. As the budgetary consolidation policy is modelled as temporary (although over a fairly long time horizon of 12 years), in the long run the economies return to the baseline path rather quickly after these 12 years. Only public debt remains well below baseline values for many years, inducing a (very modest) long-run increase of real GDP over its baseline values. By contrast, a permanent reduction of public consumption and hence the budget deficit can lead to substantial permanent gains in output.

Although the general behaviour of the variables of the countries directly affected by the policy shock is the same in all simulations considered, there are some differences in detail. Comparing the three methods of reducing the budget deficit, we can see that lowering public consumption and taxes simultaneously gives the strongest effects, followed by decreasing public consumption only, while lump-sum (net) tax increases result in the weakest reactions.

An interesting distinction can be made between the simulations where only one country implements the budgetary consolidation policy and those where the entire Euro Area consolidates. In the case of a coordinated budgetary consolidation for the entire Euro Area, there are gains from coordination: Negative short-run Keynesian effects on GDP and employment are weaker, deficit and debt reductions are stronger and hence medium-run positive non-Keynesian effects on GDP and employment are also stronger than if one country only consolidates; this is true also for the country in question. Moreover, inflation oscillates less in the coordination than in the non-coordination scenarios. As for the simulations of structural policies and their effects on TFP, it turns out that coordinated policy-making brings about a “coordination dividend” for the countries participating.

In addition to implementing either only structural reforms or budget consolidation policies separately, combinations of both policies may be pursued. In the short run, such policy combinations result in almost additive combinations of the effects of the single policies combined. For instance, with respect to GDP and employment, the negative short-run effect of budgetary consolidation combines with the positive effect of structural reforms to give ambiguous results in the first periods, whereas for public deficit and debt, inflation and interest rates, the favourable effects of both policies reinforce each others. The long-run effects are probably more revealing, given the EU political objective of achieving higher growth and more jobs during the remainder of the decade and beyond. The combination of structural and budgetary consolidation policies, even when confined to one single Member State without any policy change in other countries, suffices to make higher GDP, current account improvements, lower public budget deficit and lower public debt sustainable in the long run. There are also some permanent international spillovers to the other Euro Area economies; the size of these long-run spillover effects depends primarily upon the economic size of a country and its international trade and financial flows with the other Euro Area countries and less on the effectiveness of its policies on its own economy. The ultimate coordination scenario for the Euro Area is for all Euro Area countries to implement both the structural reforms and a budgetary consolidation policy. In this area-wide common policy scenario, real GDP remains above baseline for all countries in the long run. Permanent improvements also apply to the current account, the public deficit and public debt in all Member States. The short-run interest rate is below baseline in the long run.

The most important lessons from these simulations are the following: In the long run, the effects of structural policy reforms that increase the TFP level permanently dominate and can bring about a permanent improvement of key macroeconomic target variables such as output and public finances. In the medium run, budgetary policies are stronger, but as we have assumed that the budget consolidation will be done over a limited time period, it exerts almost no permanent effects (except on public debt) unless supported by structural reforms. International spillover effects within the Euro Area are relatively small (except those from the biggest economy, Germany) and can be advantageous (mostly through the channel of the common interest rate) or disadvantageous (especially if they affect the competitiveness of some countries at the expense of other Member States within the Euro Area). As many other studies on international macroeconomic policy-making have shown, we can confirm that coordinated policies are superior to non-coordinated policies, and using two (or more) instruments is superior to relying on one instrument only. Our results show that the most effective way of achieving permanently higher output and lower public debt without undesirable side-effects is via a Euro Area-wide coordinated design of both structural and budgetary consolidation policies. How such coordination can be achieved is a political question which goes beyond the scope of the present study.

One of the effects of structural reform is increased flexibility, which turns out to be a more subtle concept than traditional analyses would lead us to believe. Blanket statements, such as "the US is a more flexible economy", mean very little. The US is not obviously more flexible in many respects. Rather, it is more flexible in a number of particular ways; and it has held on to its greater flexibility better. Also, the Euro Area economies have shown rather little flexibility in the core (France, Germany, Italy), but more in the periphery and smaller economies. They now probably have less flexibility than the US at the crucial business cycle frequency. More important, they have shown greater wage persistence; and some have a downward trend in relative flexibility. Finally, they have all shown an ability to create greater flexibility when times are bad, but they have been equally bad to hold on to that flexibility thereafter. As a result, the degree of short-run wage flexibility has fallen by as much 100%-150% since qualifying for the Euro Area, and wage flexibility is now lower than during the 1990s. The results in this volume therefore suggest the US may have now increased its flexibility advantage over the EU, due to "reform fatigue" in Europe.

References

Ahmed, S., B. Ickes, P. Wang and B. Sam Yoo (1993), International business cycles, American Economic Review, vol. 83, no. 3, p.335-359.

Ahn, S. (2002), Competition, innovation and productivity growth: A review of theory and evidence, OECD Economics Department Working Papers no.317.

Alesina, A., S. Ardagna, G. Nicoletti and F. Schiantarelli (2003), Regulation and investment, OECD Economics Department Working Papers no.352.

Allsopp, Ch., W. J. McKibbin and D. Vines (1999), Fiscal consolidation in Europe: Some empirical issues, in A. Hughes Hallett , M. Hutchinson and S. Hougaard Jensen (eds.). (1999) Fiscal aspects of European monetary integration, Cambridge University Press, p. 288–333.

Ardagna, S.; F. Caselli and T. Lane (2005), Fiscal discipline and the cost of public debt service: some estimates for OECD countries, Centre for Economic Performance, CEP Discussion Paper No. 670.

Artis, M.; H.-M. Krolzig and J. Toro (1998), The European business cycle, CEPR Discussion Paper No. 2242.

Bayoumi T. and P. Masson (1998), Liability-creating versus non-liability-creating fiscal stabilisation policies: Ricardian equivalence, fiscal stabilisation and EMU, The Economic Journal, vol. 108, p. 1026-1045.

Bayoumi, T., D. Laxton, and P. Pesenti (2004), Benefits and spillovers of greater competition in Europe: A macroeconomic assessment, NBER Working Paper 10416.

Beetsma, R. and M. M. Giuliodori (2004), What are the spillovers from fiscal shocks in Europe? An empirical analysis, ECB working paper no. 325.

Blanchard, O. and R. Perotti (2002), An empirical characterisation of the dynamic effects of changes in government spending and taxes on output, Quarterly Journal of Economics, vol. 117, no.4, p. 1329-1368.

Bruneau, C. and O. De Bandt (2003), Monetary and fiscal policy in the transition to monetary union: What do SVAR models tell us?, Economic Modelling, vol. 20, p.959-985.

Buti, M, W. Roeger and J. in 't Veld (2001), Stabilising output and inflation in EMU: Policy conflicts and co-operation under the Stability Pact, mimeo.

Canova, F. and H. Dellas (1993), Trade interdependence and the international business cycle, Journal of International Economics, vol.34, p.23-47.

Claeys P. (2004), Monetary and budgetary policy interaction: An SVAR analysis of stabilization policies in monetary union, EUI working paper, no. 22.

Cochrane, J. (2001), Long term debt and optimal policy in the FTPL, Econometrica, vol. 69, p. 69-116.

Coppens, F. and D. Vivet (2004), Liberalisation of network industries: Is the electricity sector an exception to the rule?, National Bank of Belgium, Working Paper 200409.

Dalsgaard, T. and A. de Serres (2000), Estimating prudent budgetary margins for EU countries: A simulated SVAR model approach, OECD Economic Studies, vol. 30, no. 1, p.115-147.

Daniel, B. (2001), The fiscal theory of the price level in an open economy, Journal of Monetary Economics, vol. 48, p. 293-308.

De Arcangelis, G. and S. Lamartina (2004), Fiscal shocks and policy regimes in some OECD countries, in: Beetsma et al. (eds.), Fiscal policies, monetary policies and labour markets, key aspects of European macroeconomic policies after monetary unification, Cambridge: Cambridge University Press, p. 224-255.

De Grauwe, P. (1999), Discussion of Allsopp et al., (1999), in A. Hughes Hallett , M. Hutchinson and S. Hougaard Jensen (eds.). (1999) Fiscal aspects of European monetary integration, Cambridge University Press, p. 334–345.

Dupor B. (2000), Exchange rates and the fiscal theory of the price level, Journal of Monetary Economics, vol. 45, p. 613-630.

European Commission (2004), The EU economy: 2004 review, European Economy no. 6.

Fatas, A. and I. Mihov (1999), The macroeconomic effects of fiscal policy, mimeo.

Garcia, S. and A. Verdelhan (1999), Impact of the monetary and fiscal shocks in the Euro Area, mimeo.

Garcia, S. and P. Hénin (2000), Balancing budget through tax increases or expenditure cuts: Is it neutral? Economic Modelling, vol. 16, p.591-612.

Gjersem, C. (2004), Policies bearing on product market competition and growth in Europe, OECD Economics Department Working Papers no.378

Giordani, P. (2004), Evaluating New-Keynesian models of a small open economy, Oxford Bulletin of Economics and Statistics, vol. 66, Special Issue, p. 713-733.

Griffith, R. and R. Harrison (2004), The link between product market reform and macro-economic performance, European Commission, Economic Papers no.209.

Hughes Hallett, A.; P. Mooslechner and M. Schuerz (eds.) (2001), Challenges for economic policy coordination within European Monetary Union, Boston: Kluwer.

Jean, S. and G. Nicoletti (2002), Product market regulation and wage premia in Europe and North America: An empirical investigation, OECD Economics Department Working Papers no.318.

Kim, S. (1999), Do monetary policy shocks matter in the G-7 countries? Using common identifying assumptions about monetary policy across countries, Journal of International Economics, vol.48, p.387-412.

Kim, S. and N. Roubini (2000), Exchange rate anomalies in the industrial countries: A solution with a structural VAR Approach, Journal of Monetary Economics, vol.45, p.561-586.

Koren, S. and A. Stiassny (1998), Tax and spend, or spend and tax? An international study, Journal of Policy Modeling, vol.20, no.2: p.163-191.

Landon, S. and C. Smith (2000), Government debt spillovers and creditworthiness in a federation, The Canadian Journal of Economics, vol. 33, no.3, p. 364-661.

Mélitz, J. (2000), Some cross-country evidence about fiscal policy behavior and consequences for EMU, mimeo.

Muscatelli, A.; P. Tirelli and C. Trecroci (2002), Monetary and fiscal policy interactions over the cycle: Some empirical evidence, CESifo Working Paper no.817.

Prozybyla, M. and M. Roma (2005), Does product market competition reduce inflation? Evidence from EU countries and sectors, ECB Working Paper No. 453.

Rogoff, K., (1985), Can international monetary policy cooperation be counterproductive? Journal of International Economics, vol. 18, p. 199–217.

Sala, L. (2004), The Fiscal Theory of the Price Level: identifying restrictions and empirical evidence, IGIER working paper no. 257.

Sauner-Leroy, J.-B. (2003), The impact of the implementation of the Single Market Programme on productive efficiency and the mark-ups in the European Union manufacturing industry, European Economy, Economic Papers No. 192.

Semmler, W. and W. Zhang (2004), Monetary and fiscal policy interactions in the Euro Area, Empirica, vol. 31, p. 205-227.

van Aarle, B. and H. Garretsen (2003), Keynesian, Non-Keynesian or no effects of fiscal policy changes? The EMU Case, Journal of Macroeconomics, vol. 25, p. 213-240.

2 Budgetary spillovers and short-term interest rates

Bas van Aarle

2.1 Introduction

In Chapter 1, it was discussed in detail that there are various spillovers in a highly integrated economic space like the Euro Area. It was explained in which ways these spillovers manifest themselves in the Euro Area e.g. through trade flows, pass-through of inflation, adjustments caused by changes of the common short-term interest rate and the exchange rate of the euro. It was also noted that there exist several spillover effects from monetary and fiscal policies in a highly integrated monetary union like the Euro Area. Monetary and fiscal policies in the Euro Area are intrinsically linked through these spillovers. In the short run, spillovers arise from the effects that monetary policy may have on the macroeconomic conditions under which fiscal policies are undertaken, and vice versa. In the long run, these spillovers/ interdependencies arise in particular from the accumulation of government debt.

The macroeconomic spillovers constitute an important rationale for pursuing policy coordination: through spillovers, macroeconomic policies and conditions in one Euro Area country will affect other Member States. Vice versa, the economic conditions and policies in the rest of the Euro Area constitute an important factor of the macroeconomic adjustments in the individual Euro Area countries. This chapter tries to provide plausible estimates of the magnitude of short-run spillovers from fiscal policy in the Euro Area. While there is a substantial amount of literature on spillovers -see, e.g., some references in Chapter 1-, it is nevertheless fair to say that knowledge on the sign, size and timing of spillovers in the Euro Area is far from complete.

To analyse spillovers in the Euro Area, this chapter uses VAR models. In these models various channels of spillovers can be identified in a straightforward and intuitive manner. The issue of spillovers of fiscal and monetary policies in the Euro Area is studied at two levels of aggregation.

(a) The aggregate Euro Area level: Here, the following issues are addressed concerning spillovers at the aggregate Euro Area level: What are the spillover effects from fiscal policy shocks in the Euro Area on output and inflation in the Euro Area and on the short-term interest rate / monetary policy of the ECB and the euro exchange rate? What are the effects from monetary policy shocks? What are the spillover effects from "external" shocks (e.g. oil-price shocks, exchange rate shocks and shocks to output, interest rates or inflation outside the Euro Area) on macroeconomic adjustments in the Euro Area?

(b) The individual Euro Area country level: A number of issues concerning spillovers is relevant at the disaggregated Euro Area level. (i) The effects of internal spillovers : How do developments in the rest of the Euro Area affect the individual Member States? What are the spillover effects of short-term interest rates (i.e. monetary policy of the ECB) on individual counties? (ii) The effects of external spillovers: How do adjustments outside the Euro Area and the euro exchange rate affect the individual Member States? (iii) For the three largest Euro Area countries, Germany, France and Italy, we also analyse the spillovers of fiscal shocks in these countries to macroeconomic variables in the rest of the Euro Area[1].

2.2 Methodology and literature

VAR models have been used extensively to study the transmission of real and monetary shocks.[2] A VAR represents a reduced form model of the endogenous variables. The advantage of the VAR approach is that there is no need to build a structural model describing the economy in general and the mechanisms of fiscal and monetary policy design and transmission in particular. Moreover, the VAR models deliver two convenient tools in the form of impulse response functions (IRF) and variance decompositions (VD) that provide detailed information on the impact and transmission of

[1] We focus on the three large Euro Area countries since we can safely assume that the impact of shocks in one the small Euro Area countries on the rest of the Euro Area is of a minor importance.

[2] Insightful studies are e.g. Sims (1992), Bernanke and Blinder (1992), Gerlach and Smets (1995), Rudebusch (1998). Gordon and Leeper (1994) and Leeper et al. (1996) analyse in detail the difficulties with identification in VAR models of monetary policy.

macroeconomic shocks and policy innovations. IRF show the effects of different types of shocks on the various endogenous variables. VD show which fraction of the total variability of the endogenous variables is explained by each shock.

The VAR framework is particularly suited to assess the effects of fiscal and monetary policy innovations and spillovers, since it isolates the response of each variable to shocks and policy innovations and shows their macroeconomic transmissions over time. However, some limitations have to be kept in mind: the VAR model is entirely data-driven. The underlying structure is determined by the data themselves (proponents of VAR modelling, of course, argue that this is the main advantage of the VAR approach). Economic theory is only brought into the analysis when the identifying restrictions are based on economic theory.[3] This lack of theoretical and behavioural relations may, however, also result in outcomes that seem counterintuitive. In VAR models of monetary policy, counterfactual results like, e.g., the price-puzzle are well-known.

The working of the VAR approach can be briefly summarised as follows. Assume that an unrestricted VAR model,

$$x_t = A(L)e_t \tag{2.1}$$

is estimated - written here in moving average form - where x is a vector of covariance stationary (macroeconomic) variables, $A(L)$ a polynomial matrix of lag length l, L the lag operator and e a vector of reduced-form innovations in the elements of x with variance-covariance matrix $E(e_t e_t^T) = \Sigma$.

Structural VAR models impose additional identifying restrictions upon VAR estimates to recover structural ("orthogonalised") innovations from the reduced-form innovations of estimated VAR. In practice, the identification is achieved by imposing identifying short or long-run restrictions. In order to exactly identify a VAR model of n endogenous variables, $(n^2-n)/2$ restrictions need to be imposed to obtain an SVAR model.[4] These

[3] In macroeconomic SVAR models e.g., long run restrictions are often based upon small scale IS-LM-Phillips curve type models.

[4] These reduced-form innovations, however, are likely to be correlated and can, therefore, not necessarily be interpreted as purely structural innovations. The SVAR approach relates the vector x to a vector of structural innovations, u_t, $x_t = B(L)u_t$ (2.1'), where $B(L)$ is a polynomial matrix in L. In this SVAR, u_t is a vector of serially and contemporaneously uncorrelated, normalised structural residuals with $E(u_t u_t^T) = I$. From (2.1) and (2.1') it follows that the vector of reduced-form innovations can be represented as a linear combination of the struc-

restrictions can be related to economic theory. Another popular way to obtain a set of orthogonalised innovations is to use the Cholesky decomposition or a generalisation of the Cholesky decomposition.

2.3 Fiscal spillovers at the aggregate Euro Area level

Starting point of our analysis is that in an integrated like the Euro Area (EA) there operate a large number of spillovers. These spillovers are complex and therefore not easy to identify. The spillovers imply that macroeconomic conditions in individual Member States will depend to a significant extent on developments in the aggregate Euro Area economy.

At the aggregate Euro Area level a number of types of budgetary spillovers are important: the effects of a Euro Area fiscal policy shock on output, inflation, and net exports in the aggregate Euro Area, and spillovers from fiscal policies on short-term interest rates and the euro exchange rate. Fiscal policy in the Euro Area - via its impact on output and prices - is also likely to affect interest rates and exchange rates. Thereby, expansionary fiscal policies will to some extent cause crowding-out of private consumption or investment and net exports. In the Euro Area, fiscal policy thus influences the conditions for monetary policy managed by the ECB.

Spillovers from foreign variables on euro-area output and prices are also relevant. The Euro Area itself is in many ways affected by external conditions. An increase in growth of the world economy will tend to increase extra-Euro Area exports. This will raise output and improve the current account. Changes in oil prices and prices of intermediate goods will affect producer prices in the Euro Area etc. Fluctuations in the euro exchange rate will affect net exports via the effects on competitiveness of the Euro Area and inflation via the pass-through of exchange rate fluctua-

---

tural residuals, i.e., $e_t = Cu_t$ with $CC^T = \Sigma$. As a result, $x_t = A(L)Cu_t = C(L)u_t$ and $A(L)C = B(L)$, enabling the identification of the structural innovations from the reduced-form innovations of the reduced-form. The SVAR approach was pioneered by Blanchard (1990) and Blanchard and Quah (1989) who concentrated on long-run identifying restrictions in identifying demand and supply shocks in the economy. Building upon these two papers, Gali (1992) proposes a set of identifying restrictions containing a combination of short-run and long-run restrictions. In another influential analysis, Bayoumi and Eichengreen (1992) use the SVAR approach to identify aggregate demand and supply shocks in the EU and to assess to which extent the EU countries constitute an optimum currency area by distinguishing between symmetric and asymmetric shocks.

tions to prices.

To obtain insights into these aspects, this section estimates a VAR model of macroeconomic adjustments and monetary and fiscal policy transmissions in the Euro Area. The Euro Area countries, in other words, are considered as an aggregate entity. In this way, the estimated VAR model can be interpreted as representing a macroeconomic model of the Euro Area and the innovations can be viewed as macroeconomic shocks in the aggregate Euro Area economy.

The vector x of macroeconomic variables that are included in the VAR model consists of: the output gap in the Euro Area, YGAP_EA, the fiscal balance to GDP ratio, NLGY_EA, the current account to GDP ratio, CUAY_EA, the short-term interest rate, SIN_EA, the rate of depreciation of the euro to the US dollar, DEPREUR, and inflation, INF_EA. These variables were collected for the Euro Area aggregate for the period first quarter of 1980 (1980:I) to fourth quarter of 2004 (2004:IV). The dynamics of the endogenous variables are displayed in Fig. 2.1:

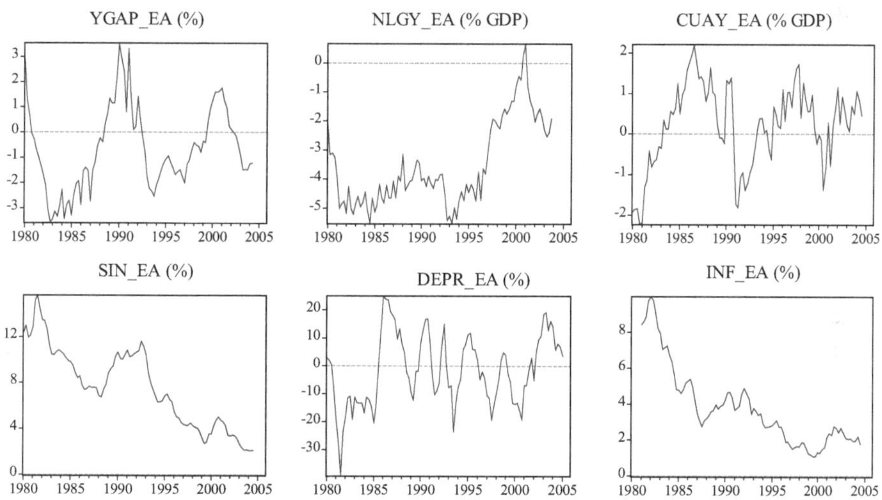

Fig. 2.1. Endogenous Euro Area variables in the Euro Area VAR

To calculate the Euro Area output gap, fiscal balance, current account and inflation we used weighted averages of the individual country variables. As weights, the GDP weights of the individual countries in Euro Area GDP were taken. This approach turns out to be useful and consistent in light of Sect. 2.4 where we define for each country aggregates of the Euro

Area which exclude the respective country in order to study the effects of developments in the rest of the Euro Area on this country. The GDP weights have fluctuated a bit over time: e.g. in 1999:I the weights were: Austria 3.1%, Belgium 3.8%, Finland 2.0%, France 21.6%, Germany 31.8%, Greece 1.8%, Ireland 1.4%, Italy 17.7%, Netherlands 6.0%, Portugal 1.7%, Spain 8.9%.

In the VAR model, the following exogenous variables are also included: the % increase in the oil price (in euro), OIL, the % growth rate of world trade, WTR, the short-term interest rate in the US, SIN_US, and DUM_EUR, a time dummy that takes a value of 1 from 1999:I onwards and a value of 0 before to capture any shift effect from the official start of EMU on January 1, 1999. The Appendix lists the exact definitions, data-availability and other details of the data set. The model is estimated with one lag in its specification. Lag lengths tests find that one lag in the specification is optimal and that increasing the number of lags is not useful. This also applies to the country-specific models estimated in the next section, implying that for all countries the same model structure is imposed. From the point of view of consistency this also seems preferable.

The VAR model is given in eq. (2.2). It is driven by six macroeconomic shocks: an output shock, e^{YGAP_EA}, a fiscal shock, e^{NLGY_EA}, a current account shock, e^{CUAY_EA}, a monetary shock, e^{SIN_EA}, an exchange rate shock, e^{DEPR_EA}, and an inflation shock, e^{INF_EA}.

$$\begin{bmatrix} YGAP\_EA \\ NLGY\_EA \\ CUAY\_EA \\ SIN\_EA \\ DEPREUR \\ INF\_EA \end{bmatrix} = A(L) \begin{bmatrix} e^{YGAP\_EA} \\ e^{NLGY\_EA} \\ e^{CUAY\_EA} \\ e^{SIN\_EA} \\ e^{DEPREUR} \\ e^{INF\_EA} \end{bmatrix} + D \begin{bmatrix} OIL \\ WTR \\ SIN\_US \\ DUM\_EUR \end{bmatrix} \tag{2.2}$$

The VAR part estimates a reduced form model of output, the fiscal balance, net exports, interest rates, inflation and the exchange rate depreciation for the Euro Area. The matrices $A(L)$ capture all relations between the endogenous variables. The matrix D contains the short-run elasticities of the endogenous variables to the exogenous variables. The output equation is interpreted as a reduced form "IS curve" and gives e.g. estimates of output persistence, output determinants (where we are interested especially in the fiscal multiplier), the interest rate channel of monetary policy and the effects of oil prices and world trade. The VAR estimations for the fiscal balance and interest rate equations can be interpreted as systematic (or automatic / anticipated) fiscal and monetary policy responses to the endogenous variables in the VAR (sometimes also interpreted as policy rules), providing information, e.g., about fiscal stabilisers, persistence of fiscal and monetary policies and the effects of oil price changes on the fiscal balance and interest rates. In this interpretation, the monetary and deficit shocks represent unanticipated monetary and fiscal policy innovations[5]. The trade balance estimation provides insights into the adjustment dynamics of the Euro Area trade balance, into the expenditure switching effect and the J-curve effect of exchange rate changes.[6] The exchange rate depreciation equation shows the adjustment of the euro/US dollar exchange rate as a function of the various shocks and macroeconomic fluctuations. The inflation equation estimates a Euro Area "Phillips curve" and provides estimates of, e.g., inflation persistence and the exchange rate pass-through.

Fig. 2.2 provides the estimated one percent impulse response functions of the VAR model for the aggregate Euro Area economy, including the plus and minus two standard deviations confidence bands.

[5] This interpretation of the fiscal and monetary innovations in the SVAR approach as representing deliberate policy actions is subject to some criticism.

[6] Kim (2001) uses a VAR model to estimate the effects of monetary policy shocks on the trade balance of Italy, France and the UK.

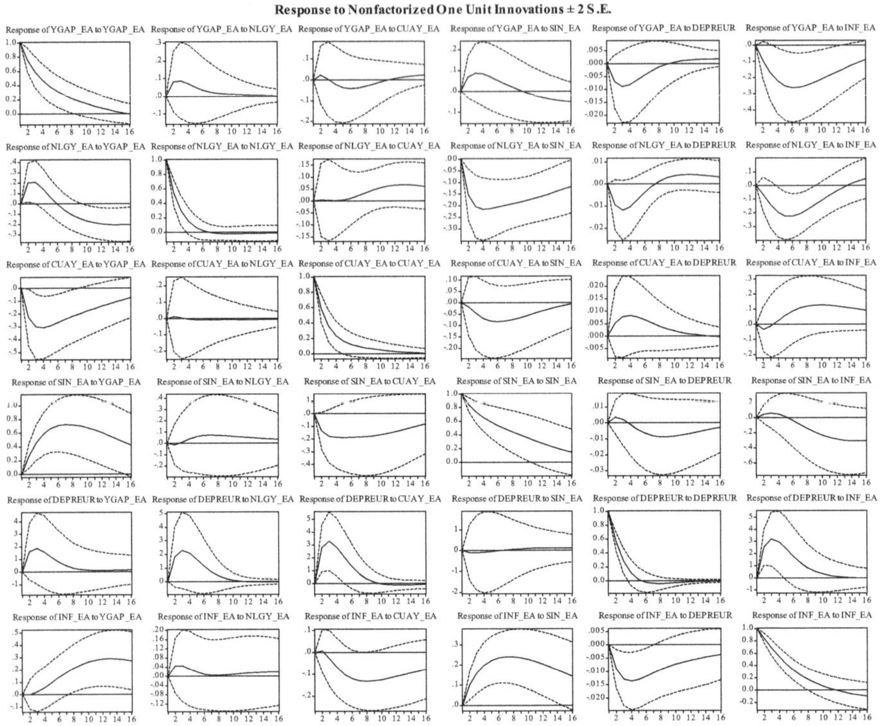

Fig. 2.2. Impulse response functions of macroeconomic shocks in the Euro Area model

The first column displays the effects of a positive output (gap) shock: it tends to improve the fiscal balance in the short run, decrease the current account balance, and increase interest rates and inflation. Also the quantitative impact can be determined straightforwardly since all shocks are 1% in size: an initial increase of output by 1 percent raises the fiscal balance on average by 0.25 percent initially and raises interest rates by about 0.4 percent. We are interested especially also in column 2 and 4 which shows the effects of a fiscal innovation (i.e. an increase in the fiscal balance) and a monetary innovation (i.e. an increase in the short-term interest rate). An improvement of the fiscal balance increases output, suggesting the prevalence of positive non-Keynesian style effects from fiscal consolidation. The observed absence of effects on the trade balance suggests that the "twin deficits" hypothesis does not hold for the Euro Area: changes in the fiscal balance tend not to affect the external balance in the same direction. Furthermore, the fiscal balance shock induces a depreciation of the euro and a small increase in inflation.

The VAR model can be used to study the important issue of the short-run interaction of fiscal and monetary policies: these interactions are measured by the impact of interest rate shocks on the fiscal variables and the impact of fiscal shocks on the interest rate. A positive innovation in the fiscal balance has a rather small positive effect on the short term interest rate. On the other hand, a positive shock to the short term interest rate has a stronger effect on fiscal balances which deteriorate by about 0.25 percent from a 1 percent interest rate increase. This suggests that in particular monetary policy affects the conditions for fiscal policy and that this mechanism constitutes an important source of spillover effects. A plausible explanation for this result seems to be the increasing interest rate burden on government debt when interest rates rise.

Another potential source of spillovers in the aggregate Euro Area model comes from shocks to the euro exchange rate: the estimated effects of a depreciation shock of the euro on output, inflation and interest rates are, however, rather small in size, suggesting that these shocks –as long as they are small in size- are not the most important source of fluctuations in the Euro Area. Concerning the effects of the exogenous variables it is found that the growth of world trade initiates a significant positive effect on the Euro Area output gap and current account. The oil price has a negative effect on the output gap and the current account and a positive effect on inflation, but the effects are relatively imprecisely estimated. The US interest rate has a positive effect on he Euro Area short term interest rate and leads to an appreciation of the euro. The EMU dummy has a significant positive effect on the fiscal balance and significant negative effect on the interest rate suggesting that the establishment of the monetary union had an effect of lowering fiscal deficits and interest rates even when considering the effects of all macroeconomic variables in the model. There is no evidence that the dummy affected other variables in the Euro Area aggregate economy: in that sense, the introduction of EMU does not seem to have had a significant independent impact on output growth, depreciation, the current account or inflation.

Summarising, in the aggregate model there is some -albeit weak- evidence of direct spillovers between monetary and fiscal policies in the Euro Area. Apart from these direct spillovers there are a number of indirect connections between monetary and fiscal policies. In addition, external factors - fluctuations in the exchange rate of the euro, oil prices and US output - initiate various spillover effects in the Euro Area economy.

2.4 Fiscal spillovers in the Euro Area at the country level

The aggregate analysis of the previous section analyzed spillover effects in the Euro Area at an aggregate level. It did not provide insights into spillovers at a more disaggregate level, between individual Member States. In this section, we therefore investigate spillovers on the level of individual countries in the Euro Area. To achieve this, in this section VARs of individual Euro Area countries are used to estimate the effects of shocks in the rest of the Euro Area on the individual Member States. In addition, we estimate how shocks in the three largest Member States (Germany, France and Italy) affect the rest of the Euro Area. We focus the analysis on spillovers from fiscal policies.

A number of issues concerning spillovers are relevant at the disaggregated level in the Euro Area: (i) How do developments in the rest of the euro-area affect the individual Member States? This regards in particular the spillovers from output, inflation and fiscal shocks in the rest of the Euro Area. (ii) What are the spillovers from the short-term interest rate / monetary policy changes by the ECB / changes in the euro exchange rate on individual counties? (iii) How do adjustments outside the Euro Area affect the individual Member States? For the three largest Euro Area countries, Germany, France and Italy, we also analyse (iv) the spillovers from fiscal shocks in these countries on macroeconomic variables in the rest of the Euro Area.

To analyse these issues, it is necessary to define for each country j the output gap, fiscal balance and inflation rate in the rest of the Euro Area (i.e. the Euro Area aggregate excluding country j). These variables were calculated using the set of (time-varying) GDP weights referred to above when discussing Euro Area aggregates. Obviously, for small countries the difference between Euro Area aggregates and their country "rest of the Euro Area" aggregates are very small; only for the set of the three large Euro Area countries, this distinction between total Euro Area and rest of the Euro Area is more substantial as each of the large countries forms a significant part of the Euro Area. This point is also seen in Table 2.3 of the Appendix that provides the contemporaneous correlations between Euro Area countries (suffix _J) and correlations between Euro Area countries and the Euro Area aggregate (suffix_EA) vis-à-vis the rest of the Euro Area aggregates of each country (suffix_REA) for the output gap, inflation and fiscal balances.

The correlations of a country's output gap with the rest of the Euro Area aggregate varies between 0.30 in the case of Finland and 0.84 in

France, according to panel (a). The degree of inflation co-movement is in many countries even higher than output co-movement as can be seen from the correlations between inflation in the Euro Area countries and inflation in the rest of the Euro Area according to panel (b). Fiscal policy displays the lowest correlations (see panel (c)): not only are the correlations between countries in most cases relatively low, also the correlation between the fiscal balance of country j and that in the rest of the Euro Area is typically lower than in the cases of output and inflation. The lowest correlation is seen for Germany. Idiosyncratic factors such as German reunification may explain this observation to some extent.

To determine the spillovers outlined in Chapter 1, for each Euro Area country a VAR model was estimated that includes as endogenous variables the output gap, the fiscal balance, the current account and inflation of country j together with the output gap, fiscal balance and inflation in the rest of the Euro Area as well as the Euro Area short-term interest rate. Exogenous variables in the individual country VAR models are: the increase in oil prices, OIL, the growth in world trade, WTR, the depreciation of the euro exchange rate, DEPREUR, and the time dummy DUM_EUR that captures any shift effects from the start of EMU on January 1, 1999. In the case of Germany, in addition a shift dummy for German reunification is included, taking a value of 1 as of January 1, 1990.

$$\begin{bmatrix} \mathrm{YGAP\_J} \\ \mathrm{NLGY\_J} \\ \mathrm{CUAY\_J} \\ \mathrm{INF\_J} \\ \mathrm{YGAPREA\_J} \\ \mathrm{NLGYREA\_J} \\ \mathrm{SIN\_EA} \\ \mathrm{INFREA\_J} \end{bmatrix} = A(L) \begin{bmatrix} e^{\mathrm{YGAP\_J}} \\ e^{\mathrm{NLGY\_J}} \\ e^{\mathrm{CUAY\_J}} \\ e^{\mathrm{INF\_J}} \\ e^{\mathrm{YGAPREA\_J}} \\ e^{\mathrm{NLGYREA\_J}} \\ e^{\mathrm{SIN\_EA}} \\ e^{\mathrm{INFREA\_J}} \end{bmatrix} + D \begin{bmatrix} \mathrm{OIL} \\ \mathrm{WTR} \\ \mathrm{DEPREUR} \\ \mathrm{DUM\_EUR} \end{bmatrix} \tag{2.3}$$

Lag lengths tests find that in practically all cases a VAR model with one lag is preferred and for simplicity and consistency, the model with one lag is therefore estimated for all countries, so that for all Member States exactly the same model structure is used, as noted earlier. Any difference between countries is therefore the result of different transmissions of shocks, rather than different model structures (e.g. lags, variables).

Fig. 2.3 shows for each country in the Euro Area the IRFs of 1% shocks to (i) output in the rest of the Euro Area (YGAPREA, column 1), (ii) the fiscal balance in the rest of the Euro Area (NLGYREA, column 2), (iii) the Euro Area short-term interest rate (SIN_EA, column 3), (iv) inflation in the rest of the Euro Area (INFREA, column 4). We are interested in the effects of these shocks on country j's output (YGAP, row 1), fiscal balance (NLGY, row 2), current account (CUAY, row 3) and inflation (INF, row 4).

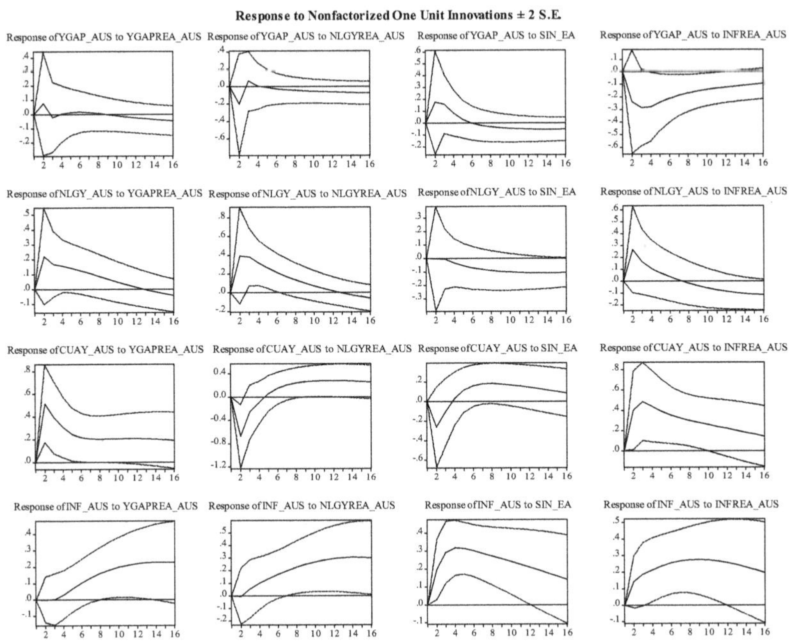

(a) Austria

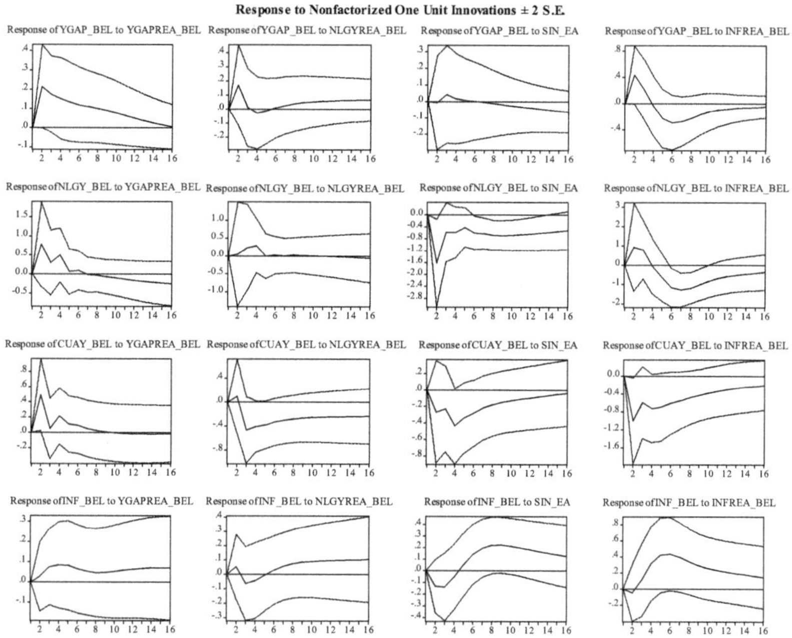

(b) Belgium

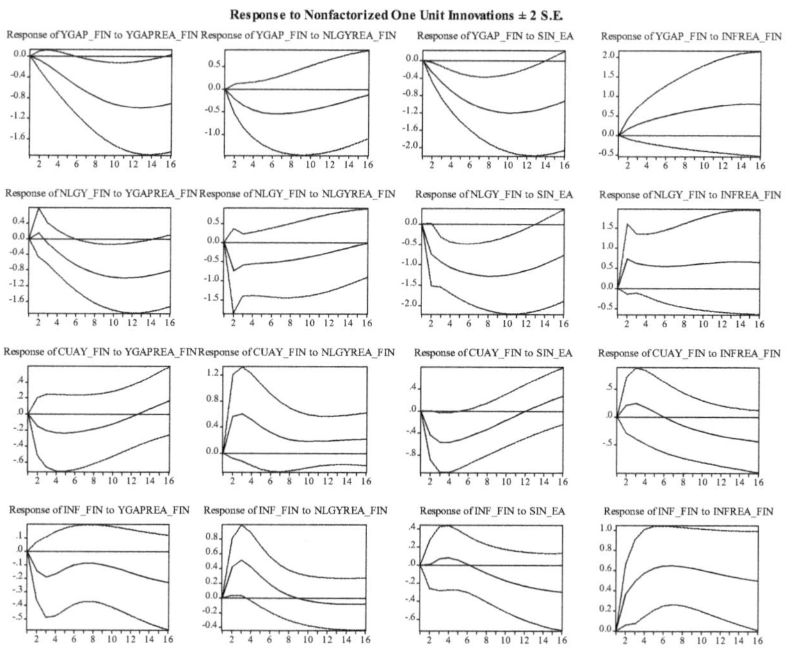

(c) Finland

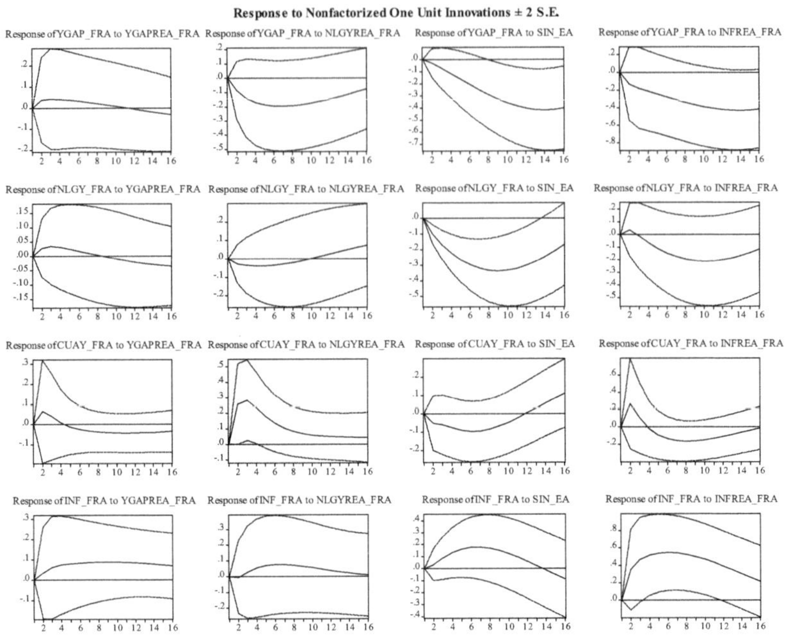

(d) France

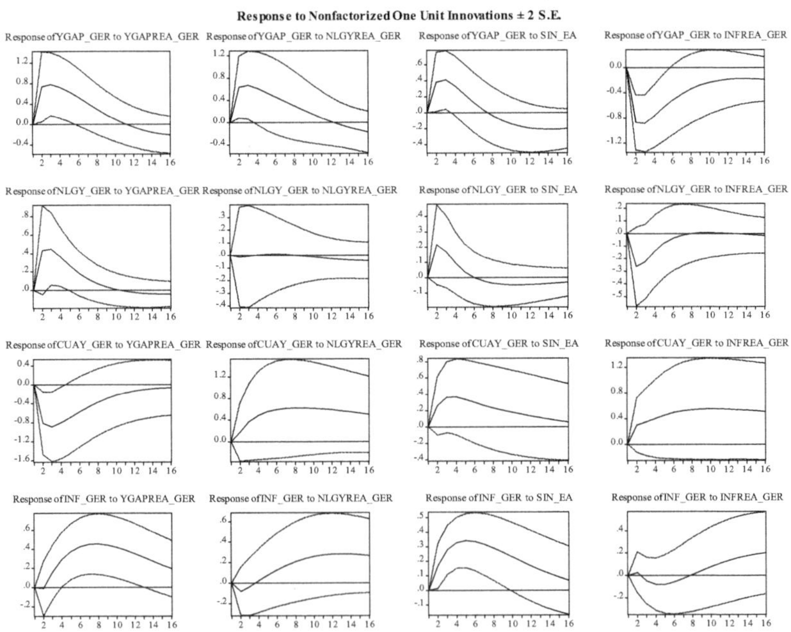

(e) Germany

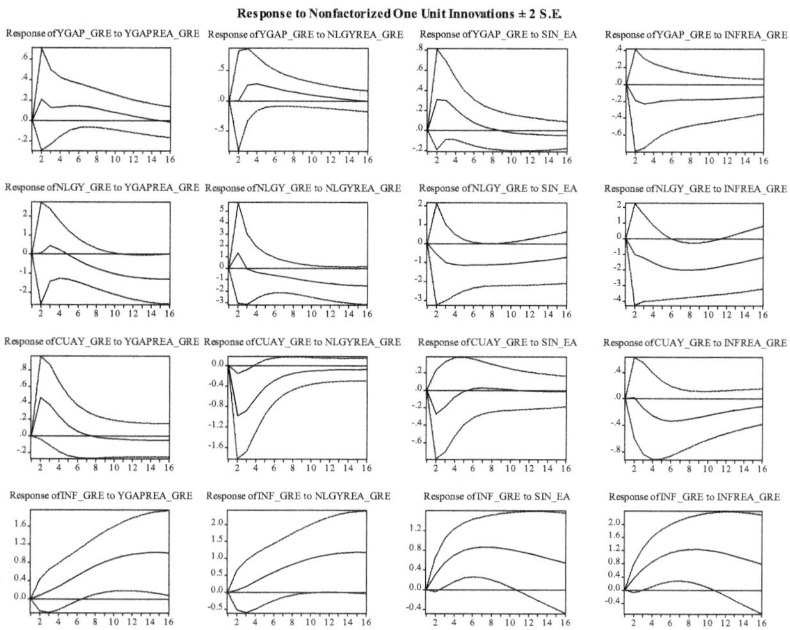

(f) Greece

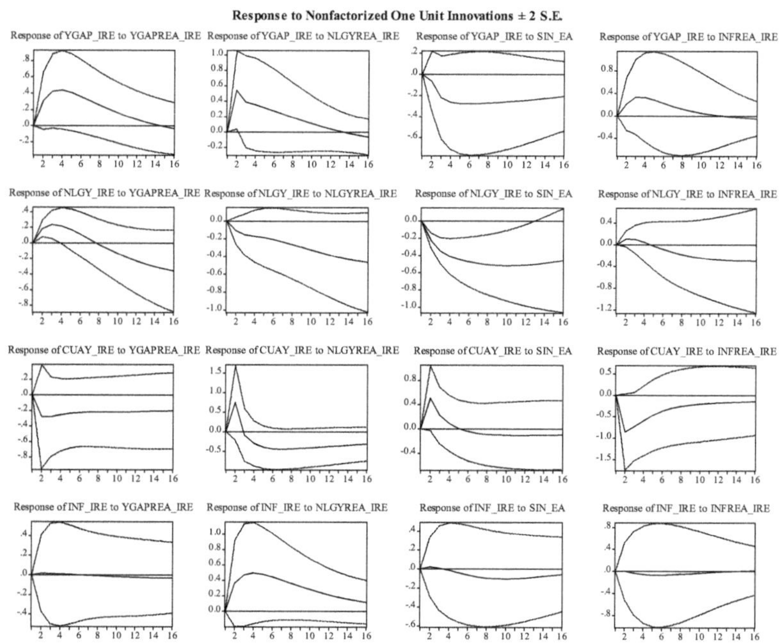

(g) Ireland

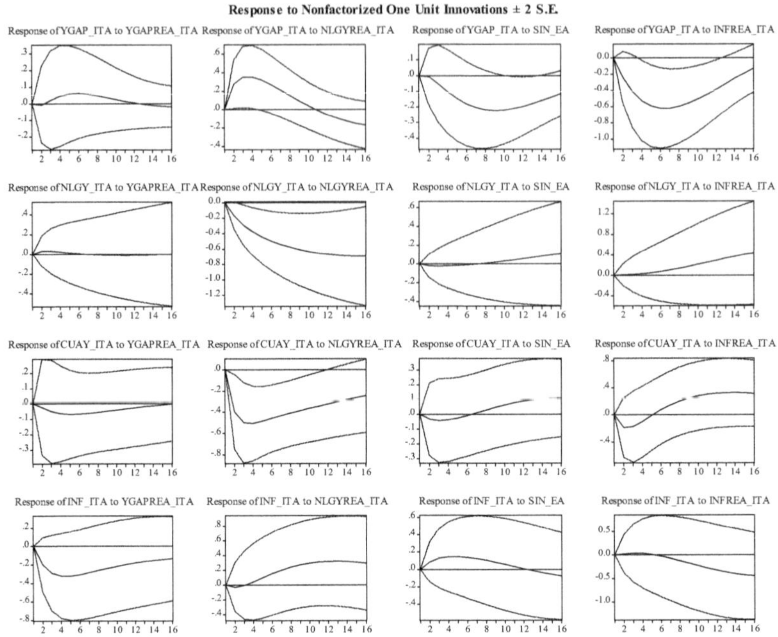

(h) Italy

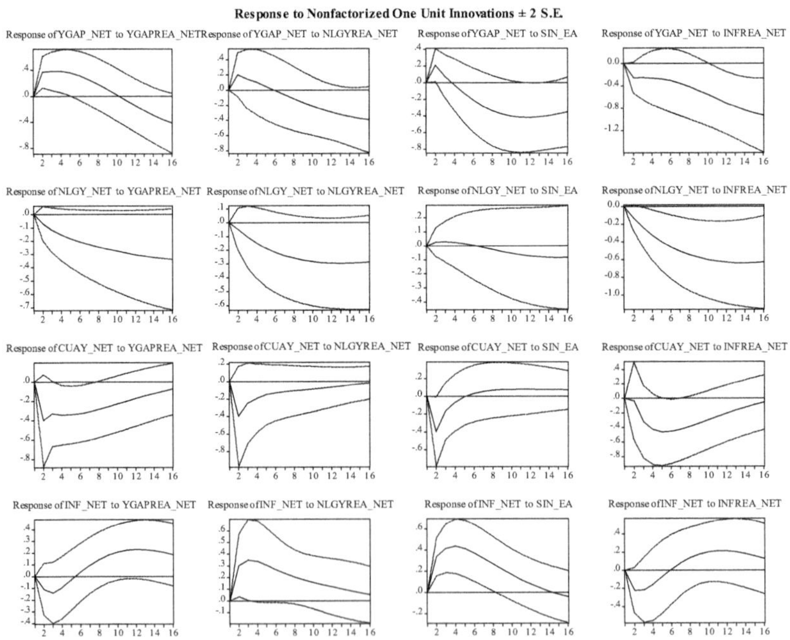

(i) Netherlands

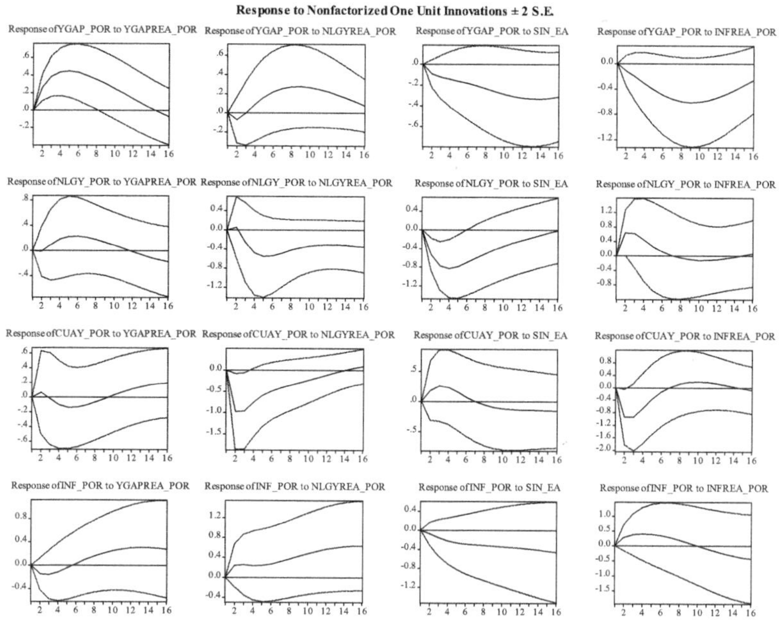

(j) Portugal

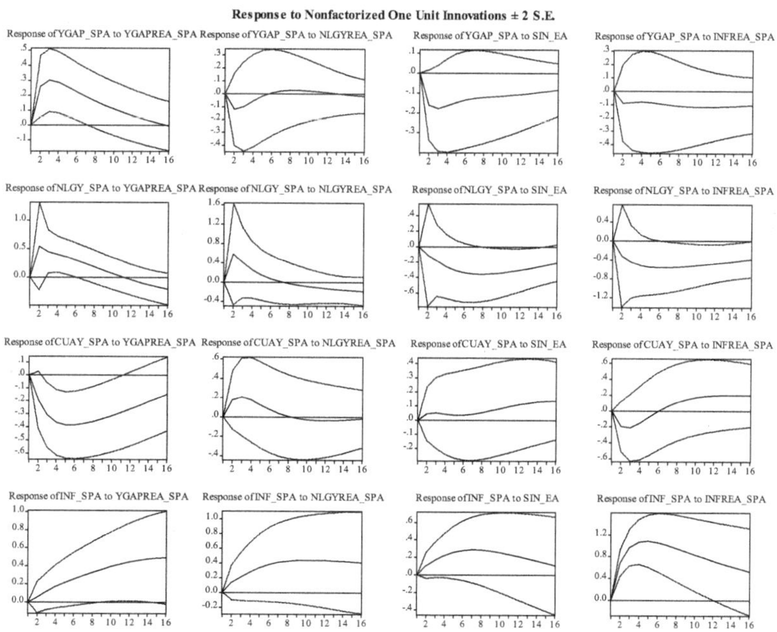

(k) Spain

Fig. 2.3. Spillovers from the (rest of the) Euro Area on individual countries

Fig. 2.3 provides a number of insights into the various spillovers that have been identified in Chapter 1. In particular, we obtain (i) in almost all cases positive output spillovers of an output shock in the rest of the Euro Area on domestic output, fiscal balances (reflecting the workings of automatic stabilizers) and domestic net exports (reflecting the spillover effects through intra-Euro Area trade). Next, we also find in most cases, (ii) positive spillovers of an increase in inflation in the rest of the Euro Area on domestic inflation. Also, the effects of (iii) an increase in the fiscal balance in the rest of the Euro Area and (iv) an increase of the common short-term interest rate on domestic output, inflation and the fiscal balance can be assessed, here we see considerably more cross-country differences in effects produced by fiscal shocks in the rest of the Euro Area and shocks to the common interest rate. Shocks to the common short-term interest rate have in most cases a negative effect on fiscal balances, suggesting an important spillover effect from this mechanism.

In the case of *Austria*, in particular positive inflation spillovers are present. Interest rate shocks mainly affect inflation: the effects on output or the fiscal balance are smaller. Interestingly, a fiscal balance shock in the rest of the Euro Area tends to induce changes in the same direction to the Austrian fiscal balance. The model of *Belgium* finds substantial output and inflation spillovers. The Belgian fiscal balance improves in the short-run in response to higher output in the rest of the Euro Area, and it is strongly negatively affected by interest rate increases. Most likely, this latter effect is explained by a relatively high debt level over the sample period. Higher interest rates burden the fiscal balance because of higher interest rate payments. *Finland* is outlying in the sense that there is no evidence of positive output spillovers from the rest of the Euro Area on Finnish output. Compared with other countries, the evidence for spillovers on the Finnish economy from the rest of the Euro Area are weaker in most cases as suggests the observation that the sign of the effects often changes over time and that the confidence bands are rather large. The interest rate spillovers on Finnish output and inflation spillovers are, however, substantial.

In the case of *France*, there is evidence of small positive output and larger inflation spillovers. The fiscal balance is also positively affected by output, fiscal shocks and inflation shocks in the rest of the Euro Area. Higher interest rates tend to reduce the fiscal balance substantially. The model of *Germany* finds positive spillovers from the rest of the Euro Area on German output and (to a lesser extent) inflation. In contrast to the other countries, higher interest rates tend to improve the German fiscal balance in the short run, as if the German fiscal policy-makers were disciplined by higher interest rates. German fiscal balances are also irresponsive to changes in the fiscal balance in the rest of the Euro Area. The improvement of German net exports after an inflation shock in the rest of the Euro Area may reflect the improved competitiveness from such a shock makes German products more competitive and which boosts its intra-Euro Area exports. *Greece* displays also considerable output, fiscal and interest rate spillovers. The effect of inflation spillovers is relatively strong: inflation in the rest of the Euro Area seems to have a substantial impact on Greek inflation

Ireland as a small open-economy is in particular marked by positive output spillovers; inflation spillovers are, however, basically absent; the fiscal balance is negatively affected by an increase in the short-term interest rate as we have seen in most other countries. For *Italy*, we find relatively small spillovers, when compared to most other countries the output and inflation spillovers, and the interest rate fiscal spillovers are quite small. The model of the *Netherlands* displays robust output and inflation spillovers. Interest rate increases tend to deteriorate output but hardly affect the fiscal balance. Spillovers are also important in the case of *Portugal.* Output, inflation and interest shocks in the rest of the Euro Area spillover quite strongly to the Portugese economy. In the case of *Spain*, there is again evidence of strong positive output and inflation spillovers. In addition, there is evidence of a small negative effect from interest rates on output and the fiscal balance as well as a negative effect from interest rate increases on the *Spain*'s fiscal balance.

Summarising, positive inflation and output shocks in the rest of the Euro Area also lead often to higher inflation and output in the domestic economy. The evidence of these positive output and inflation spillovers is found to be relatively consistent and convincing. In a number of cases restrictive fiscal policies in the rest of the Euro Area reduce output in the domestic economy; in some cases there is hardly any effect or the effect is positive. This is also the case for a restrictive monetary policy shock that raises the common interest rate. There is in several cases evidence of a spillover from interest rates on fiscal balances.

Interestingly, there are not only important similarities but also considerable differences between countries in terms of signs and sizes of the various spillover effects - note, moreover, that for each Member State the same model structure (exogenous variables, lags of the VAR) and practically the same sample period was used in the estimation, so that differences cannot be due to these factors -. This suggests that there are strong heterogeneities between Euro Area countries in the spillovers, reflecting differences in economic structures, macroeconomic shock characteristics and fiscal policy reactions. E.g. for the fiscal spillovers many factors such as the size and openness of a country, the size of the fiscal multipliers and the estimated persistence of the fiscal shock may be important. The heterogeneities between countries suggest that caution is needed when analysing the effects of shocks at the aggregate Euro Area level as in Sect. 2.3 and extending the conclusions of the aggregate analysis to the individual Member States. Also more in general, the heterogeneities indicate that a common monetary policy and harmonized fiscal policies in the Euro Area affect individual countries quite differently and are necessarily second best to a set of monetary and fiscal policies that would be set based optimally from a perspective of the individual Member State.

In the model, external spillovers are also present and measured by the impact of a depreciation of the euro, the change in oil prices and world trade on the output, fiscal balance, current account balance and inflation in the Euro Area countries. It is assumed that for the individual countries these variables are exogenous. In most cases an increase in the oil price tends to decrease output, the current account balance and the fiscal balance and contribute to higher inflation. A depreciation of the euro has in most countries a small positive effect on output and inflation. In addition, in a significant number of countries output increases if world trade increases. Apart from a few exceptions, the general picture suggests that such external spillovers on individual Euro Area countries from oil price changes, changes in the euro exchange rate and output outside the Euro Area (here represented by the US) is a source of spillovers that does matter also at the disaggregated level and, moreover, that countries vary to some degree in the sign and size of these spillovers.

A final aspect that needs to be addressed in this chapter concerns the spillovers from shocks in the three largest Euro Area countries on the rest of the Euro Area. The country VARs that were estimated in (2.2) can also be used to analyse these spillovers since they determine how shocks in Germany, Italy and France affect the respective rest of the Euro Area. Fig. 2.4 displays the spillovers from output, the fiscal balance and inflation shocks in, respectively, Germany, France and Italy on output (row 1), the fiscal balance (row 2), and inflation (row 4) in the respective rest of the Euro Area. Also the effect on the short-run interest rate in the Euro Area is shown (row 3).

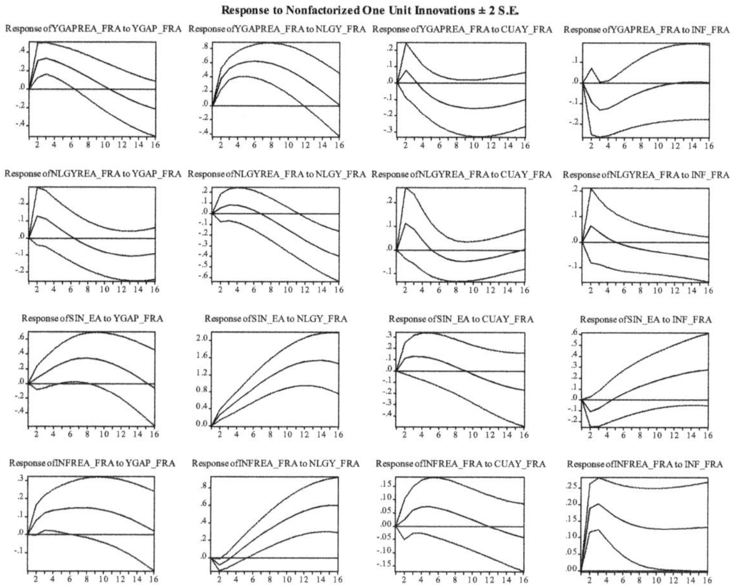

(a) France

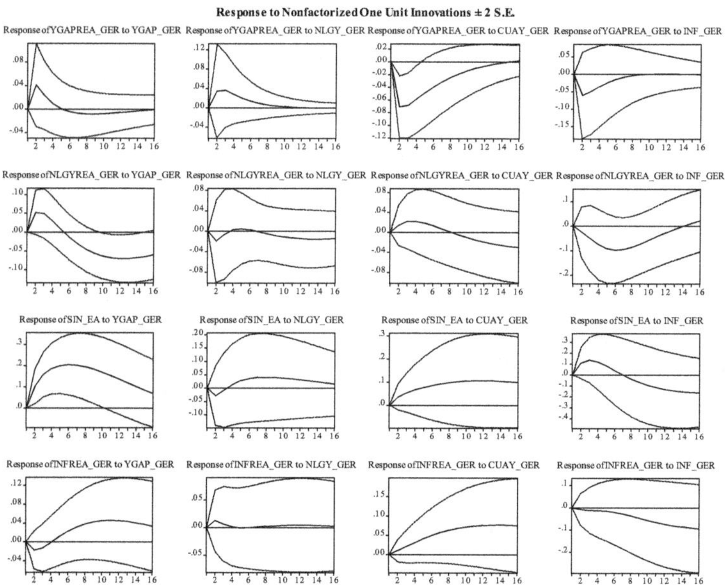

(b) Germany

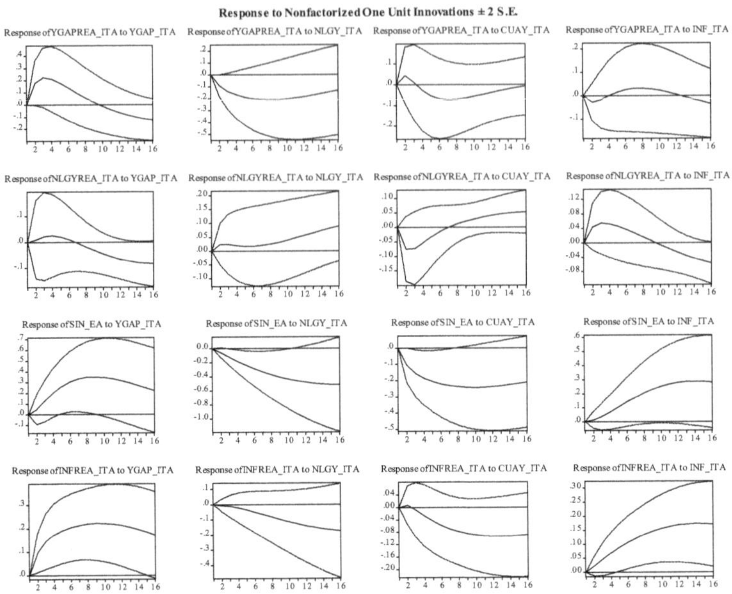

(c) Italy

Fig. 2.4. Spillovers from France, Germany and Italy on the rest of the Euro Area

According to these estimations, the output and inflation spillovers from shocks in France and Italy to the rest of the Euro Area appear to be larger than those from Germany. We observe that the spillovers from France and Italy are often comparable and somewhat larger than the spill-overs produced by the same German shocks. Possible explanations for this seemingly counterintuitive outcome could lay in the possibility possible that German reunification and the subsequent fiscal adjustments as well as the fundamental process of reforms and restructuring in the German economy caused diverging developments in Germany as compared to the rest of the Euro Area during the sample. Also the stronger orientation of the German economy towards world markets may reduce the intra Euro Area spillovers produced by German shocks when compared to the same French or Italian shock. The short-term interest rate in the Euro Area does not seem to be strongly affected by individual fiscal balance shocks in Germany. This is in line with the conclusion of the aggregate model where we also did not see a substantial effect of aggregate fiscal shocks on interest rates.

2.5 Conclusion

In an integrated monetary and economic union such as the Euro Area, budgetary and other types of spillovers are likely to be important and complex. The short-run transmissions and spillovers of budgetary policy in the Euro Area are working through several different channels. These include not only the traditional direct output and inflation spillovers via net trade flows, but also channels operating via the common interest rate (and monetary policy) and the euro exchange rate.

The multitude of spillovers and complex dynamics suggests that in particular a flexible econometric approach like VAR models is useful if one is seeking to estimate spillovers in the Euro Area. In this chapter we have therefore estimated VAR models to analyse a number of spillovers effects that were considered important in the Euro Area.

First, the spillovers at the level of the aggregate Euro Area are analysed. The effects of a change in the Euro Area fiscal balance on output, net exports, interest rates, the euro exchange rate and inflation in the Euro Area are estimated. In the aggregate model there is some - albeit weak - evidence of direct spillovers between monetary and fiscal policies in the Euro Area. In particular, a positive interest rate shock reduces the fiscal balance. A positive shock to the fiscal balance tends to reduce the interest rates in the short run, but this effect is rather small and imprecisely estimated. Apart from such direct spillovers, there are a number of indirect connections between monetary and fiscal policies, running e.g. through output, inflation and depreciation of the euro. These indirect interdependencies are also analysed in the model. Finally, external factors -oil prices and US output- are another important source of spillovers on the aggregate Euro Area economy.

Second, the disaggregated analysis indicates that behind the aggregate analysis of the Euro Area economy, there is a whole multitude of country-specific adjustments at work. The analysis at the disaggregated level finds that the effects of fiscal policy in the Euro Area differ substantially between countries. The most important results are: (i) there are positive direct output and inflation spillovers from the rest of the Euro Area on individual Member States. (ii) The spillovers from a fiscal policy shock in the rest of the Euro Area varies largely across Member States. (iii) External shocks in the form of oil price changes, changes in the euro exchange rate and fluctuations in the US output gap induce spillovers to individual countries. The timing and size of effects varies across countries. (iv) For the three large Euro Area countries, Germany, France and Italy, spillover effects of fiscal policy on the rest of the Euro Area were estimated. In this way, the effects of a fiscal shock in e.g. Germany on the rest of the Euro

Area were determined. Spillovers from a fiscal shock in Germany on the rest of the Euro Area seem to be somewhat smaller than spillovers from a fiscal shock in France or Italy, but this result might be driven by significant changes not only to the economic structure but also to fiscal polices in Germany after reunification.

Appendix: Characteristics of the dataset

The definitions of the variables used in the analysis and the data sources that have been used are given in the following table.

Table 2.1. Data definitions and sources

Variable	Definition	Unit	Source
GDP	Gross Domestic Product	Mio EUR	OECD MEI, QNA
PGDP	GDP deflator	Index (1995=100)	OECD MEI, QNA
SIN	Short Term Interest Rate	%	OECD MEI, QNA
OIL	Oil price	US dollar per barrel	IMF IFS
CUA	Current account	Mio EUR	OECD MEI, QNA
NLG	Net Lending Government	Mio EUR	IMF IFS
YGAP	Output gap	%	OECD MEI, QNA
INF	Inflation Rate	%	OECD MEI, QNA
DEPREUR	Depreciation euro exch .rate	% p.a. EUR/USD	OECD MEI, QNA
DUM_EUR	EMU dummy	= 1 after 99:I	
WTR	World Trade	Billion USD	IMF IFS

The following sample period was used when estimating the SVAR for the various countries:

Table 2.2. Sample period VAR model estimations

Country	Sample / number of observations
Euro Area	1981:III - 2003:IV, 90 observations
Austria	1981:II - 2003:IV, 91 observations
Belgium	1981:II - 2003:IV, 91 observations
Finland	1981:II - 2003:IV, 91 observations
France	1981:II - 2003:IV, 91 observations
Germany	1981:II - 2003:IV, 91 observations
Greece	1981:IV - 2003:IV, 89 observations
Ireland	1981:II - 2003:IV, 90 observations
Italy	1981:II - 2003:IV, 90 observations
Netherlands	1981:II - 2003:IV, 91 observations
Portugal	1981:III - 2003:IV, 90 observations
Spain	1981:II - 2003:IV, 91 observations

Table 2.3. Cross-country correlations of output, inflation and fiscal deficits in the Euro Area

	AUS	BEL	EA	FIN	FRA	GER	GRE	IRE	ITA	NET	POR	SPA
AUS	1.00	0.24	0.37	-0.08	0.24	0.34	0.28	0.14	0.36	0.22	0.10	0.07
BEL	0.24	1.00	0.68	0.31	0.70	0.57	0.36	0.60	0.58	0.41	0.53	0.52
EA	0.37	0.68	1.00	0.35	0.90	0.95	0.37	0.71	0.81	0.69	0.63	0.68
REA	**0.33**	**0.67**	**-**	**0.30**	**0.84**	**0.82**	**0.36**	**0.70**	**0.75**	**0.62**	**0.62**	**0.65**
FIN	-0.08	0.31	0.35	1.00	0.23	0.28	0.07	0.52	0.46	-0.05	0.31	0.47
FRA	0.24	0.70	0.90	0.23	1.00	0.79	0.31	0.65	0.74	0.54	0.76	0.67
GER	0.34	0.57	0.95	0.28	0.79	1.00	0.33	0.56	0.65	0.64	0.49	0.57
GRE	0.28	0.36	0.37	0.07	0.31	0.33	1.00	0.22	0.30	0.23	0.19	0.16
IRE	0.14	0.60	0.71	0.52	0.65	0.56	0.22	1.00	0.79	0.46	0.58	0.56
ITA	0.36	0.58	0.81	0.46	0.74	0.65	0.30	0.79	1.00	0.44	0.66	0.54
NET	0.22	0.41	0.69	-0.05	0.54	0.64	0.23	0.46	0.44	1.00	0.25	0.42
POR	0.10	0.53	0.63	0.31	0.76	0.49	0.19	0.58	0.66	0.25	1.00	0.62
SPA	0.07	0.52	0.68	0.47	0.67	0.57	0.16	0.56	0.54	0.42	0.62	1.00

(a) correlations of output gaps

	AUS	BEL	EA	FIN	FRA	GER	GRE	IRE	ITA	NET	POR	SPA
AUS	1.00	0.74	0.83	0.59	0.76	0.70	0.74	0.59	0.79	0.39	0.66	0.78
BEL	0.74	1.00	0.88	0.67	0.86	0.68	0.77	0.68	0.81	0.27	0.81	0.85
EA	0.83	0.88	1.00	0.78	0.97	0.78	0.86	0.75	0.97	0.34	0.84	0.95
REA	**0.83**	**0.87**	**-**	**0.77**	**0.92**	**0.66**	**0.85**	**0.74**	**0.93**	**0.30**	**0.84**	**0.94**
FIN	0.59	0.67	0.78	1.00	0.79	0.45	0.74	0.63	0.81	0.20	0.73	0.76
FRA	0.76	0.86	0.97	0.79	1.00	0.62	0.78	0.82	0.96	0.35	0.83	0.93
GER	0.70	0.68	0.78	0.45	0.62	1.00	0.71	0.45	0.63	0.19	0.60	0.69
GRE	0.74	0.77	0.86	0.74	0.78	0.71	1.00	0.43	0.84	0.04	0.87	0.86
IRE	0.59	0.68	0.75	0.63	0.82	0.45	0.43	1.00	0.74	0.49	0.52	0.67
ITA	0.79	0.81	0.97	0.81	0.96	0.63	0.84	0.74	1.00	0.30	0.82	0.92
NET	0.39	0.27	0.34	0.20	0.35	0.19	0.04	0.49	0.30	1.00	0.00	0.21
POR	0.66	0.81	0.84	0.73	0.83	0.60	0.87	0.52	0.82	0.00	1.00	0.91
SPA	0.78	0.85	0.95	0.76	0.93	0.69	0.86	0.67	0.92	0.21	0.91	1.00

(b) correlations of inflation rates

	AUS	BEL	EA	FIN	FRA	GER	GRE	IRE	ITA	NET	POR	SPA
AUS	1.00	0.36	0.65	0.33	0.36	0.10	0.29	0.31	0.60	0.46	0.10	0.34
BEL	0.36	1.00	0.71	0.09	-0.06	0.22	0.57	0.82	0.72	0.69	0.72	0.49
EA	0.65	0.71	1.00	0.45	0.44	0.45	0.53	0.67	0.87	0.80	0.45	0.63
REA	**0.62**	**0.62**	**-**	**0.40**	**0.25**	**0.22**	**0.48**	**0.66**	**0.68**	**0.76**	**0.44**	**0.52**
FIN	0.33	0.09	0.45	1.00	0.67	0.09	-0.16	0.00	0.24	0.15	-0.13	0.29
FRA	0.36	-0.06	0.44	0.67	1.00	0.13	-0.14	-0.14	0.13	0.14	-0.29	0.28
GER	0.10	0.22	0.45	0.09	0.13	1.00	0.18	0.27	0.16	0.27	0.26	0.16
GRE	0.29	0.57	0.53	-0.16	-0.14	0.18	1.00	0.61	0.58	0.53	0.60	0.28
IRE	0.31	0.82	0.67	0.00	-0.14	0.27	0.61	1.00	0.71	0.78	0.91	0.49
ITA	0.60	0.72	0.87	0.24	0.13	0.16	0.58	0.71	1.00	0.82	0.48	0.44
NET	0.46	0.69	0.80	0.15	0.14	0.27	0.53	0.78	0.82	1.00	0.54	0.44
POR	0.10	0.72	0.45	-0.13	-0.29	0.26	0.60	0.91	0.48	0.54	1.00	0.39
SPA	0.34	0.49	0.63	0.29	0.28	0.16	0.28	0.49	0.44	0.44	0.39	1.00

(c) correlations of fiscal balances

References

Bayoumi, T. and B. Eichengreen (1992), Shocking aspects of European monetary integration. In F. Torres and F. Giavazzi (eds.), Adjustment and growth in the European Monetary Union. Cambridge University Press, 1993, p.193-229.

Bernanke, B. and A. Blinder (1992), The federal funds rate and the channels of monetary transmission, American Economic Review, vol.82 (4), p.901-921.

Blanchard, O. (1990), A traditional interpretation of macroeconomic fluctuations, American Economic Review, vol.79, no. 5, p.1146-1164.

Blanchard, O. and D. Quah (1989), The dynamic effects of aggregate demand and aggregate supply shocks, American Economic Review, vol.79, no. 4, p.655-673.

Gali, J. (1992), How well does the IS-LM model fit post-war U.S. data, Quarterly Journal of Economics, vol.107, p.975–1009.

Gerlach, S. and F. Smets (1995), The monetary transmission mechanism: Evidence from the G7 Countries, BIS Discussion Paper no.26.

Gordon, D. and E. Leeper (1994), The dynamic impacts of monetary policy: An exercise in tentative identification, Journal of Political Economy, vol.102(6), p.1228-1247.

Kim, S. (2001), Effects of monetary policy shocks on the trade balance in small open European countries, Economic Letters, vol.71, p.197-203.

Leeper, E., C. Sims and T. Zha (1996), What does monetary policy do? Brookings Papers on Economic Activity, vol.1996, no.2, p.1-63.

Rudebusch, G. (1998), Do measures of monetary policy in a VAR make sense?, International Economic Review, vol.39, no.4, p.933-940.

Sims, C. (1992), Interpreting the macroeconomic time series facts: The effects of monetary policy, European Economic Review, vol.36, no.5, p.975-1000.

3 Budgetary spillovers and long-term interest rates

Peter Claeys

3.1 Introduction

The effect of fiscal expansions on interest rates has commanded enormous theoretical interest, but the hypothesis of crowding out has received only some – albeit not very robust – empirical endorsement. Most economists would nevertheless agree with the position that consolidating public finances reduces pressure on long-term interest rates and will be conducive to economic growth in the long run by stimulating private investment (Gale and Orszag, 2003). The crowding out premise is also an important motivation for the consolidation of public finances, as is evident from the policies advocated by both the European Commission and the European Central Bank.

Underlying the policy paradigm in the Economic and Monetary Union is the fear of a spillover of undisciplined fiscal policies on other Member States' policies. Capital flows between economically integrated economies offset interest rate differentials that follow upon an increase in the supply of government bonds. Fiscal deficits need not be financed by domestic financial resources. The budgetary decision of one government therefore affects the financing conditions of other governments. This spillover is a purely pecuniary externality, and would not really command international coordination. Nonetheless, fiscal authorities face different incentives in a monetary union. Basically, free riding between governments distorts any disciplinary incentive of higher interest rates on the issuance of more government bonds. This could lead to excessive debt accumulation, and eventually higher interest rates and inflation in the case of a monetary bailout (Beetsma and Bovenberg, 1999). Budget constraints indeed soften when the fiscal relations between governments are not clearly spelled out. In EMU, these indirect effects of debt spillover have been contained with the no bailout clause, which is enshrined in Articles 101 and 103 of the Treaty of Nice, and prohibits overdraft facilities from the ECB or the assumption of national commitments, by other Member States. Keeping the national fiscal houses in order is probably a sufficient condition to eliminate the distortion caused by free riding and to discipline national fiscal policy. The numerical rules of the Stability and Growth Pact imply a debt target, and some reform proposals on the Pact have argued for a stronger focus on debt consolidation. But the negative coordination mechanism of deficit reduction should probably be conceived of as preempting fiscal bailouts.

There is little evidence for European countries, and there are even fewer studies that examine the spillover that fiscal expansions have on long-term interest rates across borders. Little headway has been made in the modelling of open economies with a relevant role for fiscal stabilisation policies. New Keynesian models of this guise have mainly been developed for the purpose of analysing monetary policy issues. Only recently has the analysis been extended to more elaborate specifications of fiscal policy (Beetsma and Jensen, 2004; Ganelli, 2005). Hence, we have little theoretical guidance as to the interest rate effects of fiscal policy across borders. The aim of this chapter is to offer an empirical framework to test both the crowding out and spillover hypotheses.

We do so by building on the literature that examines the effects of fiscal policy with small VAR models. We analyse the gross effects that fiscal shocks have on domestic long-term interest rates. Accordingly, we specify a simple dynamic empirical VAR that is supplemented with rules-based fiscal policy -by including both deficits and debt- and long-term interest rates. We examine crowding out with this 'domestic' SVAR in a couple of European countries and the Euro Area as a whole. We find crowding out effects to be insignificant. We argue that this is due to a misspecification of the 'domestic' model that ignores the spillover of fiscal policy. We modify the empirical model accordingly. Basically, we net out the spillover effects of public deficit and debt accumulation on a country's interest rate by benchmarking the model on aggregate Euro Area conditions. Spillover indeed masks the effects of fiscal policy on long-term interest rates, even if its size is small and mostly related to financial markets. Due to data limitations, we cannot examine the effects of EMU on the relations between Member States' fiscal policies.

The chapter is structured as follows. Sect. 3.2 makes the case for our VAR modelling choice on the basis of a critical literature review. The pro and cons of the specification and identification of the SVAR model are detailed in Sect. 3.3. The empirical results on gross crowding out effects of fiscal expansion follow in Sect. 3.4, while Sect. 3.5 investigates the spillover of fiscal policies. The final section summarises the main results, discusses some implications for the design of fiscal policy coordination in EMU, and ends with some policy recommendations.

3.2 Deficits and interest rates: is there any robust evidence?

Many economists probably consider Ricardian Equivalence as a reasonable starting point for the theoretical analysis of the effects of fiscal policy. Few would endorse it as a realistic description of fiscal policy, however. The view that private savings do not fully offset the change in public savings is not based on a firm empirical rejection of Ricardian Equivalence, for this hypothesis is not directly testable. Plenty of empirical studies have therefore examined the alternative hypothesis as to whether fiscal policy has any real economic effects.

In the causal chain from budgetary deficits to private investment only the first link running from a fiscal expansion to interest rates has usually been examined. Recent evidence seems to converge on at least some crowding out effect in practice of fiscal expansions on long-term interest rates. However, no consensus has been reached (Elmendorf and Mankiw, 1999). The effect of higher interest rates on capital accumulation has been much less the object of study. The evidence for this second link in the chain has remained much more problematic.[1] In the following, we take the usual shortcut in this literature of looking into the intermediate effect of fiscal policy on interest rates, and not the final effect on private investment.

3.2.1 Static versus dynamic models

Interest rates have typically been explained by including fiscal balances among the regressors in a single equation – next to short-term interest rates, inflation and other relevant variables – often in a panel framework. This specification derives from a partial equilibrium 'loanable funds' model in which the interest rate adjusts so as to maintain equality between the supply and demand of bonds (Cebula, 1998). Alternative specifications are based on intertemporal models of saving behaviour (Laubach, 2003). The large number of studies that employ various definitions of government deficit or debt, interest rates, econometric approach and data sets can basi-

---

[1] See Alesina et al. (1999) or Friedman (2005) though.

cally give support for any possible view on crowding out.[2] Most of the empirical work has been done on US data, but some of the studies on EU countries reach similar conclusions (Knot and De Haan, 1995; Knot, 1996).

The factors that determine interest rates are of course plenty, and long-term structural factors probably account for much more of the variation in interest rates. But a major reason for the ambiguous effect is due to the static specification of the relation between deficits and interest rates in these models. Government bonds are actually traded on financial markets that are forward-looking. The anticipation of upcoming deficits may therefore result in higher long-term rates, as the direct crowding out on short-term rates accumulates in long-term rates via the expectations hypothesis. As a consequence, the exclusion of the shorter end of the term structure could bias the findings (Bernheim, 1987). Expectations of higher future deficits would show up directly in a steeper yield curve, as future short-term rates rise. Correspondingly, the correct measure of the deficit need be employed. Those studies that include expectations of future fiscal developments – for example, by using the fiscal forecasts of the Congressional Budget Office (CBO) in the United States – unanimously find significantly positive effects of expected deficits on expectations of interest rate moves (Laubach, 2003).[3] Some studies capture interest rate expectations by modelling the effects on the entire term structure, and thereby obviate the need for modelling the determinants of interest rates (Reinhart and Sack, 2000; Lindé, 2001 or Canzoneri et al., 2002). Another way of capturing agents' expectations is through the 'news' approach to public announcements of fiscal policy changes (Afonso and Strauch, 2003). Event studies try to detect the impact of unexpected changes in fiscal policy on financial markets, much like the narrative VAR approach of Ramey and Shapiro (1998).[4]

Any direct relation between interest rates and fiscal balances is

[2] See the references in Barth et al. (1991), Gale and Orszag (2003) or the European Commission (2004).

[3] The scarcity of such data for European countries prohibits a straightforward extension. The European Commission produces forecasts for year $t+2$ at most. Heppke-Falk and Hüffner (2004) examine the effect on interest swap spreads of deficit forecasts of financial market dealers.

[4] For the USA, Wachtel and Young (1987), Elmendorf (1996) and Kitchen (1996) give a good overview, while Knot (1996) gives a survey of findings for European countries. The literature based on event analyses or micro evidence on the behaviour of bond spreads typically concludes that fiscal policy does matter but its effects are quite small. A one per cent increase in the deficit ratio would raise interest rates on government bonds by about 10 basis points on average in the EU.

also obscured by the contemporaneous influence of countercyclical monetary policy, the workings of automatic fiscal stabilisers and any economic effects of fiscal policy itself. In addition, the endogeneity of the fiscal balance to interest rates, via the higher interest payments on outstanding debt obligations, further clouds the direction of causality. For these reasons, the econometric evidence of most reduced form empirical models remains rather inconclusive.[5]

Such effects can only be uncovered in dynamic models. Large macroeconomic models can account for the endogeneity of fiscal balances, but usually embed the consensus opinion of a positive crowding out effect of fiscal deficits on long-term interest rates already. VAR-models have only recently received attention for the analysis of fiscal policy. Importantly, these models control for the contemporaneous effect on interest rates of other macroeconomic variables that are correlated with deficits. Some early VAR applications that rely on Cholesky orderings can be found in Evans (1987a,b), Orr et al. (1995) or Miller and Russek (1996). Evans and Marshall (2002), who investigate the determinants of the variability in the nominal Treasury yield curve with this method, do not find significant contributions of fiscal shocks to interest rates. A more recent application is found in Ardagna et al. (2004), who find rather large crowding out effects in a panel of OECD countries, leading to cumulative 150 basis points rise at a horizon of 10 years. Approaches that identify fiscal shocks following the Blanchard and Perotti (2002) methodology do not always find significant effects on interest rates either. In these studies, only short-term interest rates are examined. However, in models that include both long- and short-term interest rates, significant crowding out effects are obtained. Tavares and Valkanov (2001) do find robust evidence for the impact of fiscal policy on relative bond returns, expressed as the spread of long-term rates over 3-month Treasury bills. Similarly, Canzoneri et al. (2002) include both the Federal Funds rate and the 10 year bond yield in their structural VAR, and find significant and large impact and long-term effects in response to government spending shocks.

The main hurdle in detecting changes in fiscal policy in VARs is that policy shocks need not affect fiscal variables first. The implementation of announced policy changes is subject to lengthy and visible political negotiations that are anticipated by the financial markets and the public at large (Perotti, 2005). Therefore, it is hard to pin down all the information concerning future government actions the public has available. The unexpected component of changes in fiscal variables may bear little relation

[5] The use of fiscal projections or cyclically adjusted balances as in Cebula and Koch (1989) or Kitchen (2002) can remove these effects.

then to projections of future fiscal policies. As the expected fiscal variables are merely extrapolations from past data, they do not account sufficiently for newly available information. Elmendorf (1993) demonstrates the poor performance of VAR-forecasts relative to fiscal projections.

This problem is even more pronounced for the analysis of effects on financial markets. A promising approach is to use financial market information to identify fiscal shocks. Dai and Philippon (2005) impose no-arbitrage restrictions on government bonds markets over the entire term structure and link the latent factors to macroeconomic policies in a structural VAR. An increase in the deficit by one per cent of GDP is found to increase the 10-year rate on government bonds by 41 points.

Another problem in the identification of fiscal policy relates to the strong persistence of fiscal policy changes that consequently build up in the stock of public debt. One way around this problem is to include the fiscal stock variable. The accumulation of deficits in public debt that raise debt permanently would crowd out interest rates considerably, whereas temporary changes that are expected to be undone afterwards may have little impact (Feldstein, 1986; Friedman, 2005). This allows the inclusion of different degrees of persistence of fiscal deficits. VAR models that include debt usually find the direct crowding out effect of debt to be small relative to the impact of deficits (Engen and Hubbard, 2004).[6] Actually, in specifications with public debt the effect on interest rates is often found to be negative (Ardagna et al., 2004). This owes to a portfolio effect and an associated decline in the liquidity premium when the supply of government bonds increases.[7]

If we interpret the higher interest rates following fiscal expansions as the higher rates the government has to offer investors to willingly hold more bonds, the interest rate becomes a direct – probably non-linear – function of debt. There is indeed some evidence for non-linear effects in specifications with debt. Only at higher debt levels do interest rates move significantly (O'Donovan et al., 1996; Conway and Orr, 2002).[8]

---

[6] Paesani et al. (2006) exploit the integration properties of public debt in the USA, Germany and Italy to distinguish the impact on bond yields of persistent trends in fiscal policy from transitory developments.

[7] Caporale and Williams (2002) argue that this portfolio effect is even more pronounced when investors switch from bad quality debt issues to those of more creditworthy issuers, decreasing the yield even if total outstanding debt rises.

[8] Evidence on default premia can be found in Alesina et al. (1992), Favero et al. (1997), Copeland and Jones (2001) or Codogno et al. (2003).

3.2.2 Capital flows and crowding out in open economies

Most of the empirical analysis pertains to US data, and this may provide few insights for EU countries. In open economies that are economically integrated and do not impede trade or financial flows, capital flows move massively so as to offset any domestic interest rate rises following higher bond-financed deficits. In the limit of total capital mobility, these increases are proportional to each country's total indebtedness on the relevant market (Chang, 1990). Yardstick comparisons across governments of bond traders may partially undo this spillover. The accumulation of debt by one government increases the relative creditworthiness of comparable governments.

There is little empirical evidence on these spillover effects. Two different strategies have been adopted. In the first approach, the effect of capital inflows or fiscal developments abroad is netted out from the total domestic crowding out effect. The reasoning is that the domestic effect of fiscal expansions will likely be larger once these international linkages are controlled for. In the reduced form approach, Cebula and Koch (1989) condition the relation between interest rates and deficits on capital inflows. Ardagna et al. (2004) find significant crowding out effects from both domestic and average foreign fiscal expansions in a panel of OECD countries. Faini (2006) considers the fiscal effect on interest rates at home and at EMU level contemporaneously. On a global scale, all spillover effects should cancel out and a significant crowding out effect restored. Tanzi and Lutz (1993) or Ford and Laxton (1999) look into the effects of domestic deficits and debt on global rates.

Alternatively, the spillover can be assessed directly from the effects of deficits and debt on interest rates abroad. Studies in the VAR-tradition have rather looked into the effect of domestic fiscal policy changes on economic variables abroad. Marcellino (2002) or Giuliodori and Beetsma (2005) consider the impact of German fiscal policy on the French and Italian economy[9]. Paesani et al. (2006) take a somewhat different approach by identifying spillover from shocks to bond markets on internationally linked capital markets. This allows the authors to test the direction of the spillover. Changes in fiscal policy in the United States are argued to have a greater influence on bond yields in Europe than vice versa. A similar argument is found in Brook (2003).

---

[9] In a further study, Beetsma et al. (2005) explicitly model the trade channel of fiscal spillover in EU countries.

3.2.3 Monetary integration and crowding out

The spillover of domestic fiscal policies can only be enhanced if different governments borrow in the same currency. In the absence of agreements specifying the fiscal relations among these governments, the crowding out effect depends – *ceteris paribus* – on the aggregate fiscal policy stance of all tiers of government. The free-riding problem between the various tiers makes each fiscal authority disregard its own intertemporal solvency constraint (Beetsma and Bovenberg, 1999). A variety of reasons may be invoked for the lack of credibility of a no bail-out clause that prevents other governments (or the central bank) from saving the insolvent government.[10] Political and economic cohesion calls for fiscal solidarity. Systemic risk increases if government revenues are interdependent: tax bases may be very mobile or elastic in highly synchronised and integrated economies. Contagion effects may further amplify the debt accumulation spillover when lenders interpret the difficulties of one debtor as signalling impending problems for similar governments. The offsetting interest rate effects do not need to materialise then, as default premia are spread out over the n members of the union. This price distortion of the bond market is one way to read a possible insignificant reaction of domestic interest rates to debt accumulation. Monetary unification not only affects spreads, but may also raise the level of interest rates. Beetsma and Vermeylen (2002) argue that as the substitutability of public debt of various Member States increases with monetary unification, the average expected real debt return rises as well.

Disentangling empirically the spillover effects that come from capital mobility from those induced by monetary union is difficult, however. Some of the evidence based on an examination of the default and liquidity premia on government bonds is inconclusive on the effect of EMU (Bernoth et al., 2004; Codogno et al., 2003). Studies that look into the aggregate effect on the level of interest rates are even fewer. Landon and Smith (2000) compare the significant cross-effects of federal and provincial debt in Canada. Giuliodori and Beetsma (2005) simulate the effects of monetary union in their fiscal VAR for the three main Euro Area economies. By setting to zero exchange rate adjustments, they find that the cross-country spillover from a fiscal expansion is amplified.

[10] See Bayoumi et al. (1995) for a discussion.

3.3 A stock-flow fiscal VAR for open economies

We propose using the VAR-approach to examine crowding out of long-term interest rates induced by changes in fiscal policy. We first set up the empirical model for inferring on crowding out in a closed economy, and then extend this model by controlling for open economy variables, to indirectly infer on spillover effects of fiscal policy. The central question of interest in the empirical analysis of the closed economy is: *What is the gross crowding out effect of shocks to deficits – and the accumulation of debt – on long-term interest rates within a country?*

In other words, what is the overall crowding out effect on domestic long-term interest rates from fiscal expansions at home? To answer this hypothesis, we suggest specifying an empirical model that contains both the deficit flow and the stock of public debt. Bohn (1998) attributes to the reaction of deficits to debt the meaning of a systematic fiscal rule. A negative reaction of the primary deficit to debt accumulation is considered a sufficient condition for government solvency. Rules have become an increasingly popular method of describing policy behaviour, as well as a means of constraining discretionary policy interventions. Deviations from the fiscal rule signal likely fiscal corrections in the near to short-term future. Consequently, fiscal shocks are identified as an unusual change in fiscal policy setting as might be anticipated from the systematic behaviour of the fiscal policymaker. Including such a rule in the VAR tackles the anticipation problem in other VAR models of fiscal policy. I.e., the shock we identify occurs at the moment the public perceives a change in the behaviour of fiscal policy, and is also the moment at which the economic effects of the shock take place. In contrast to other studies, there is no discrepancy between the timing of the shock and the effects of this shock. Nonetheless, the distinction between the effective change in fiscal policy and the economic effects remains.

The inclusion of debt moreover lets us distinguish the crowding out effects of both deficits and debt. Deficits typically are highly persistent. Permanent changes in deficits accrue in public debt and may be argued to have stronger permanent effects on interest rates than temporary reversals of cyclically induced deficits (Feldstein, 1986). We could thus label our shock to debt as a 'Permanent deficit' shock, and the shock to net lending as a 'Temporary deficit' shock. We can indeed discriminate both as we supplement the rules-based modelling of the government sector with a small economic system, as in Favero (2003), that captures the cyclical movements in the fiscal variables. Government sets deficits in reaction not only to debt developments, but also as a function of the output gap and inflation. This again helps identification, as the automatic stabilisers can be filtered from the structural changes in policy.

The inclusion of the stock of debt in the VAR is not unproblematic. First, the inclusion of debt may cause inference problems if there are non-linear effects of fiscal policy. For the high-debt countries in our sample, this may be a problem. Formal stability tests on the VAR model are not possible due to the small number of degrees of freedom.[11] Second, deficits and debt are linked via the flow budget constraint, and hence the stock of debt is just the accumulation of past deficits. Including both flow and stock variables is not unproblematic for the specification of a VAR, but this should nonetheless not be overstated. Under some weak economic assumptions, it can be shown that the stationarity of the quasi-difference of debt is a necessary and a sufficient condition for the intertemporal government budget constraint to hold if and only if debt and the primary surplus are cointegrated. (Trehan and Walsh, 1991). Current public debt is then equal to the present value of current and future primary surpluses. Hence, all outstanding debt is eventually paid off. Hansen et al. (1991) show that this sustainability condition imposes some cross-restrictions on the joint process of deficit and debt. We do not impose these restrictions on the VAR. We are not interested in testing sustainability, and moreover believe that fiscal policies in some countries in the sample might have been unsustainable.[12] An alternative necessary and sufficient condition for sustainability is that government spending and revenues are cointegrated (Ahmed and Rogers, 1995). We ignore possible cointegration between both sides of the budget, and analyse only the aggregate deficit. Standard asymptotic tests remain valid if the VAR is estimated in levels, even in the presence of unit roots (Sims et al., 1990). Finally, in the VAR specification of the joint process of stock and flow variables, lags of the stock variable do enter into the equation of the flow variable because (Fry and Pagan, 2005).[13]

---

[11] In Sect. 3.4, we indeed find stronger responses of interest rates to fiscal shocks in countries with higher debt ratios.

[12] A VAR in primary surpluses and debt has been suggested as a means to test the Fiscal Theory of the Price Level. Canzoneri et al. (2001) distinguish Ricardian from non-Ricardian regimes in fiscal policy by examining the sign of serial correlations in deficits following shocks to debt in a bivariate model. They find the combination of an active fiscal policy and passive monetary policy rather implausible for describing US macroeconomic policies.

[13] This stock-flow relation is in reality more complicated because of the denomination and the maturity structure of public debt. Hence, the stock of debt enters into the equation of the flow-deficit when other variables like interest rates or inflation are included in the empirical model that have an impact on interest payments.

We look at the effect of fiscal policy shocks on real long-term interest rates. One may argue that the direct effect on short-term interest rates is the more relevant one. A larger deficit directly crowds out other demands for funding on financial markets. If the expectations hypothesis holds, the effect on the short-term rate accumulates over the entire term structure. However, there are two problems with analysing the effect of fiscal shocks on short-term interest rates. First, the short-term rate is mainly influenced by day-to-day monetary policy decisions, and its reaction to fiscal imbalances has hardly ever been found significant (Blanchard and Perotti, 2002; Mountford and Uhlig, 2005). In many studies, changes in the 3-months T-bill rate are considered as monetary policy shocks. We did not want to simultaneously identify fiscal and monetary policy shocks as this requires a different set of assumptions.[14] Second, it has been common to analyse the effect of fiscal policy expansions on exchange rate, default and liquidity premia on government bonds (Favero et al., 1997; Bernoth et al., 2004). The reaction of short-term interest rates to an increase in government bonds has often been found to be negative, owing to a portfolio effect and an associated decline in the liquidity premium. We do not want to look into the pricing of specific fiscal instruments to decompose the effect of fiscal shocks. In order to compare the crowding out effect across countries, we examine the aggregate effect on the level of long-term interest rates. We do not completely disregard short-term interest rates, however. In the Appendix we specify a VAR model that spans the full term structure of interest rates by including the yield between both long and short-term rates.

The inclusion of aggregate economic conditions accounts for the endogeneity problem of fiscal policy setting. The equations for inflation and output gap can then be seen as summarising the economy in a very generic version of a Phillips curve and an IS-equation.

We thus have a complete model of fiscal policy and the economic system to analyse the effects on interest rates that can be summarised in the following VAR representation (3.1):

[14] The interaction of both policies throws up some major problems in identification. The anticipation of a monetary bailout of the fiscal authority, which has inflationary consequences, makes it difficult to distinguish short-term reactions from policy interaction in the long term (Canzoneri et al., 2001).

$$B(L)\begin{bmatrix} B_t \\ d_t \\ i_i \\ \pi_t \\ y_t \end{bmatrix} = \begin{bmatrix} \varepsilon_t^B \\ \varepsilon_t^d \\ \varepsilon_t^i \\ \varepsilon_t^\pi \\ \varepsilon_t^y \end{bmatrix} \tag{3.1}$$

where $B(L)$ is the lag operator with length p, and ε_t the (white noise) reduced form residual with variance-covariance matrix Σ. To simplify notation, we divide this system in three blocks of variables. Henceforth, we refer to: (a) the fiscal block F that includes the debt ratio B_t and deficit ratio d_t, $F = [B_t \quad d_t]'$; (b) the monetary block M that includes some different specifications for interest rates, $M = [i_t]'$; and (c) the economic block Y that summarises economic conditions in the output gap y_t and inflation p_t, $Y = [y_t \quad p_t]'$.

This specification suffices for characterising the effect of fiscal shocks in a closed economy. The identification strategy that will be used in this chapter is based on a simple Cholesky ordering, as in Giuliodori and Beetsma (2005) or Ardagna et al. (2004). There is no obvious choice on placing debt before or after deficits. Debt is the accumulation of deficits over time, and is arguably more endogenous than deficits. The initial conditions of debt can also be a constraint on current fiscal actions. We therefore decide to put debt before deficit so as to allow for the strongest possible reaction of deficits for maintaining sustainability ($F = [B_t \quad d_t]'$). We do not take a position on the monetary block following the economic block or vice versa, but will experiment with both possibilities. Placing the fiscal block first

$$[F \quad M \quad Y]' \text{ or } [F \quad Y \quad M]' \tag{3.2a}$$

implies no contemporaneous reaction of F to the economic variables or to interest rates. The reaction of the other variables to fiscal policy is maximised though. But the reverse order

$$[Y \quad M \quad F]' \text{ or } [M \quad Y \quad F]' \tag{3.2b}$$

implies a complete crowding out effect of government spending on GDP and interest rates. Either of these assumptions is too extreme. The range between the most 'liberal' and the most 'conservative' estimate of the effects of fiscal policy then gives an indication on how robust our findings are. To that end, the impulse response functions of the interest rate variable following upon a shock of 1% to the fiscal deficit or debt to GDP ratio are summarised in a single graph for all four possible Cholesky orders in (3.2a-b). They are plotted over a 10-year horizon, together with the maximum and averages of the four bootstrapped 90% confidence intervals.[15]

The detection of crowding out would be consistent with the literature that finds real effects of fiscal expansions, also in EU countries. It would moreover be favourable to the no bailout clause, as financial markets succeed in separating different bond markets. A necessary condition for market discipline to work is then fulfilled. A non-significant response on the other hand might be consistent with no interest effects of fiscal imbalances at all – in support of Ricardian equivalence. However, this reaction accrues the responses in a closed economy with any attenuating influences of international capital flows and monetary union. A non-significant response could also be consistent with strong spillover effects, and hence a misspecification of model (3.2a-b). We therefore model an open economy fiscal VAR to net out the spillover of fiscal policy settings abroad on domestic long-term rates. This answers the second question of this chapter: *What is the net crowding out effect of shocks to deficits – and the accumulation of debt – on domestic long-term interest rates, next to the spillover effect of other countries' deficits and debt accumulation?*

Alternatively phrased, is there any relevant crowding out effect of deficit accumulation on a country's long-term interest rates, once the effects of foreign fiscal policies are accounted for? The simple VAR-model we propose only controls for the complete crowding out effect for foreign debt and interest rate spillover. We do not attempt to distinguish the spillover that arises from financial integration from those coming from the moral-hazard channel of no bailout or contagion effects via economic channels. A significantly positive response to fiscal expansion at home is consistent with the existence of each of these spillovers. An insignificant crowding out effect is evidence for the Ricardian Equivalence proposition.[16]

To examine this second hypothesis, we adopt the same specification for the VAR, and consider two strategies for modelling open econo-

---

[15] The VAR model always includes a constant and two lags of each endogenous variable.

[16] Only the yardstick comparison of relative debt levels would also mitigate crowding out effects.

mies. Empirical open economy models have to struggle with the burden of overparametrisation. Ideally, one would analyse the reciprocal interest rate effects of changes in fiscal policies in both the home and foreign country. The paucity of fiscal data for European countries renders this unfeasible, and we need to make some simplifying assumptions. The direction of the spillover is in both cases assumed to run from the country to the benchmark aggregate. We assume that this benchmark for the offsetting spillover effects come from intra-Euro Area capital flows only. This is a debatable choice. First, there is some evidence for global linkages rather than regional spillover (Tanzi and Lutz, 1993). Second, the fiscal framework of EMU pertains to both Euro Area and other Member States of the EU. The Stability and Growth Pact and the no bailout clause apply to both groups of EU Member States. Nevertheless, the consequences of fiscal free riding carry more weight for those countries that share the same currency.

In the first instance, we scale down the model by assuming identical transmission mechanisms in all countries. We express all variables in country i as a difference to the same variable for the Euro Area.[17] This identifies asymmetric shocks across countries only. It expresses the idea that only country-specific deviations from average economic and fiscal conditions in the Euro Area matter for the effect of changes in fiscal policies on interest rates. We can write the model concisely, as in (3.3a), for the various orderings of the fiscal, interest rate and economic bloc. The asterisk indicates Euro Area variables:

$$\begin{gathered}\left[F-F^* \quad M-M^* \quad Y-Y^*\right]' \text{ or } \left[F-F^* \quad Y-Y^* \quad M-M^*\right]' \text{ or} \\ \left[Y-Y^* \quad M-M^* \quad F-F^*\right]' \text{ or } \left[M-M^* \quad Y-Y^* \quad F-F^*\right]'. \end{gathered} \tag{3.3a}$$

We can then indirectly assess the importance of spillover from finding any domestic crowding out effect that is stronger than in the 'domestic' version of the VAR model. Note that the interpretation of the results differs from the 'closed economy' version. In the latter model, fiscal shocks lead to some percentage point change in interest rates. In this model, fiscal shocks are relative to Euro Area fiscal developments, and have domestic interest rate effects that are relative to Euro Area wide interest rate changes. We therefore measure the relative change in interest rates. Furthermore, shocks cannot be scaled to GDP and the impulse responses follow upon a one standard deviation shock now.

In second instance, we take a 'small open economy' assumption

[17] The own country's contribution to the Euro Area aggregate has been taken out.

by adding the benchmark Euro Area interest rate i^* and/or public debt B^* as exogenous variables to the VAR of country i. That is, we control for the marginal effect of domestic fiscal policies on interest rates, and do not allow for a feedback effect of aggregate Euro Area variables on any domestic series. We take the benchmark variables i^* and/or B^* as exogenous, but leave the order of the other variables otherwise unchanged, as in (3.3b):

$$[i* \quad B* \mid F \quad M \quad Y]' \text{ or } [i* \quad B* \mid F \quad Y \quad M]' \text{ or } [i* \quad B* \mid Y \quad M \quad F]' \text{ or } [i* \quad B* \mid M \quad Y \quad F]' \tag{3.3b}$$

This benchmarking method loosens the restriction that all data enter in differences, but becomes less realistic for larger economies. The variation in domestic interest rates is due to shocks in domestic fiscal policy, for given conditions at the Euro Area level. In other words, it tells us by how much domestic rates would increase, given unchanged rates at the Euro Area level.[18]

Seen in combination with model (3.3a), this then allows us to infer upon the importance of spillover. If – for given Euro Area rates – fiscal shocks change the country spread (model 3.3b), but do not lead to significant responses in relative interest rates following country-specific fiscal shocks (model 3.3a), then this interest gap measures the attenuation of crowding out due to spillover.

Notice that we are not able to infer on the effects of EMU on the spillover of fiscal policy. Formal stability tests on the VAR model are not possible due to the small number of degrees of freedom. We also do not model specific transmission channels of spillover to evaluate contagion or yardstick comparison effects to evaluate the importance of monetary union. Given the increasing integration of goods and financial markets, our estimates probably provide a lower bound on the spillover effect of fiscal policy.

It suffices to look at the large number of studies to see that many various choices on the data specification are possible. Limited availability of fiscal data constrains the choice of sample and frequency in our case.

---

18 Under an alternative assumption, a subset of countries could be analysed. This limits spillover and the role of common shocks (Prasad and Lumsdaine, 2003). One may also restrict the VAR coefficients for all countries. With heterogeneous fiscal stances, this may not be realistic.

The data that we use in the empirical models mainly come from the annual database of AMECO of the European Commission. This is the highest frequency at which a standardised dataset covering fiscal data for EU countries over a maximum time span from 1960 to 2004 is available. See Tables 3.1 and 3.2 for details on the construction of the data and sample length. The analysis focuses on the entire Euro Area, the largest EMU economies (Germany, France and Italy) and a group of smaller ones (Austria, Belgium, Finland and The Netherlands). We also consider the United Kingdom, for it provides a check against the results for the Euro Area.

Regarding the deficit, we consider total net lending of the general government expressed as a ratio to GDP for at least three reasons.[19] First, total net lending is of direct interest to fiscal policy-makers. Second, the spurious relation that exists between the overall deficit and interest rates is taken account of in the specification of the VAR.

[19] General government data consolidate across government levels, regardless the country-specific devolution of fiscal powers.

Table 3.1. Data definitions and sources

Series	code	description	source
i) EU countries			
total net lending	GLN	ratio to GDP	AMECO
public debt	UDGGL	ratio to GDP	OECD
long-term interest	ILNN	%	
short-term interest	ISN	%	AMECO
CPI inflation	ZCPIN	growth rate	
output gap	GAP	% of potential GDP	
ii) Euro Area			
total net lending	GLN	ratio to GDP	AMECO
public debt	UDGGL	ratio to GDP	AMECO
long-term interest	LTN	%	
short-term interest	STN	%	
CPI inflation	HICP	growth rate	ECB
output gap	-	% of potential GDP	
Potential GDP	-	HP-filtered real GDP	
real GDP	YER	Level	

Table 3.2. Data sample

Country	sample	sources
Germany	1970-2004	AMECO
France	1977-2004	AMECO
Italy	1964-2004	AMECO
Euro Area	1970-2004	AMECO (for net lending, public debt); ECB-EAS (for interest rates, inflation and output gap)
United Kingdom	1970-2004	AMECO
Austria	1970-2004	AMECO OECD (for net lending)
Belgium	1970-2004	AMECO
Finland	1970-2004	AMECO OECD (for net lending)
Netherlands	1969-2004	AMECO

The ECB-EAS database constructs synthetic Euro Area aggregate statistics since 1970 on a quarterly basis. See Fagan et al. (2001).

The reverse causality problem of rising interest rates that induce a compensation for higher interest payments on outstanding debt with other budget categories is entirely included in our specification. The same argument holds for the endogenous cyclical variations in the budget. We can still consider the reaction of the total deficit to debt as a fiscal rule then. Third, debt –which we take to be the general government debt ratio to GDP– is arguably a more endogenous variable than the primary deficit. The latter reacts to output and perhaps inflation, whereas debt and total deficits are also influenced by interest rates. Placing debt before total deficits in (3.2a-b) is then less problematic.

The variables describing the economy are taken to be the CPI based inflation rate, and the output gap relative to potential GDP. As inflation is already included in the model as a separate variable, the long-term interest rate on 10-year government bonds is deflated by realised CPI inflation. One might prefer using expectations of inflation in order to maintain consistency with the term structure of interest rates. Surveys or forecasts for inflation are not available at that horizon for European countries. Ardagna et al. (2004) use trend inflation to approximate inflation expectations but find little difference in their results between nominal, real or expected long-term rates. We therefore use the current realised interest rate.

For the open economy model, we also need to specify the benchmark Euro Area data. As we assume that spillover effects are limited to the Euro Area, we limit attention to data for EMU. The benchmark open economy variable is a Euro Area aggregate. The data for this artificial Euro Area economy come from both the AMECO and the quarterly ECB-EAS database.[20] A given country i cannot always be taken as small relative to EMU. The larger the country, the smaller the difference with the Euro Area average will be. We therefore need to correct the Euro Area aggregate. For net lending and public debt, we simply subtract the country i's series from the Euro Area aggregate, and scale it with the corresponding output series. Unfortunately, aggregate data is not always available. In particular, data on French public debt before 1978 is simply absent. The aggregate public debt has therefore been constructed from those countries that represent together two thirds of Euro Area GDP. The other variables for this hypothetical EMU *minus one* are obtained by subtracting series i and then rescaling the GDP-weighted aggregate.

[20] End of period data have been used to construct yearly data.

3.4 Crowding-out effects of fiscal policies

This section first discusses the results on the crowding out effects in closed economies. We then assess these effects for the entire EMU so as to prepare the ground for the discussion of spillover between Euro Area countries.

Let us consider first the results of model (3.2a-b). For the various Cholesky orderings, Fig. 3.1 summarises the effects of a 1% shock to the net lending and debt ratio. The gross effect of a positive 1% shock to the deficit is to temporarily increase long-term interest rates by about 20 basis points in all countries, except Finland. This increase is insignificant in the very first years after the expansion, except in the Netherlands.[21] The crowding out effect is much more relevant for a shock to the public debt ratio, particularly so in the long run. Its size is nevertheless generally smaller, and the reaction is only really significant in the more indebted countries as Belgium, the Netherlands and Italy. When debt has clearly derailed, rates rise much more over a longer horizon. This is a result that is common to the literature. Ardagna et al. (2004) also find large effects on interest rates only in countries with above-average levels of debt.[22] The contrast between the larger – but insignificant – short run impact of deficits, and the smaller long run impact of debt, is also consistent with most evidence in the literature (Engen and Hubbard, 2004). Our evidence supports the hypothesis of Feldstein (1986) that interest rates should respond to the permanent creation of deficits that accumulate in higher debt in the long term, but not to temporary changes in fiscal policies. Having included both deficit and debt probably explains why we do not find the (counterintuitive) negative impact of debt on long-term interest rates that other authors have documented. Ardagna et al. (2004) find a cumulative reaction to shocks in (primary) deficits of up to 66 basis points, but owe the decline in interest rates following debt shocks to liquidity effects on financial markets.

We do not really document a strong crowding out effect domestically. But even if the spillover between open economies within in the Euro Area is large, in a relatively homogeneous and closed area as EMU these

[21] All results are rather robust to the ordering of the variables in the VAR, as all responses follow the same pattern.

[22] In contrast to some other studies that examine the consumption and saving responses (Nicoletti, 1989), we find that at higher levels of public debt, fiscal policy expansions invoke a less Ricardian response. An alternative explanation for this finding is that the default premium for highly indebted countries rises by more, while the risk-adjusted rate is unaffected by fiscal policy.

would cancel out on aggregate. Any crowding out effects could become more evident again at the Euro Area level. To gain some insight into the relevance of the spillover channels internal to EMU, the first question on the gross crowding out effect can be re-examined for the entire Euro Area. However, as can be seen in Fig. 3.2, crowding out effects on European interest rates do not become much more pronounced. The impulse responses to debt shocks in the same domestic VAR model show a robust long-term rise in the interest rate. Its size is small, however, and not significant at any horizon. Deficit shocks have a shorter run impact in the order of 20 basis points, but these results are hardly significant. This result tells that there is hardly any difference between individual Member States of the Euro Area. This could imply that the effects of fiscal policy are Ricardian. As we have modelled the offsetting effects from intra-European capital flows only, we cannot exclude that global spillover on international financial markets is more relevant. This result thus indicates that spillover may rather be due to financial integration than to an incredible no bailout clause *per se*.

What about the role of fiscal policy in explaining variability in interest rates? Table 3.3 displays the percentual contribution of deficit and debt shocks in explaining the variance of the real long-term interest rate at various horizons (1, 5 and 10 years). The overall contribution of fiscal policy is rather small, but gets larger at longer horizons. In the Euro Area as a whole, only 7% is explained by deficits and public debt. The latter outcome is to a large extent determined by German fiscal policy, whose contribution is also rather small. The picture for other countries is less clear. There is no evidence for a larger driving role of deficits behind interest rates in highly indebted countries. Similarly, there is no larger role for debt in these countries. Rather, the deficit may signal incipient problems in highly indebted countries (Drudi and Prati, 2000). This then provokes a stronger reaction of interest rates to deficits, as in the case of Italy for example.

3.5 Spillovers of fiscal policies

We are now ready to look into the crowding out effects in an open economy. By concentrating on the deviation of fiscal and economic conditions from the Euro Area benchmark, we may recover a significant domestic crowding out effect, and indirectly infer the importance of the spillover.

3.5.1 Relative fiscal shocks and relative crowding out

The results from expressing the data in differences to the Euro Area base, following model (3.3a), are summarised in Fig. 3.3. As we examine Euro Area aggregates, we do not consider the United Kingdom any longer. The crowding out effect is even more mitigated than the response for the closed economy. Neither deficit nor debt shocks produce any significant response. This result tells us that any deviation from the average fiscal conditions specific to that country do not affect the relative country spread. In other words, asymmetric fiscal shocks do not translate in relative changes in financing conditions. Given that we detected some small but significant crowding out effect in closed economies, this would indicate rather strong spillover effects of any fiscal shock onto the aggregate interest rates, and little to no effect on country-specific variables. This result is reminiscent of Faini (2006). As differences to the Euro Area benchmark are taken, the forecast error variance decomposition attributes a somewhat larger role to fiscal policy deviations in explaining long-term rates. Again, the contribution of deficits is larger than the one of debt for the highly indebted countries (Table 3.3).

shock to net lending ratio *shock to debt ratio*

Austria

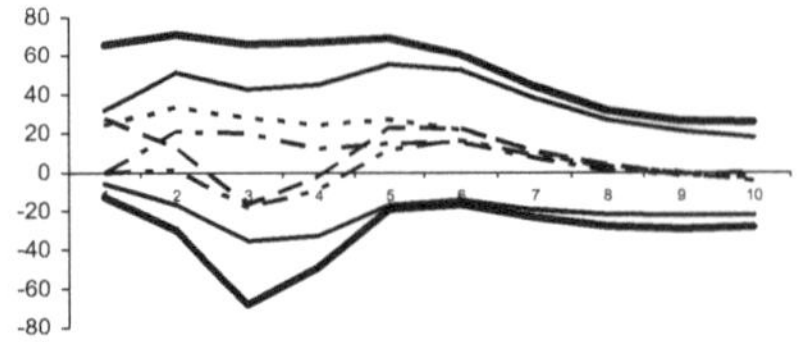

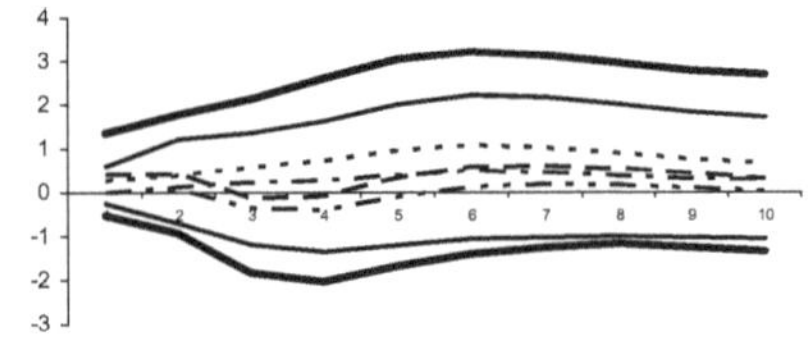

Belgium

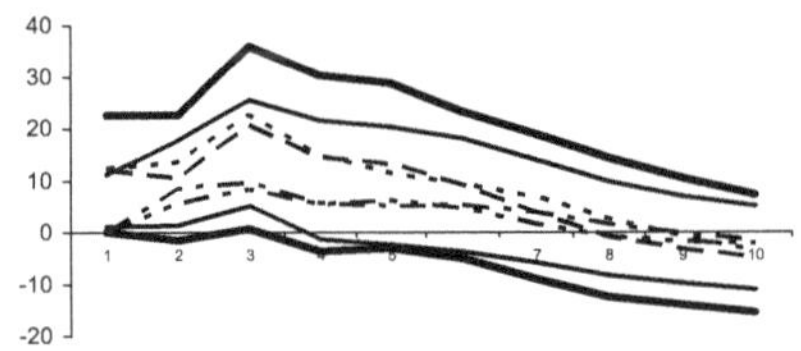

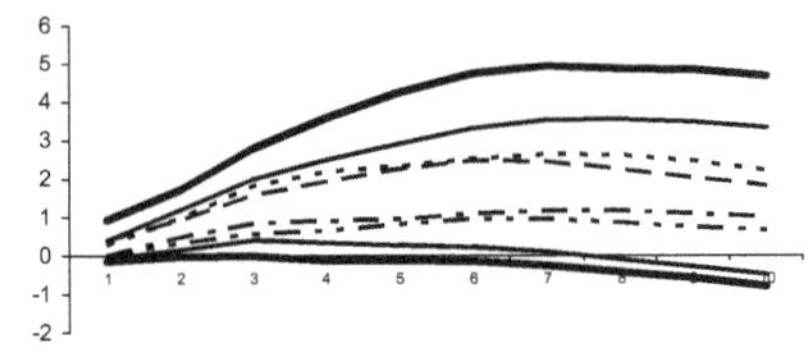

Germany

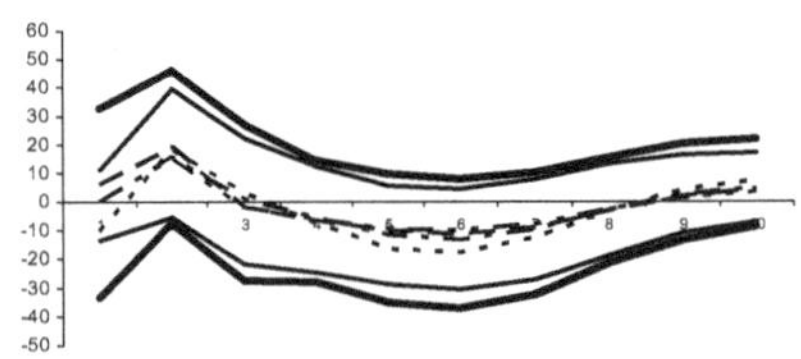

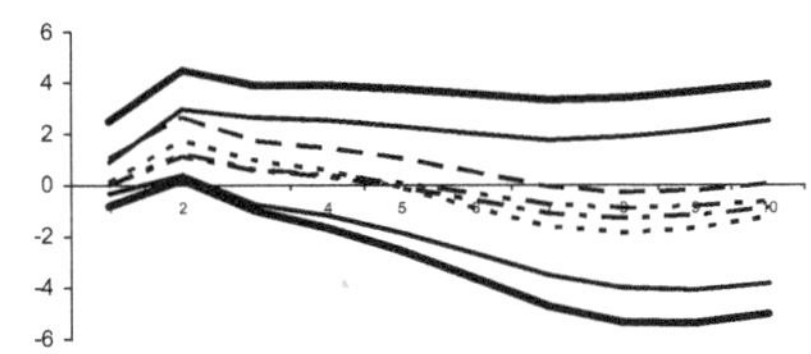

Finland

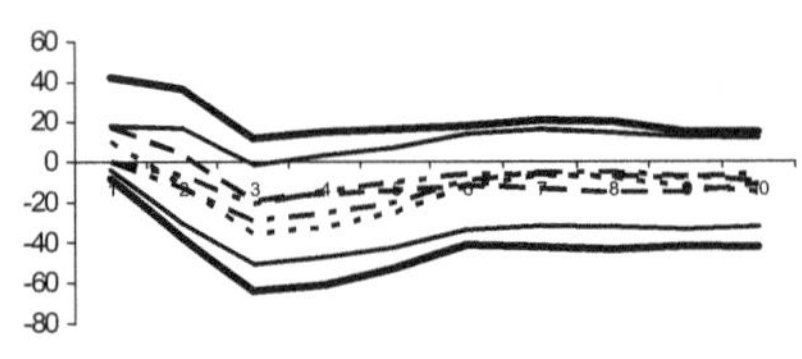

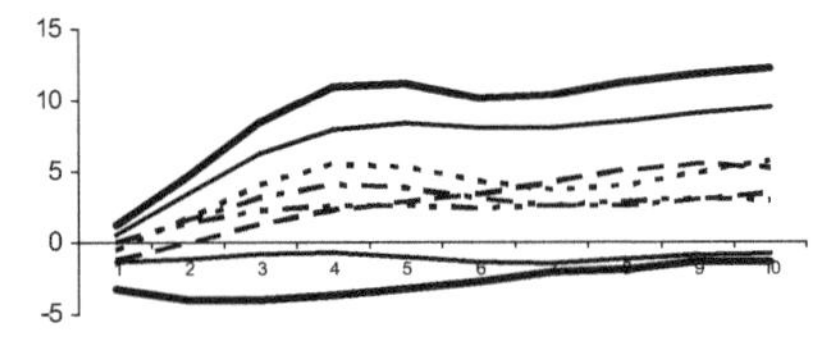

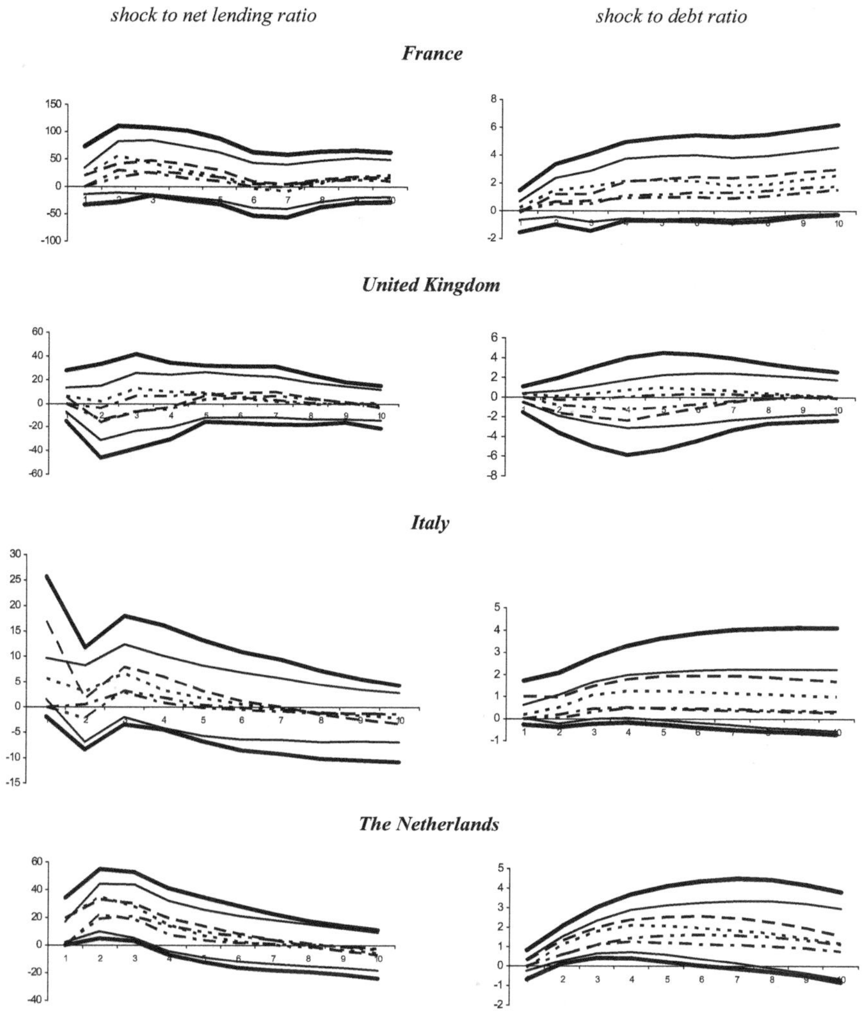

Fig. 3.1. Domestic economy, SVAR model (3.2a-b): impulse responses of real long-term interest rates to shocks of 1% of GDP in net lending and debt ratio.

Notes: (a) graphs display the percentage point impulse responses of the interest rate measure, in response to a fiscal shock, for each of the four Cholesky orders in (3.2a-b), ----- is $[Y \quad M \quad F]'$, — — — is $[M \quad Y \quad F]'$; — - — - is $[F \quad Y \quad M]'$ and — - - - — is $[F \quad M \quad Y]'$; (b) 90% confidence intervals from bootstrapped model – with 1000 draws – are the average (normal continuous line) and maximum (bold continuous line) of all four Cholesky orders.

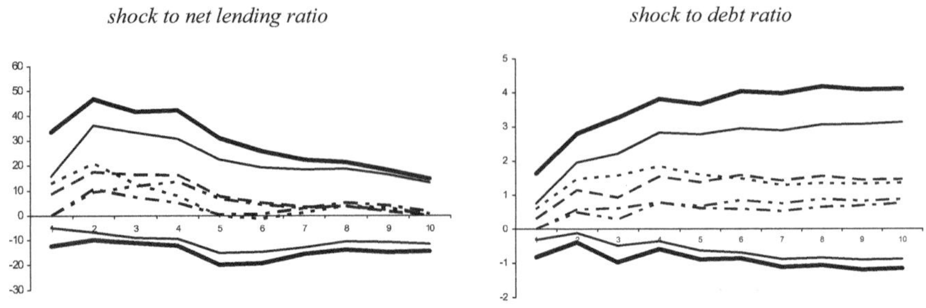

Fig. 3.2. Euro Area economy, SVAR model (3.2a-b): impulse responses of real long-term interest rates to shocks of 1% of GDP in net lending and debt ratio.

Notes: (a) graphs display the percentage impulse responses of the interest rate measure, in response to a shock, for each of the four Cholesky orders in (3.2a-b), ----- is $[Y \quad M \quad F]'$, ——— is $[M \quad Y \quad F]'$; —-—- is $[F \quad Y \quad M]'$ and —-—- is $[F \quad M \quad Y]'$; (b) 90% confidence intervals from bootstrapped model – with 1000 draws – are the average (normal continuous line) and maximum (bold continuous line) of all four Cholesky orders.

Table 3.3. Domestic economy, SVAR model (3.2a-b): forecast error variance decomposition of real long-term interest rates (see Fig. 3.1 and 3.2)

	horizon	debt endogenous	
country	year	debt	net lending
Euro Area	1	3.60	4.39
	5	2.09	3.34
	10	2.69	4.83
Germany	1	0.20	2.57
	5	0.31	3.70
	10	0.37	3.49
France	1	24.02	4.07
	5	22.47	4.59
	10	25.53	4.98
Italy	1	2.84	1.14
	5	4.20	7.06
	10	4.30	17.01
United Kingdom	1	1.37	0.23
	5	2.65	4.60
	10	4.15	4.42
Austria	1	1.28	1.77
	5	14.38	2.35
	10	14.23	1.93
Belgium	1	0.23	0.39
	5	1.98	0.67
	10	1.71	0.64
Finland	1	1.21	8.99
	5	6.53	7.47
	10	6.02	6.35
Netherlands	1	4.82	2.31
	5	5.45	2.71
	10	9.37	2.03

3.5.2 Crowding out in small open economies

The latter results can give a somewhat misleading picture if asymmetric fiscal shocks do not play an important role. Instead of imposing the restriction of variables entering in differences, we now consider the 'small open economy' model. As specified in (3.3b), we control for the Euro Area debt ratio, the Euro Area real long-term interest rates (or both), by adding these to the domestic model. Figs. 3.4 to 3.6 display the results for the 'open economy' SVAR.

Controlling for aggregate public debt seems to matter little: we nearly replicate the results of the domestic model (3.2a-b). Debt shocks have large cumulative effects on interest rates, but these are again significant in highly indebted countries only (Fig. 3.4). A more promising approach seems to benchmark the domestic interest rate to the corresponding Euro Area rate. Table 3.5 sums up the graphical evidence from Fig. 3.5, by setting out the point estimate and the error bounds, as well as the peak effects, for a horizon of up to 5 years. There now is a significant increase in the long-term rates in response to a 1% shock in the debt ratio in all countries. The effect is also rather precisely estimated, and robust to any of the chosen Cholesky orders. It can be seen that this effect is again more pronounced for the highly indebted countries, but is also much stronger for the other countries. The scale of the effect is moreover substantial. For most countries, the peak effect is between 30 and 40 basis points, and is reached after 4 years. For the highly indebted countries, this goes even up to 60 or 70 basis points, as for example in the Netherlands and Belgium. On the other hand, no crowding out is found in Germany and Austria at all. This indiscernible effect may be explained by the weight of Germany in the Euro Area. Deficit shocks do not have significant effects as the 'small open economy' VAR-model is not valid for Germany.

shock to net lending ratio *shock to debt ratio*

Austria

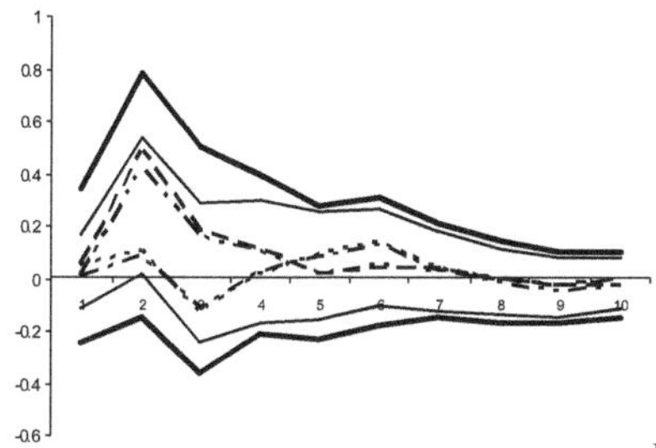

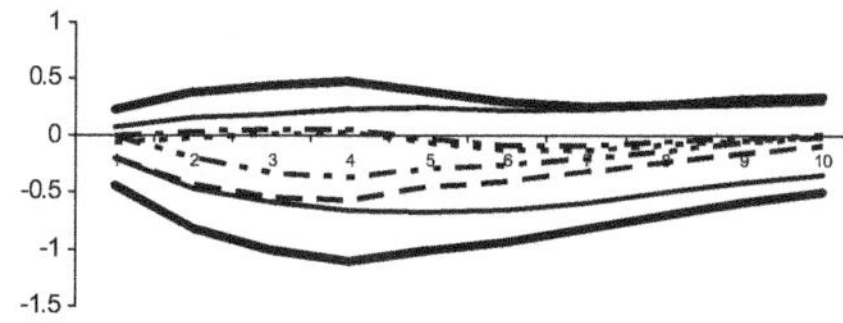

Belgium

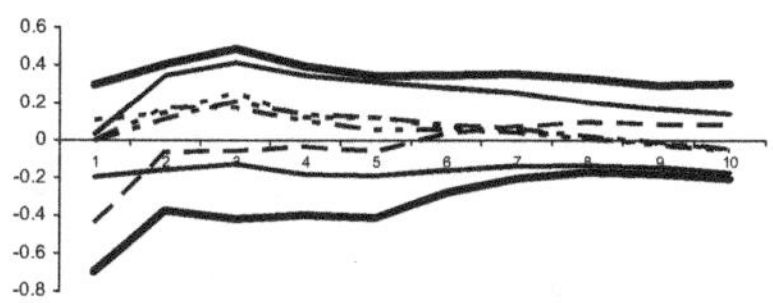

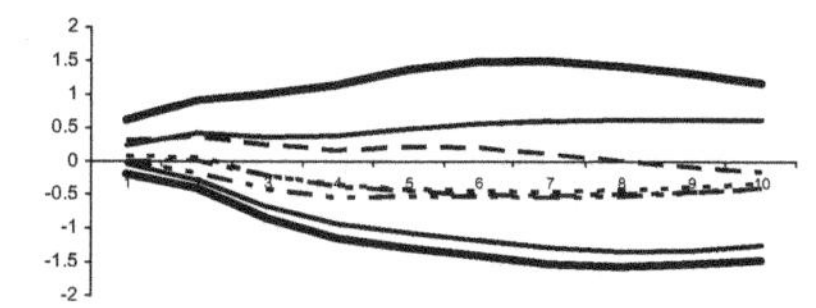

Germany

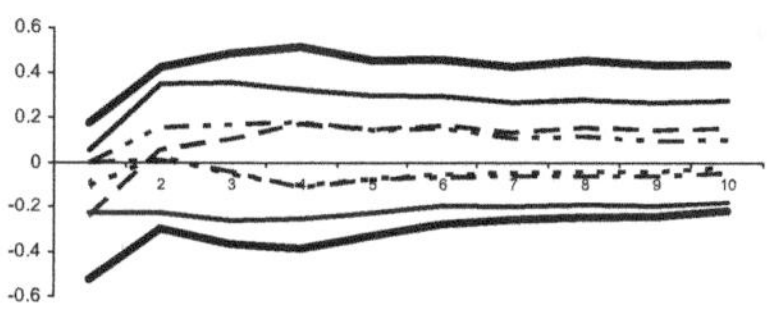

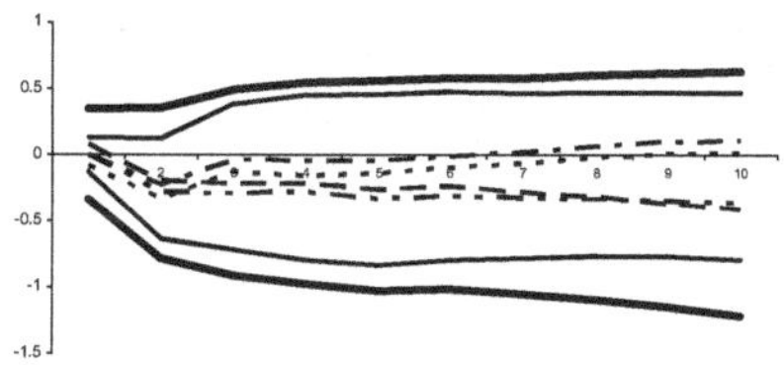

Finland

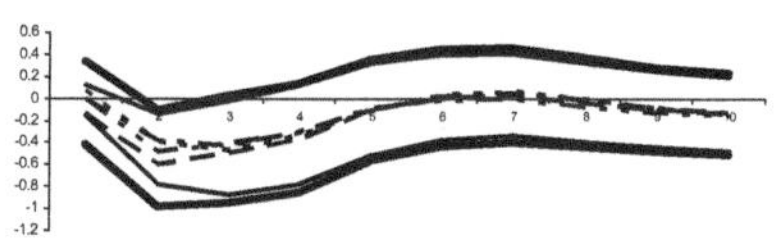

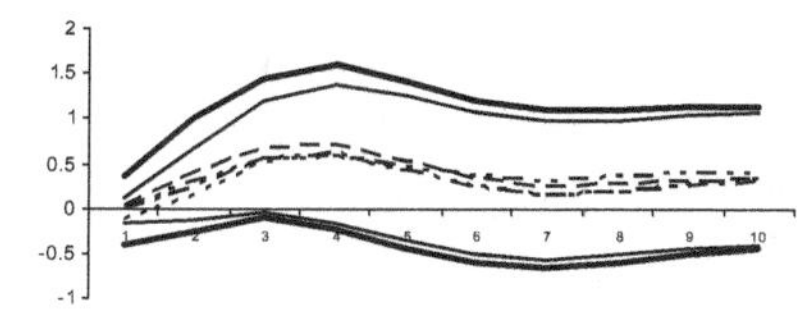

France

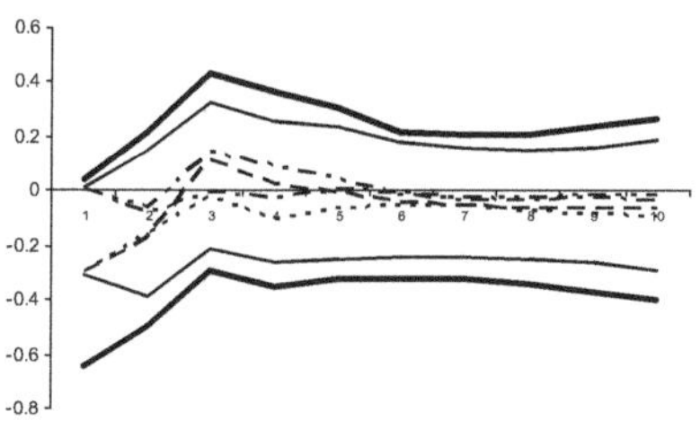

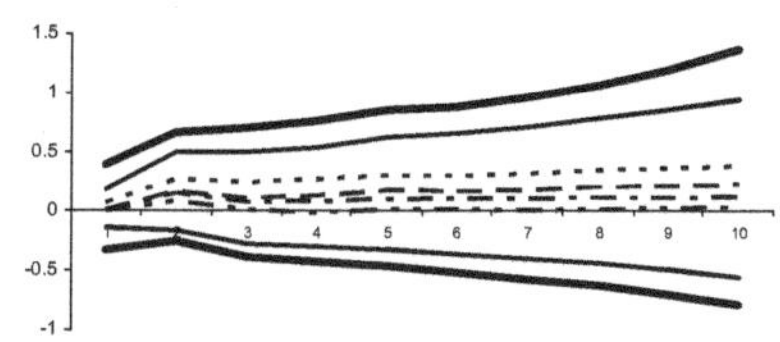

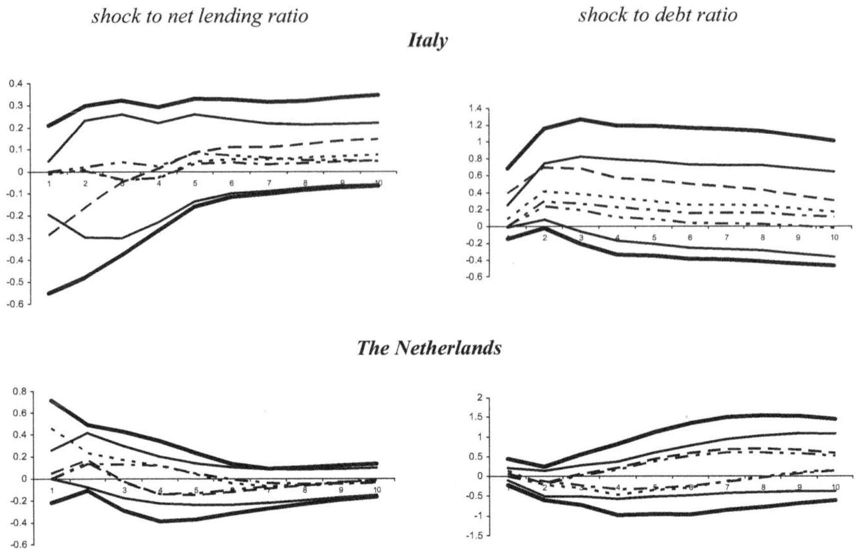

Fig. 3.3. Open economy, SVAR model (3.3a): difference of country i to Euro Area; impulse responses of real long-term interest rate to standard deviation shock in net lending and debt ratio

Notes: (a) graphs display the impulse responses of the interest rate measure, in response to a 1 standard deviation shock, for each of the four Cholesky orders in (3.3a), individual impulse responses follow the order in Fig. 3.1, except for the scaling to the Euro Area wide variable; (b) 90% confidence intervals from bootstrapped model – with 1000 draws – are the average (normal continuous line) and maximum (bold continuous line) of all four Cholesky orders.

Table 3.4. Open economy, SVAR model (3.3a): difference of country i to Euro Area; forecast error variance decomposition of real long-term interest rates (see Fig. 3.3)

country	horizon year	debt endogenous debt	debt endogenous net lending
Germany	1	0.60	1.17
	5	5.76	12.34
	10	18.24	10.03
France	1	0.43	5.77
	5	4.78	8.64
	10	7.08	8.44
Italy	1	5.04	2.49
	5	11.02	10.06
	10	12.96	17.77
Austria	1	1.75	0.12
	5	8.77	2.81
	10	14.51	5.25
Belgium	1	0.01	0.03
	5	3.72	7.65
	10	6.93	7.11
Finland	1	0.06	0.15
	5	1.25	7.37
	10	1.34	8.20
Netherlands	1	1.63	10.97
	5	0.93	4.50
	10	2.50	3.90

shock to net lending ratio *shock to debt ratio*

Austria

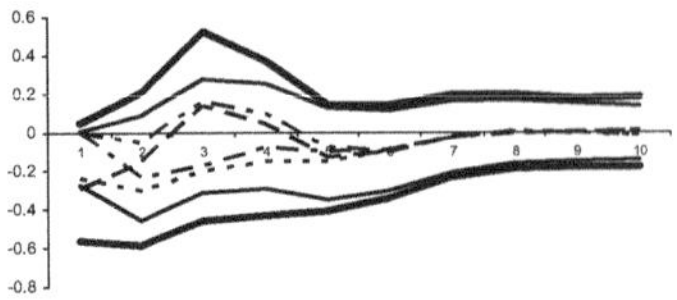

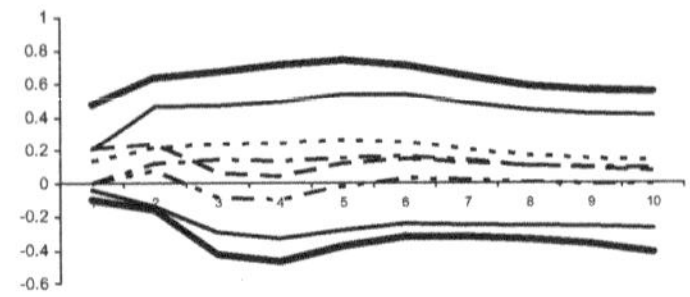

Belgium

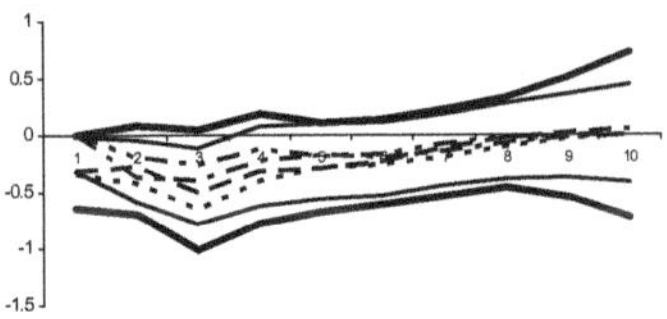

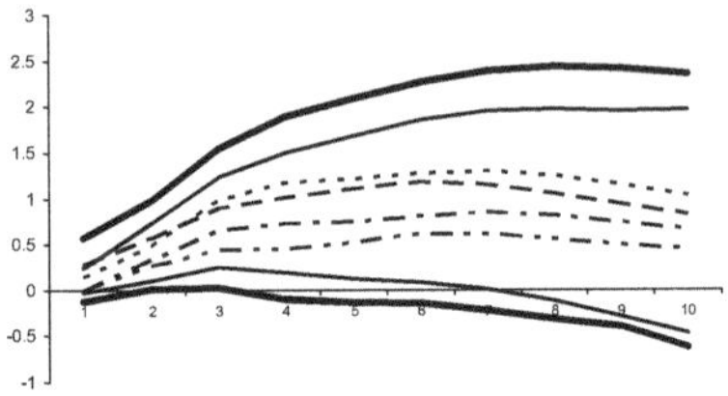

Germany

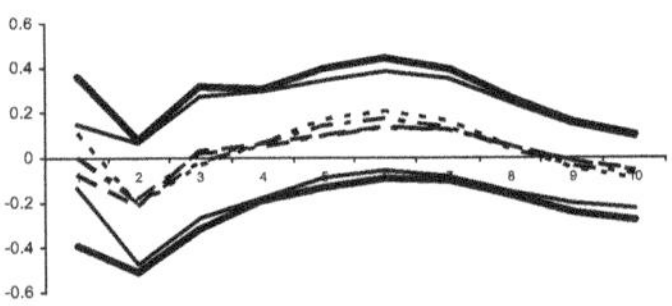

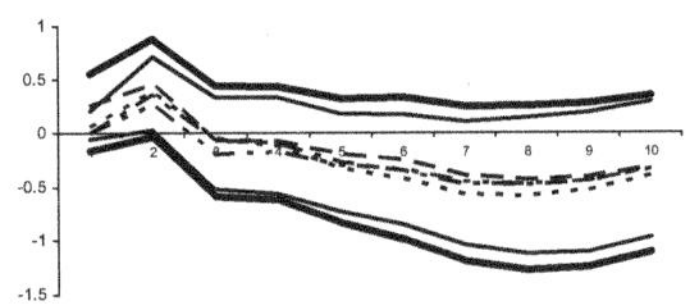

Finland

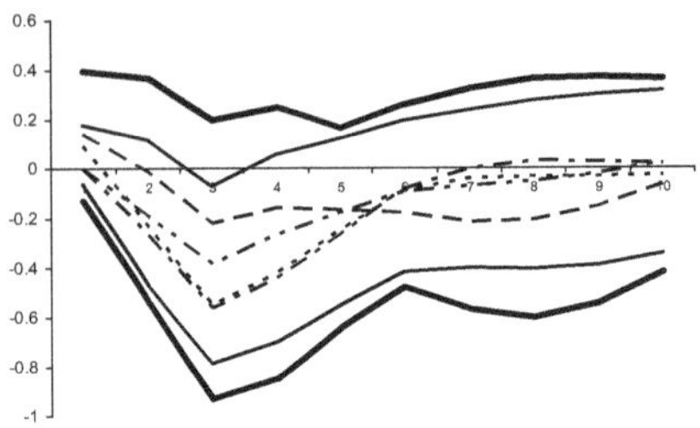

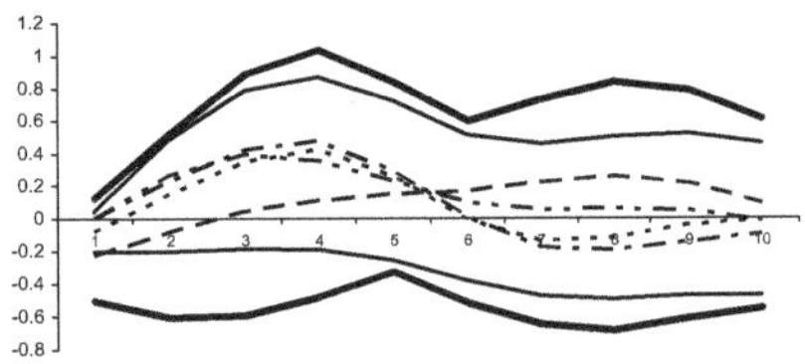

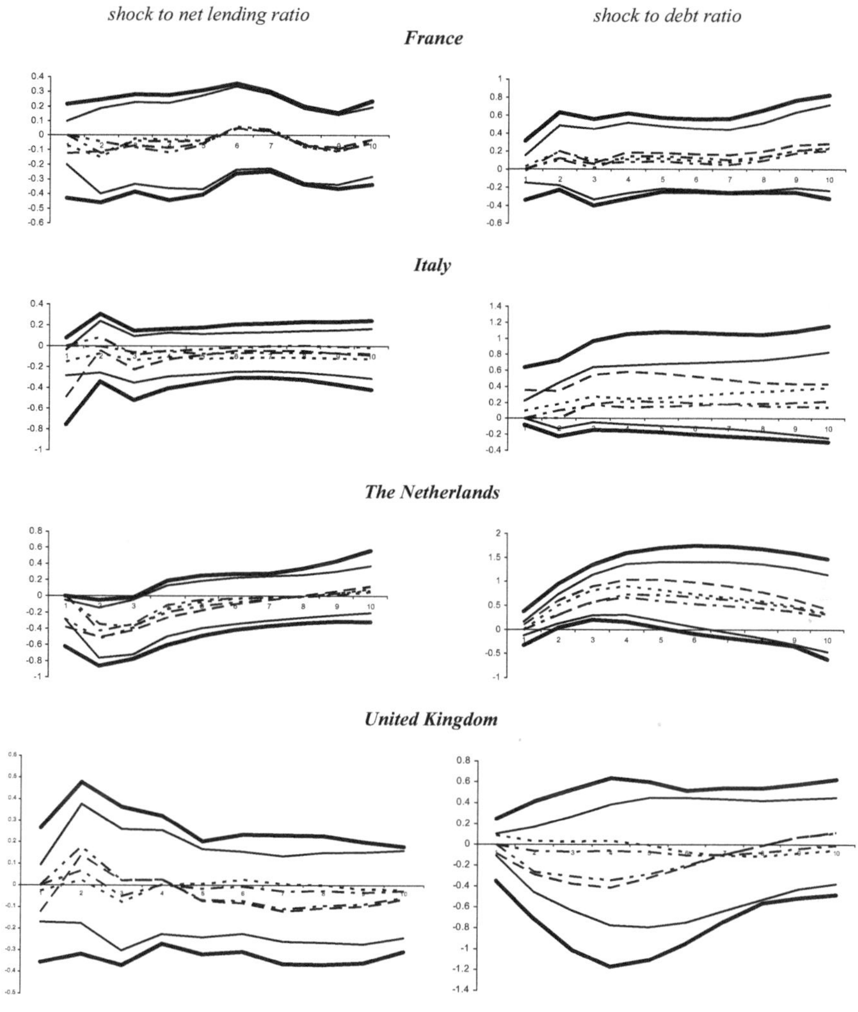

Fig. 3.4. Open economy, 'marginal method', SVAR model (3.3b): conditioned on Euro Area debt ratio; impulse responses of real long-term interest rates to shocks of 1% of GDP in net lending and debt ratio

Notes: (a) graphs display the impulse responses of the interest rate measure, in response to a 1 standard deviation shock, for each of the four Cholesky orders in (3.3a), individual impulse responses follow the order in Fig. 3.1, except for the scaling to the Euro Area wide variable; (b) 90% confidence intervals from bootstrapped model – with 1000 draws – are the average (normal continuous line) and maximum (bold continuous line) of all four Cholesky orders.

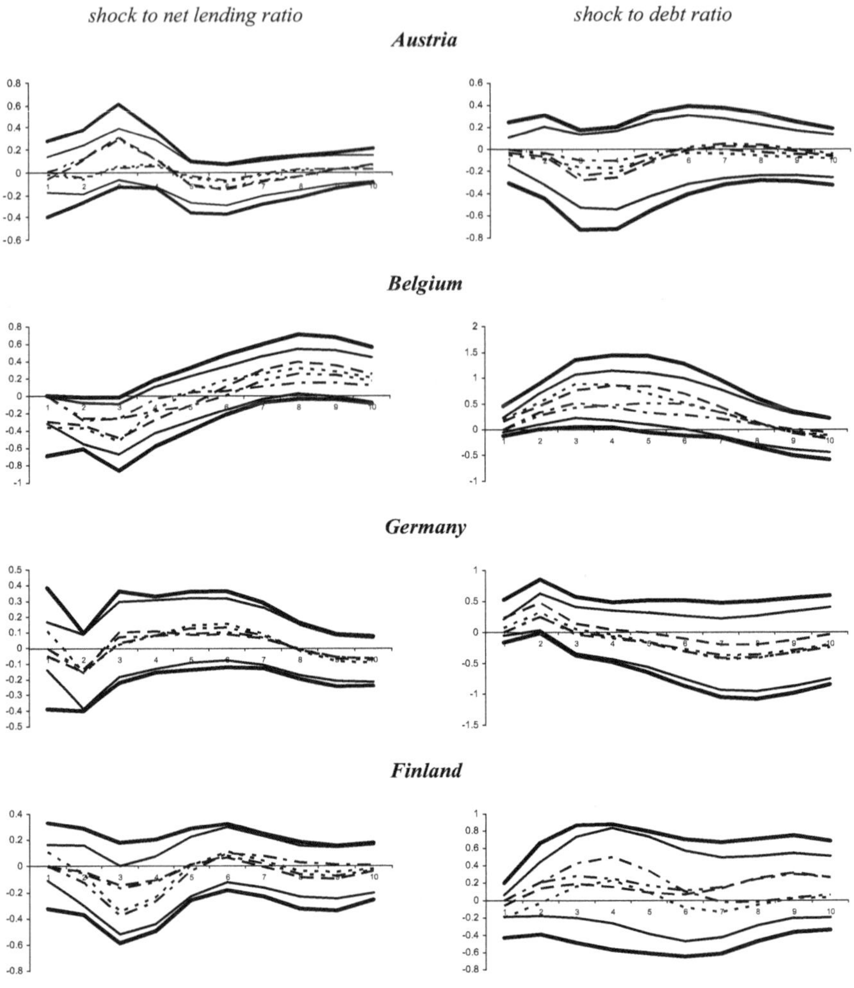
shock to net lending ratio
shock to debt ratio
Austria
Belgium
Germany
Finland

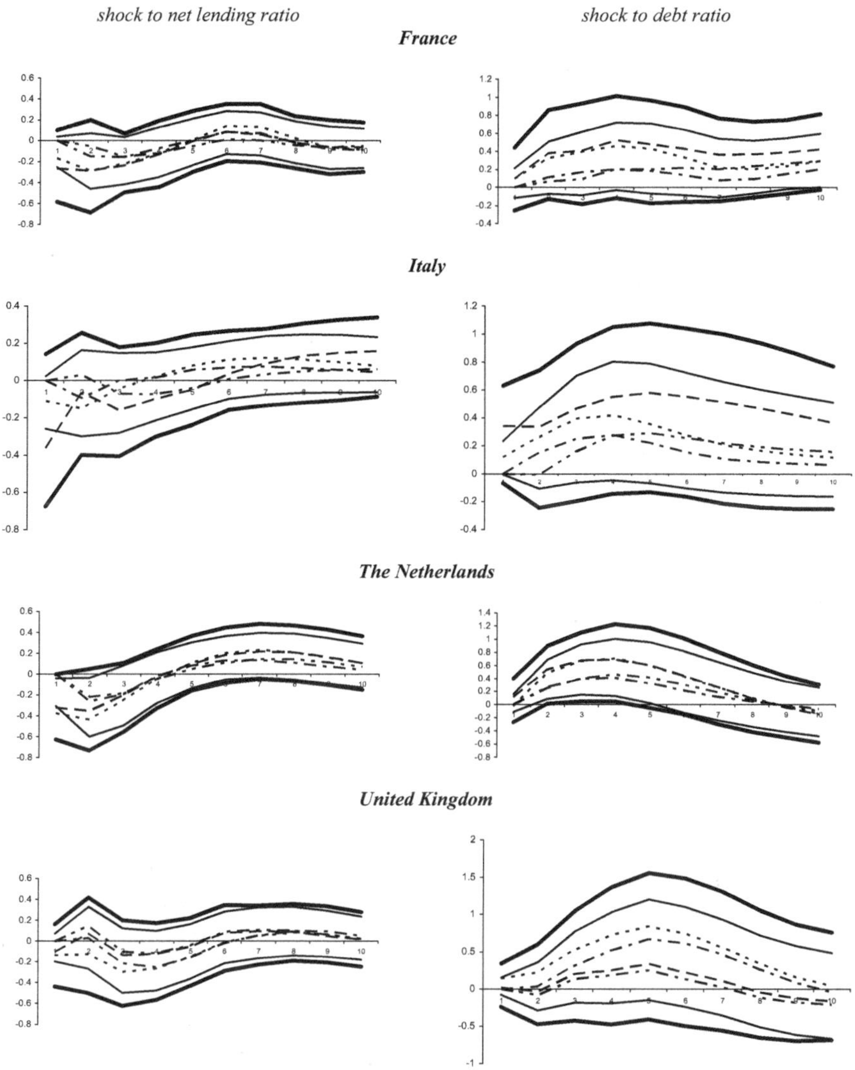

Fig. 3.5 Open economy, 'marginal method', SVAR model (3.3b): conditioned on Euro Area real long-term interest rate; impulse responses of real long-term interest rates to shocks of 1% of GDP in net lending and debt ratio

Notes: (a) graphs display the percentage impulse responses of the interest rate measure, in response to a shock, for each of the four Cholesky orders in (3.3b), individual impulse responses follow the order in Fig. 3.1, except for the scaling to the Euro Area wide variable; (b) 90% confidence intervals from bootstrapped model – with 1000 draws – are the average (normal continuous line) and maximum (bold continuous line) of all four Cholesky orders.

Table 3.5. Open economy, 'marginal method': average point estimated response +/- 1.95 standard error bounds of impulse response to a 1% shock to the debt ratio (from Fig.3.5)

horizon				horizon			
		Austria				**France**	
1	-0.15	**-0.02**	0.11	1	-0.12	**0.05**	0.21
2	-0.32	**-0.06**	0.20	2	-0.07	**0.22**	0.51
3	-0.53	**-0.20**	0.14	3	-0.08	**0.27**	0.62
4	-0.54	**-0.19**	0.17	4	-0.03	**0.35**	0.72
5	-0.42	**-0.08**	0.26	5	-0.06	**0.32**	0.71
		Belgium				**Italy**	
1	-0.05	**0.09**	0.23	1	0.00	**0.11**	0.23
2	0.09	**0.40**	0.71	2	-0.11	**0.19**	0.48
3	0.22	**0.65**	1.08	3	-0.07	**0.32**	0.70
4	0.17	**0.66**	1.15	4	-0.05	**0.38**	0.80
5	0.09	**0.60**	1.10	5	-0.07	**0.36**	0.79
		Germany				**The Nether-lands**	
1	-0.05	**0.08**	0.21	1	-0.11	**0.02**	0.16
2	0.03	**0.33**	0.62	2	0.09	**0.39**	0.69
3	-0.34	**0.04**	0.42	3	0.15	**0.54**	0.92
4	-0.43	**-0.04**	0.35	4	0.13	**0.57**	1.01
5	-0.56	**-0.12**	0.31	5	0.02	**0.49**	0.95
		Finland				**United King-dom**	
1	-0.19	**-0.06**	0.06	1	-0.08	**0.04**	0.15
2	-0.18	**0.13**	0.45	2	-0.29	**0.04**	0.36
3	-0.20	**0.26**	0.73	3	-0.18	**0.30**	0.78
4	-0.26	**0.28**	0.83	4	-0.19	**0.42**	1.03
5	-0.39	**0.17**	0.73	5	-0.15	**0.52**	1.20

Notes: bold entries are point estimates; shaded cells indicate the peak effect.

shock to net lending ratio *shock to debt ratio*

Austria

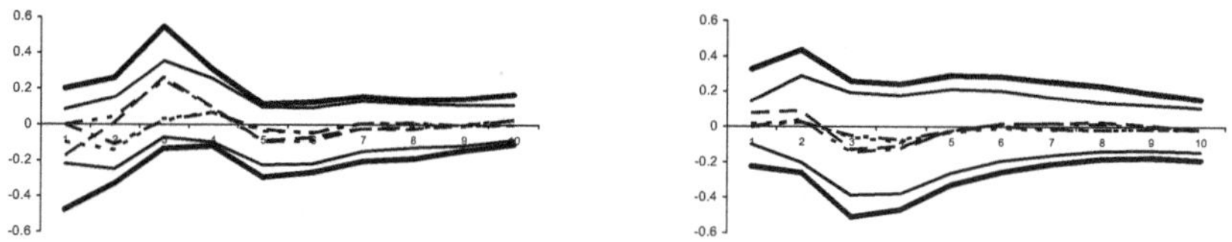

Belgium

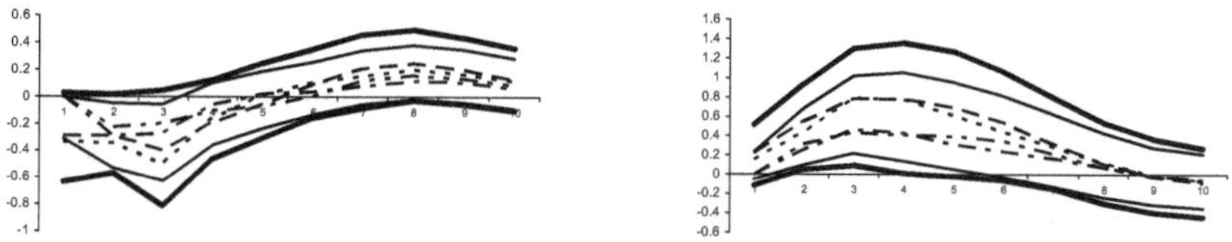

Germany

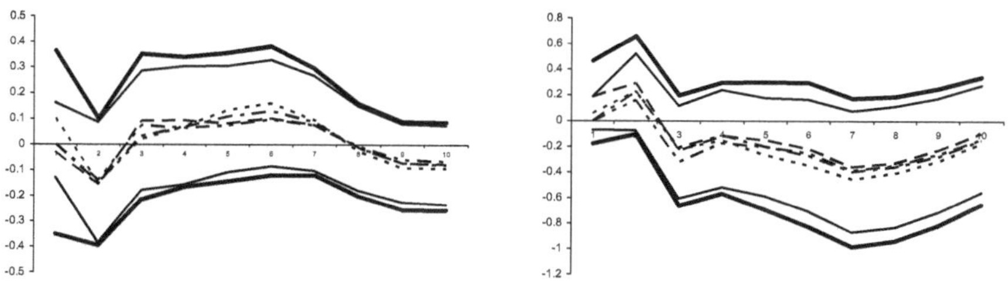

Finland

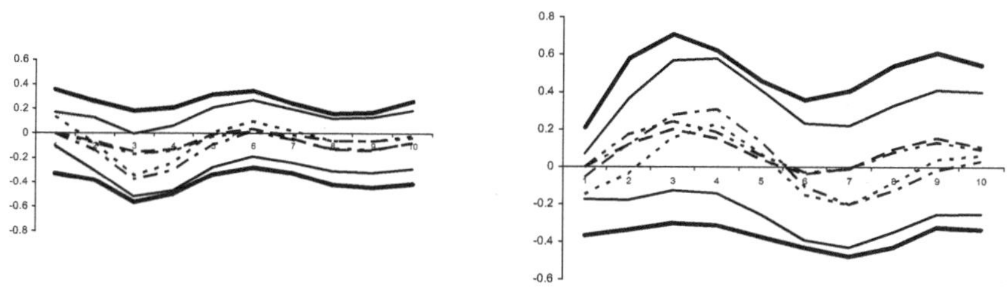

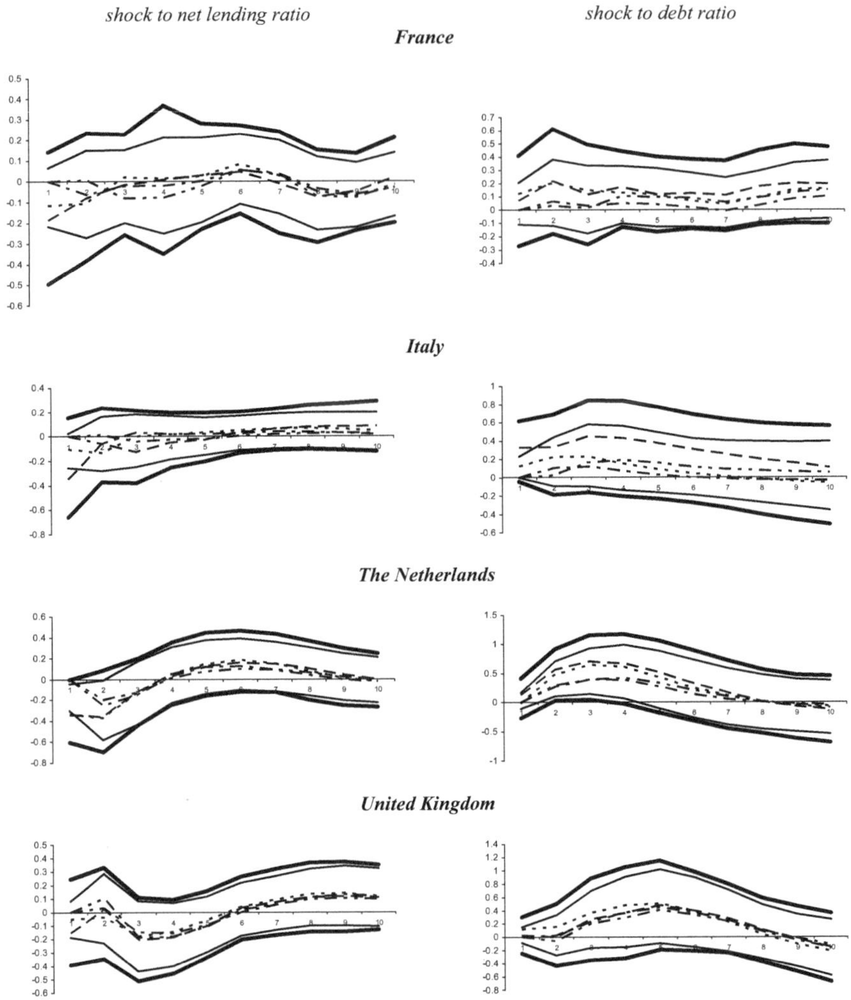

Fig. 3.6. Open economy, 'marginal method', SVAR model (3.3b): conditioned on Euro Area debt ratio and Euro Area real long-term interest rates; impulse responses of real long-term interest rates to shocks of 1% of GDP in net lending and debt ratio

Notes: (a) graphs display the percentage impulse responses of the interest rate measure, in response to a shock, for each of the four Cholesky orders in (3.3b), individual impulse responses follow the order in Fig. 3.2, except for the scaling to the Euro Area wide variable; (b) 90% confidence intervals from bootstrapped model – with 1000 draws – are the average (normal continuous line) and maximum (bold continuous line) of all four Cholesky orders.

Similar results are obtained for a combination of Euro Area debt and interest rates (Fig. 3.6). Euro Area debt adds little in explaining crowding out domestically. This again favours the hypothesis that capital market linkages are crucial for the spillover of fiscal policies, rather than the fiscal rules of the Treaty and the Pact.

The results for the United Kingdom also give an indirect answer as to whether spillover is more relevant for EMU than EU. The open economy model is only slightly less successful for the United Kingdom in finding significant effects of debt accumulation than in other countries (Figs. 3.4-3.6). There is nevertheless a change similar to other EU countries. A tentative conclusion is again that the spillover of financial integration is relatively more important than those related to EMU.

Not surprisingly, debt contributes relatively more to explaining the variance of interest rates when it is the only variable added to the domestic VAR (Table 3.6). When Euro Area interest rates are incorporated, its contribution to the variance of the long-term rates is much smaller than that of deficits. This holds even if the effects of net lending shocks are not relevant. It rather gives some support to an interpretation of a signalling effect of deficits for unsustainable longer-term fiscal policies. Overall, neither net lending nor public debt is an important determinant of real long-term rates, and certainly not at short-term horizons.

How do we square the significant effect in the marginal open economy VAR with the evidence for strong spillover effects in the first open economy model? In the first case, we consider a relative fiscal shock that has a non-significant impact on relative spreads. If we keep the benchmark interest rate fixed, there is, *ceteris paribus*, a large impact on the domestic interest rate. This indicates that changes in the fiscal stance do not affect so much the country spread, but rather affect the aggregate level of interest rates. This confirms the interpretation in Faini (2006). Actually, the point estimates in Faini (2006) are very close to ours. A one percent expansion in EMU primary balances raises the EMU rate on average by 41 basis points in his study. Our country-specific results show such effects to lie between 30 and 70 basis points. The insignificant effect on relative spreads is also corroborated by the small 5 basis points rise in Faini (2006), or in studies that investigate the effects of fiscal policy on default premia (Favero et al., 1997; Codogno et al., 2003). Any consolidation that an individual country undertakes, will largely spillover to Euro Area interest rates. The eventual gain for each country in terms of lower interest rates is rather small, even for the highly indebted countries. A coordinated action for bringing down debt ratios across the EU would pay off with substantially lower long-term interest rates instead.

Table 3.6. Open economy, 'marginal method', SVAR model (3.3b): forecast error variance decomposition of real long-term interest rates (see Fig.s 3.4-3.6)

	horizon	domestic debt endogenous Euro Area debt exogenous		domestic debt endogenousEuro Area real long-term rate exogenous		domestic debt endogenousEuro Area debt and real long-term rate exogenous	
Country	year	Debt	net lending	debt	net lending	debt	net lending
Germany	1	0.01	1.32	3.78	5.74	0.59	2.54
	5	0.41	3.34	4.41	10.55	2.08	8.02
	10	0.37	3.29	4.52	9.96	2.01	7.52
France	1	24.72	5.09	16.30	0.00	7.72	7.37
	5	23.47	4.80	14.40	7.11	5.76	35.26
	10	25.98	4.66	13.94	8.71	5.15	31.04
Italy	1	3.77	1.95	0.75	0.57	1.11	0.40
	5	3.30	15.05	1.27	1.25	6.20	2.85
	10	15.67	10.24	1.43	1.53	13.11	2.34
United Kingdom	1	0.26	0.00	0.48	1.18	0.00	4.04
	5	1.62	5.23	1.80	6.63	1.40	8.56
	10	2.24	5.47	2.56	6.20	2.09	9.60
Austria	1	0.81	0.36	1.19	0.00	2.06	0.85
	5	19.42	1.80	0.91	13.13	3.71	13.88
	10	18.26	1.54	2.96	13.15	5.23	14.44
Belgium	1	0.81	0.12	0.33	3.42	0.00	0.89
	5	2.78	1.55	0.37	7.96	0.76	2.40
	10	1.94	1.63	0.56	8.37	1.56	2.43
Finland	1	0.40	13.53	0.04	8.82	0.64	7.75
	5	10.84	23.73	8.46	9.84	11.34	8.30
	10	24.19	12.57	7.51	11.48	11.41	10.02
Netherlands	1	6.75	3.84	5.68	2.57	6.71	2.67
	5	10.34	6.62	8.00	3.24	9.19	3.80
	10	16.46	5.22	7.45	4.20	8.05	4.77

3.5.3 Robustness checks

The results may be sensitive to the specification we have considered. A novelty we have introduced is to make debt endogenous in the empirical model. In this case, the VAR equation for debt describes the accumulation of deficits via past fiscal imbalances. Alternatively, debt could be specified as an exogenous variable to the economic model, reflecting initial fiscal conditions. The VAR equation in the deficit can then still be considered a fiscal rule. This model is examined in Appendix A. The main lesson is that imposing the stock of public debt as a control variable insufficiently accounts for the persistence of deficit and the accumulation of fiscal imbalances over time. There are hardly any significant responses to 1% shocks in the net lending ratio, except in Belgium and the Netherlands. Modelling both debt and deficits, and retrieving 'Permanent deficit' from debt and 'Temporary deficit' shocks from net lending, helps in the identification.

Another robustness check concerns the specification of the interest rate. We have chosen to include a real long-term rate, but many studies consider the yield instead. Laubach (2003) argues that taking into account both ends of the term structure may improve inference on crowding out effects. Ardagna et al. (2004) find little differences, however, for any of the various measures of interest rates that they examine. We re-estimate all the specifications of closed and open economy models by using the yield between long and short-term rates. The results are summarised in Appendix B. There is a consistent swap of the impulse response across all specifications, as is demonstrated in Fig. 3.8. That is, debt accumulation causes negative interest responses instead of positive ones, or weakens the significant response of long-term rates. This result, also found in Ardagna et al. (2004), must be due to the stronger responses of short-term rates, and can probably be explained by restrictive countercyclical responses of monetary policy or a portfolio effect. The results on spillover are relatively unaffected (Fig. 3.9). By considering spreads, fundamental determinants of interest rates are to a large extent cancelled out and are more affected by fiscal conditions. In this case, the deficit and debt shocks obviously explain more of the variance in the yield.[23] The results stand in contrast with specifications that include both short and long-term rates separately. Both Tavares and Valkanov (2001) or Canzoneri et al. (2002) find large and positive effects of fiscal policy on market returns on bonds.

---

[23] Results not reported.

3.6 Conclusion

The fiscal policy recommendations of the ECB and the EC are based on the crowding out effect of fiscal expansions on long-term interest rates. Fears of fiscal profligacy underlie the fiscal rules of EMU however. The mitigating effect of financial integration on domestic interest rates is only enhanced by the expectations of fiscal or monetary bailouts under a common currency. Such spillover effects would only exacerbate crowding out effects at the EMU level, while insufficiently disciplining fiscal policy in individual Member States.

This chapter constructs an empirical model to examine crowding out effects of deficit and debt accumulation in individual EU countries and the entire Euro Area. The VAR supplements a rules-based representation of fiscal policy with a simple economic model and interest rates. This model is then modified to examine crowding out effects in open economies and to look into the importance of this policy induced spillover.

The main result is that spillover masks the effects of fiscal policy on long-term interest rates. With the exception of some highly indebted countries, there are hardly significant interest rate responses to changes in domestic fiscal policies as such. Changes in the fiscal stance do not affect so much relative country spreads, but rather spillover to aggregate Euro Area interest rates. There is some indirect evidence that this spillover is not related to EMU but mainly derives from financial markets, casting some further doubts on market discipline. We deduce this from the responses of interest rates for the Euro Area as a bloc being only slightly stronger than for the individual Member States. Also, there is no obvious difference in the interest rate responses in the United Kingdom. Hence, the interest rate spillover must be global rather than internal to EMU.

The consequence is that any individual country would not even benefit partially from consolidation of its own public finances. The interest rate spread is only marginally affected, while the decline in interest rates is thinly spread out over all Euro Area economies. Even for the highly indebted countries, the gain is rather small. We contrast in Table 3.7 a coordinated and an individual consolidation of debt by 1% of GDP. With some exceptions, the ensuing drop in domestic interest rates is weaker if other countries do not undertake consolidation too. A coordinated action for bringing down debt ratios across the EU would pay off with overall substantially lower long-term interest rates. A permanent 1% consolidation of debt across the EU brings down interest rates by about 30 basis points, and even more so for highly indebted countries.

Table 3.7. Distribution of interest rate reductions after a debt consolidation of 1% of GDP

	1 year horizon		5 year horizon	
	individually	coordinated	individually	coordinated
Austria	0.05	0.02	0.06	0.08
Belgium	-0.05	-0.09	-0.20	-0.60
Finland	0.08	0.06	-0.35	-0.17
France	-0.02	-0.05	-0.20	-0.32
Germany	-0.08	-0.08	-0.10	0.12
Italy	-0.08	-0.11	-0.17	-0.36
The Netherlands	-0.01	-0.02	-0.20	-0.49
United Kingdom	0.03	-0.04	0.50	-0.52

The results have some further implication for the design of fiscal rules. The evidence in this chapter reveals that permanent deficits create stronger crowding out effects than temporary fiscal imbalances. Evidence for highly indebted countries is rather clear-cut on the large impact on long-term rates. Fiscal rules should focus on the long-term objective of sustainable public finances. Moreover, there are considerable benefits from concerted action of fiscal policymakers that goes beyond simply constraining fiscal discretion with rules. Coordinated action could avoid free-riding on consolidation efforts in other countries. The political and economic costs of unilateral consolidation may well be larger than the longer run benefits from lower interest rates. Joint consolidation of public finances could bring about quicker the desired beneficial economic effects. However, this is subject to four important caveats.

Firstly, coordination may be difficult if the distribution of economic benefits is uneven. It is mainly the highly indebted countries that would benefit from consolidation, even if the results show that the marginal gain is negligible in these countries (about 10 basis points).[24] A more serious obstruction is that the gain in some countries, and particularly in Germany, could be nil. Whether countries are willing to suffer the short-term pains of consolidation without longer term gains in terms of lower rates is an open question. Secondly, we find that spillover mainly come from global capital markets. The eventual lowering of interest rates may be smaller than our estimates suggest and also spread to other third countries. Nevertheless, it should not be underestimated that EMU is one of the large players on global bond markets. Thirdly, the argument for coordination is

[24] This reflect the difference in the decline in interest rates when highly indebted countries undertake a unilateral domestic consolidation (as in model 3.2a-b), as compared to the spread relative to the exogenous euro are rates (as in model 3.3b).

perhaps not so convincing in cases where spillover comes from capital markets. After all, the mitigating effect of financial markets is a purely pecuniary externality that does not really require international coordination. The allocation of savings to the public or private sector, whether at home or abroad, is efficient. The ongoing integration of financial markets under EMU can only have increased this spillover. Finally, the contribution of fiscal policy to long-term interest rates is rather small, and we find this to be a robust result. Other drivers of long-term interest rates are more important. However, we have considered only the effect of the aggregate deficit or debt on interest rates. Changes in the composition of spending categories and tax instruments may have different supply side effects that also impinge on interest rates. How to achieve a coordinated fiscal consolidation with different policy instruments is an open question. The Broad Economic Policy Guidelines are a step in bringing about a virtuous circle of the coordination of fiscal policies, but do not have a specific consolidation purpose at this stage.

The results of this paper can be extended in a few directions. If spillover is mainly related to capital market integration, one hypothesis is that fiscal policies probably have global rather than regional effects. Results in Tanzi and Lutz (1993) and Ardagna et al. (2004) go in the same direction. An extension of the results to incorporate the fiscal stance in other OECD countries, especially the United States and Japan, could shed some light on this.

As financial integration has deepened substantially in the EMU, the evidence on crowding out effects in the Euro Area is probably a conservative lower bound estimate. The benefits of coordinated consolidation have probably become larger over time. Monetary union is indeed a complete overhaul of the monetary and the fiscal policy regime. The incentives on governments' financing decisions have changed completely, and are regulated by a combination of deficit rules and the no bailout clause. Evidence in Faini (2006) points to somewhat stronger spillover effects since 1999, albeit for the highly indebted countries only. In order to extrapolate the evidence to EMU, we need to construct an empirical benchmark that mimics the effect of monetary union. Moreover, uniform monetary policy settings could be simulated as in Giuliodori and Beetsma (2005).

Appendix A: Domestic economy: SVAR models with exogenous debt ratio

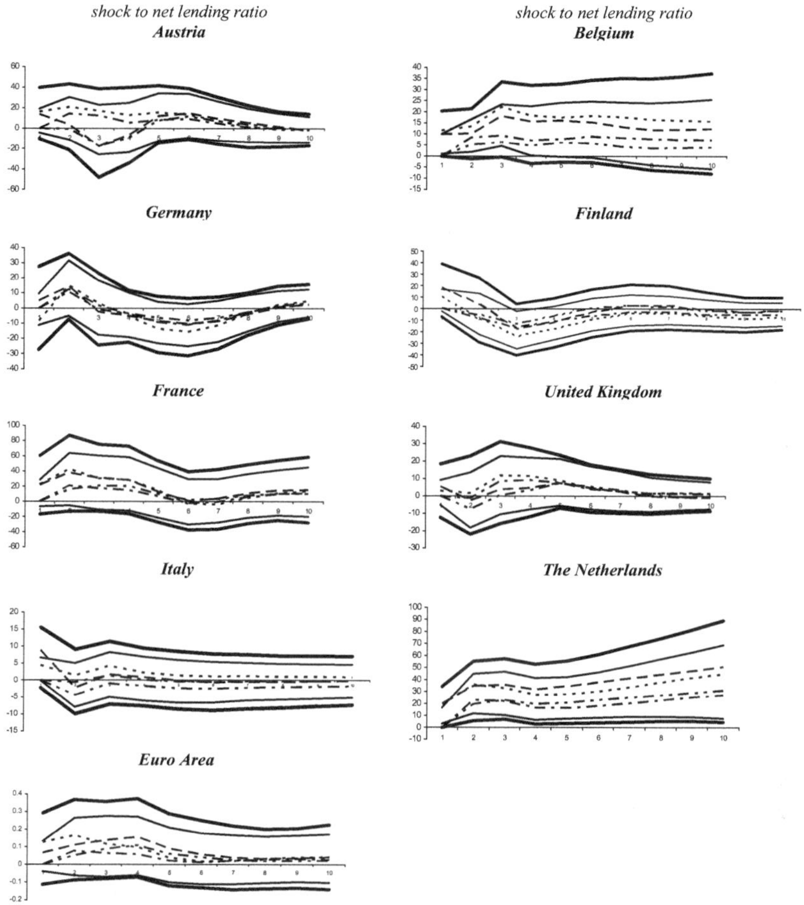

Fig. 3.7. Domestic economy, SVAR-model (3.2a-b): impulse responses of real long-term interest rates to shocks of 1% of GDP in net lending ratio

Notes: (a) graphs display the percentage point impulse responses of the interest rate measure, in response to a fiscal shock, for each of the four Cholesky orders in (3.2a-b), ----- is $[Y \quad M \quad F]'$, – – – is $[M \quad Y \quad F]'$; – - – - is $[F \quad Y \quad M]'$ and — - - - — is $[F \quad M \quad Y]'$; (b) 90% confidence intervals from bootstrapped model – with 1000 draws – are the average (normal continuous line) and maximum (bold continuous line) of all four Cholesky orders.

Appendix B: SVAR models with yield

shock to net lending ratio *shock to debt ratio*

Austria

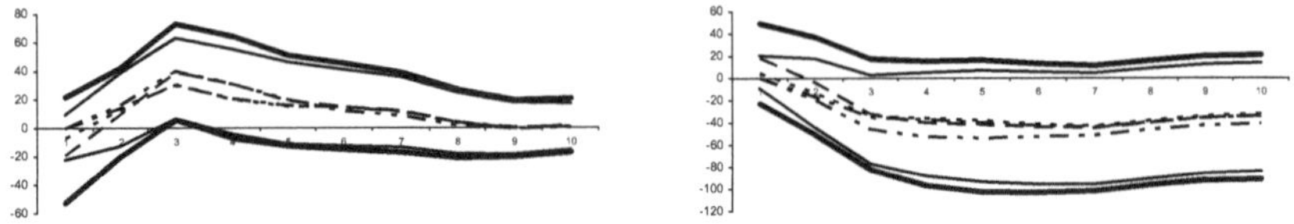

Belgium

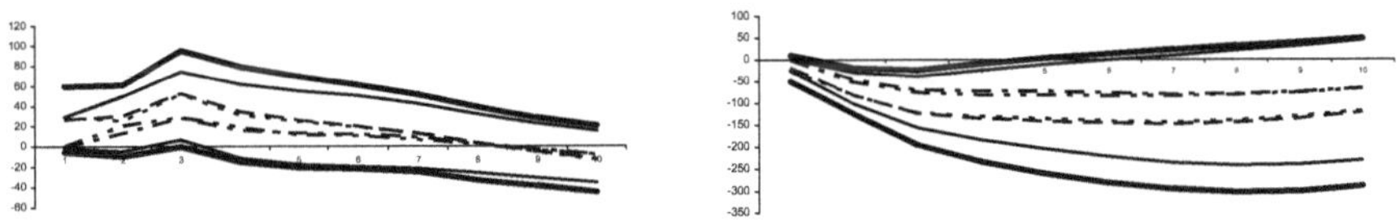

Germany

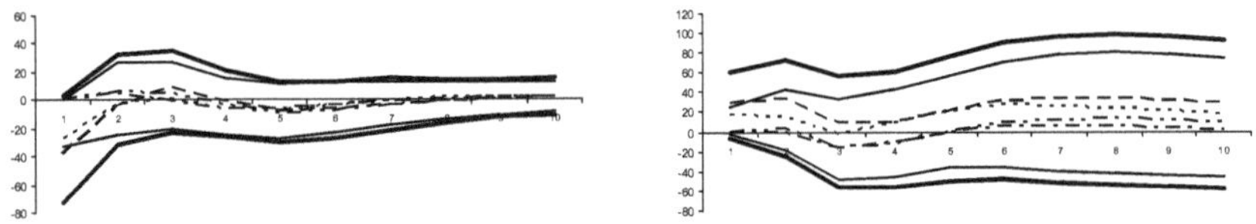

Finland

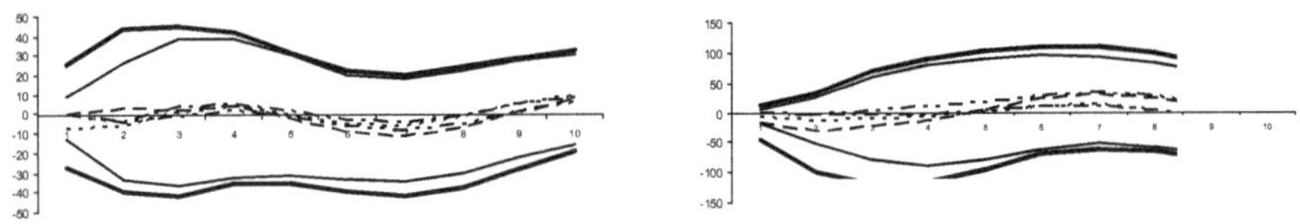

France

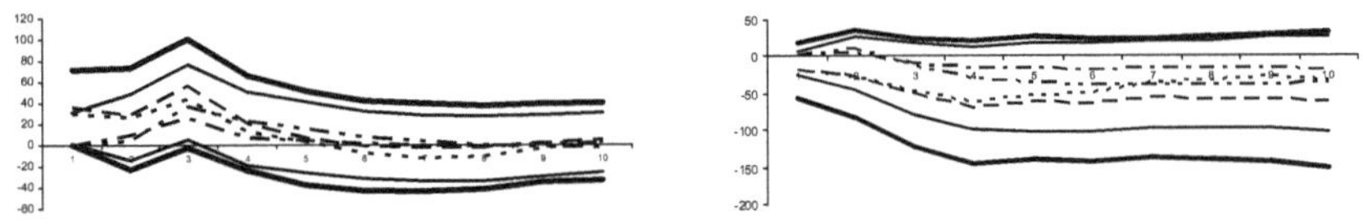

shock to net lending ratio *shock to debt ratio*

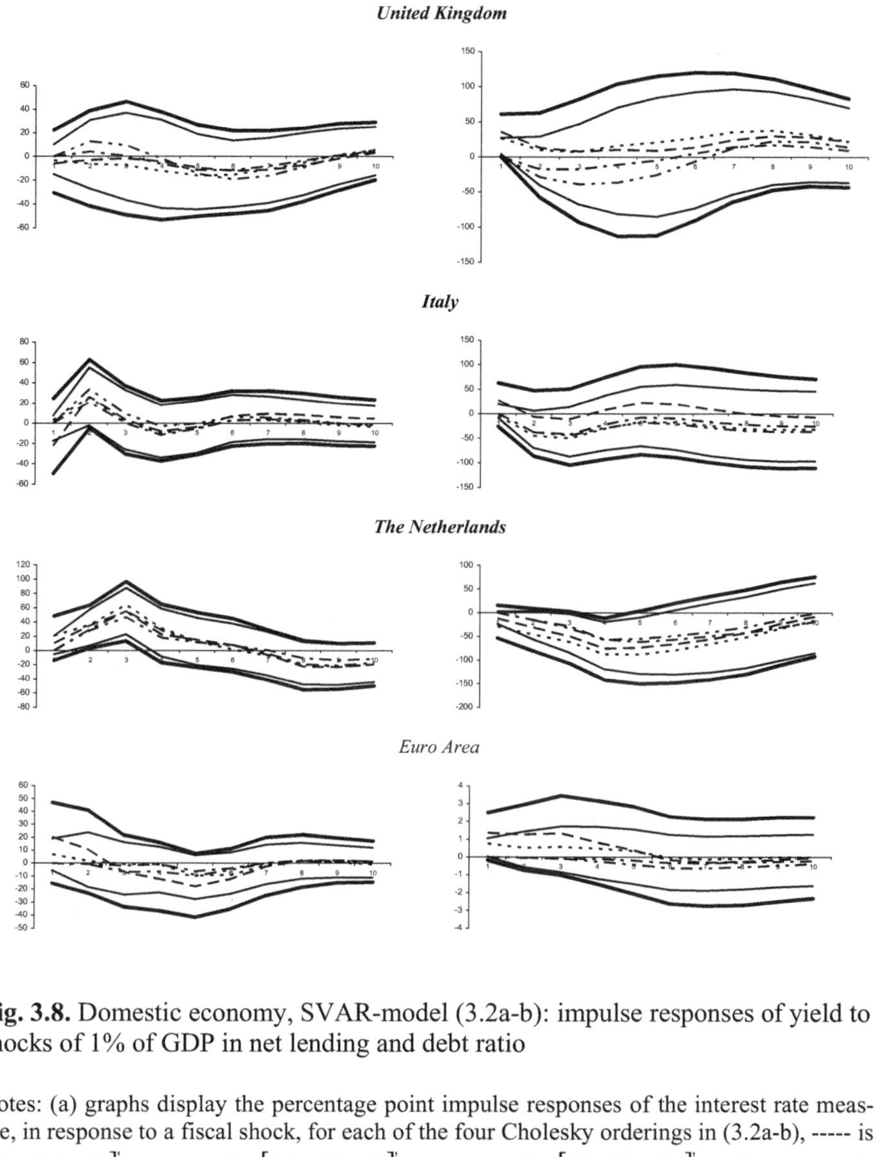

Fig. 3.8. Domestic economy, SVAR-model (3.2a-b): impulse responses of yield to shocks of 1% of GDP in net lending and debt ratio

Notes: (a) graphs display the percentage point impulse responses of the interest rate measure, in response to a fiscal shock, for each of the four Cholesky orderings in (3.2a-b), ----- is $[Y \quad M \quad F]'$, — — — is $[M \quad Y \quad F]'$; — - — — is $[F \quad Y \quad M]'$ and — - - - — is $[F \quad M \quad Y]'$; (b) 90% confidence intervals from bootstrapped model – with 1000 draws – are the average (normal continuous line) and maximum (bold continuous line) of all four Cholesky orderings.

shock to net lending ratio *shock to debt ratio*

Austria

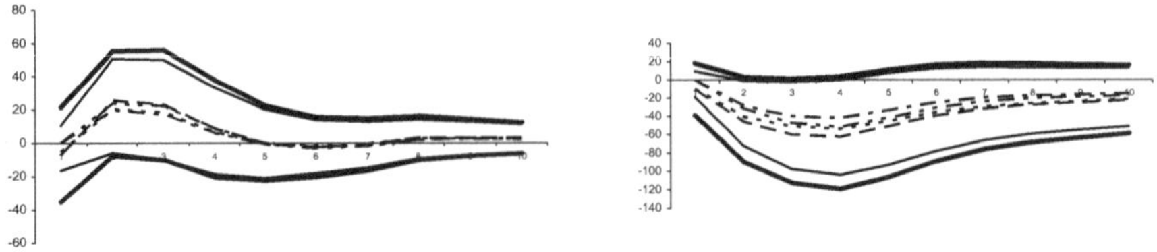

Belgium

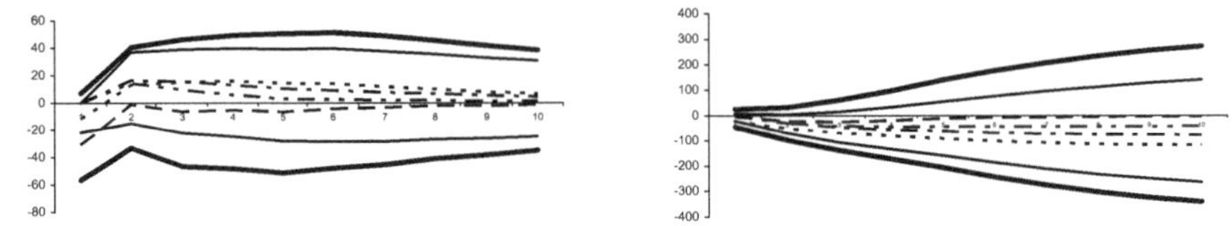

Germany

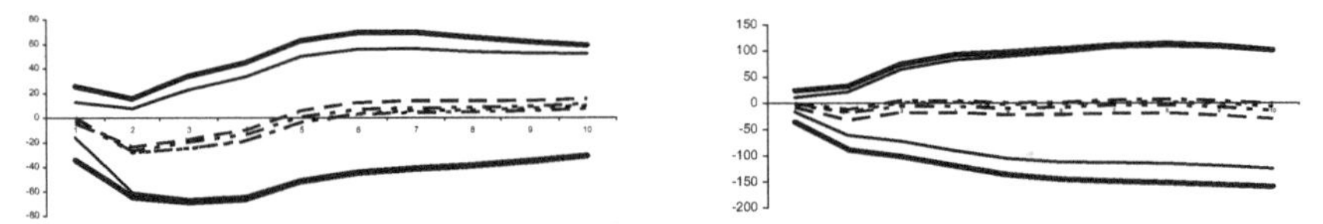

Finland

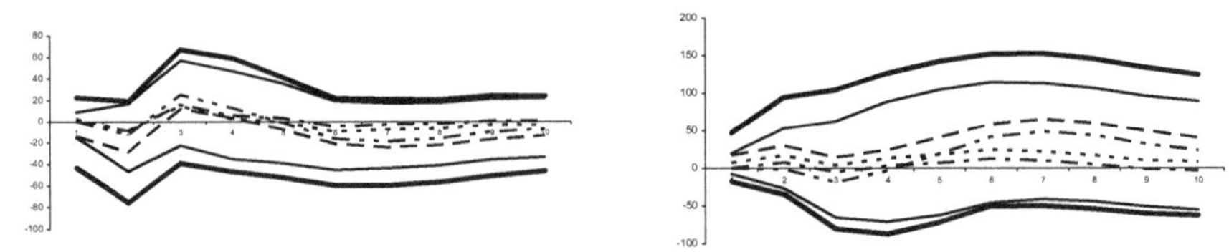

France

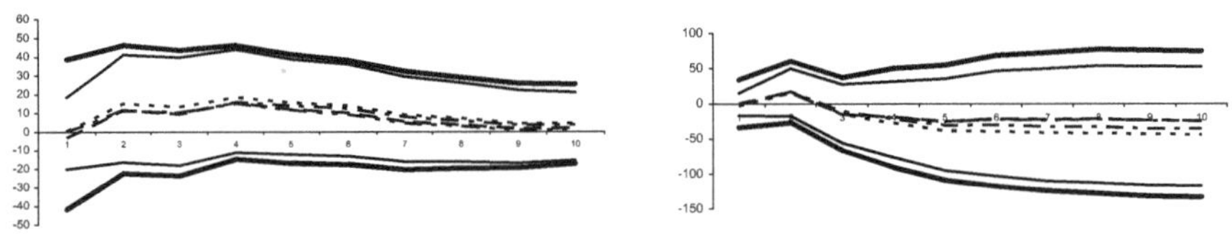

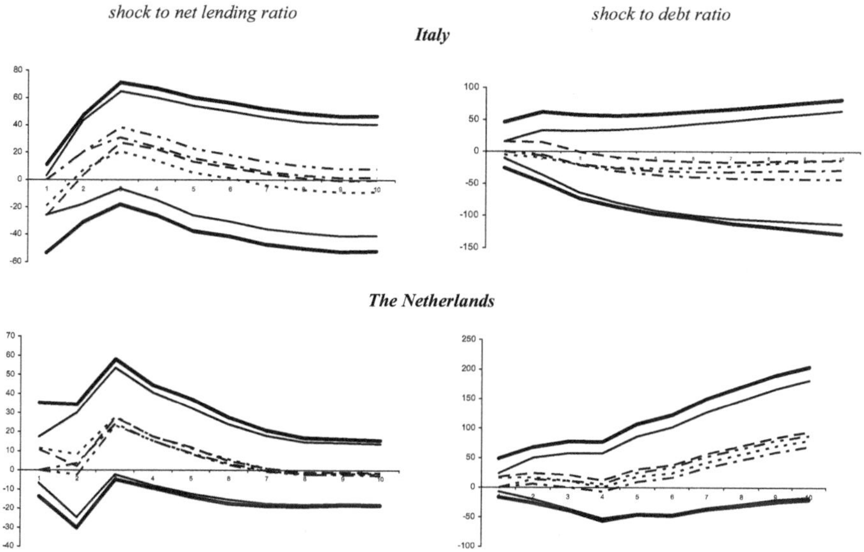

Fig. 3.9. Open economy, 'marginal method', SVAR model (3.3b): conditioned on Euro Area real long-term interest rate; impulse responses of real long-term interest rates to shocks of 1% of GDP in net lending and debt ratio.

Notes: (a) graphs display the percentage point impulse responses of the interest rate measure, in response to a fiscal shock, for each of the four Cholesky orders in (3.2a-b), ----- is $[Y \quad M \quad F]'$, — — — is $[M \quad Y \quad F]'$; — - — - is $[F \quad Y \quad M]'$ and — - - - — is $[F \quad M \quad Y]'$; 90% confidence intervals from bootstrapped model – with 1000 draws – are the average (normal continuous line) and maximum (bold continuous line) of all four Cholesky orders.

References

Afonso, A. and Strauch, R., (2003), Fiscal policy events and interest rate swaps spreads: some evidence from EU', ECB working paper no. 303.

Ahmed, S. and Rogers, J., (1995), Government budget deficits and trade deficits. Are present value constraints satisfied in long term data?, Journal of Monetary Economics, vol. 36, p. 351-374.

Alesina, A., De Broeck, M., Prati, A., and Tabellini, G., (1992), Default risk on government debt in OECD countries, Economic Policy, vol. 15, p. 427-463.

Alesina, A., Ardagna, S., Perotti, R., and Schiantarelli, F., (1999), Fiscal policy, profits and investment, American Economic Review, vol. 92(3), p. 571-589.

Ardagna, S., Caselli, F., and Lane, T., (2004), Fiscal discipline and the cost of public debt service, NBER working paper no. 10788.

Barth, J., Iden, G., Russek, F. and Wohar, M., (1991), The effects of federal budget deficits on interest rates and the composition of domestic output, in: Penner, R., (ed.), The great fiscal experiment, Washington D.C.: Urban Institute Press, p. 69-141.

Bayoumi, T., Goldstein, M. and Woglom, G., (1995), Do credit markets discipline sovereign borrowers? Evidence from the US States, Journal of Money, Credit and Banking, vol.27(4), p.1046-1059.

Beetsma, R., and Bovenberg, L., (1999), Does monetary unification lead to excessive debt accumulation?, Journal of Public Economics, vol. 74, p. 299-325.

Beetsma, R., and Jensen, H., (2004), Mark-up fluctuations and fiscal policy stabilization in a monetary union, Journal of Macroeconomics, vol. 26, p. 357-376.

Beetsma, R., and Vermeylen, K., (2002), The effect of monetary unification on public debt and its real return, CEPR discussion paper no. 3491.

Beetsma, R., Giuliodori, M., and Klaassen, F., (2005), Trade spillover of fiscal policy in the European Union: a panel analysis, CEPR discussion paper no. 5222.

Bernheim, B., (1987), Ricardian equivalence: an evaluation of theory and evidence, in: Fisher, S. (ed.), NBER Macroeconomics Annual, Cambridge, Mass.: MIT Press, p. 263-304.

Bernoth, K., Von Hagen, J. and Schuhknecht, L., (2004), The determinants of the yield differential in the EU government bond market, CEPR discussion paper no. 4465.

Blanchard, O. and Perotti, R., (2002), An empirical characterisation of the dynamic effects of changes in government spending and taxes on output, Quarterly Journal of Economics, vol. 117(4), p. 1329-1368.

Bohn, H., (1998), The behaviour of US public debt and deficits, Quarterly Journal of Economics, vol. 113(3), p. 949-963.

Brook, A., (2003), Recent and prospective trends in real long-term interest rates: fiscal policy and other drivers, OECD Economics Department working paper no. 21.

Canzoneri, M., Cumby, R., and Diba, B., (2001), Fiscal discipline and exchange rate regimes, The Economic Journal, vol. 111, p. 667-690.

Canzoneri, M., Cumby, R., and Diba, B., (2001), Is the price level determined by the needs of fiscal solvency?, American Economic Review, vol. 91(5), p. 1221-1238.

Canzoneri, M., Cumby, R., and Diba, B., (2002), Should the European Central Bank and the Federal reserve be concerned about fiscal policy?, in: Rethinking stabilization policy, Federal Reserve Bank of Kansas City, p. 333-389.

Caporale, G., and Williams, G., (2002), Long-term nominal interest rates and domestic fundamentals, Review of Financial Economics, vol. 11, p. 119-130.

Cebula, R., (1998), an empirical analysis of the impact of federal budget deficits on long-term nominal interest rate yields: using alternative expected inflation measures, Review of Financial Economics, vol. 7(1), p. 55-64.

Cebula, R., and Koch, J., (1989), An empirical note on deficits, interest rates, and international capital flows, Quarterly Review of Economics and Business, vol. 29(3), p. 121-127.

Chang, R., (1990), International coordination of fiscal deficits, Journal of Monetary Economics, vol. 25, p. 347-366.

Codogno, L., Favero, C., and Missale, A., (2003), Yield spreads on EMU government bonds, Economic Policy, p. 503-532.

Conway, P., and Orr, A., (2002), The GIRM: a global interest rate model, Westpac Institutional Bank Occasional Paper.

Copeland, L. and Jones, S., (2001), Default probabilities of European sovereign debt: market-based estimates, Applied Economics Letters, vol. 8, p. 321-324.

Dai, Q., and Phillipon, T., (2005), Fiscal policy and the term structure of interest rates, NBER working paper series no. 11574.

Drudi, F. and Prati, A., (2000), Signaling fiscal regime sustainability, European Economic Review, vol. 44(10), p. 1897-1930.

Elmendorf, D., (1993), Actual budget deficit expectations and interest rates, Harvard Institute of Economic Research.

Elmendorf, D., (1996), The effect of deficit reduction laws on real interest rates, Federal Reserve Board, Finance and Economics discussion paper no. 44.

Elmendorf, D., and Mankiw, N., (1999), Government debt, in: Taylor, J., and Woodford, M., (eds.), Handbook of Macroeconomics, Amsterdam: Elsevier Science, Chapter 25.

Engen, E., and Hubbard, G., (2004), Federal government debt and interest rates, NBER working paper no. 10681.

European Commission, (2004), Public Finances in EMU, European Economy, Directorate General for Economic and Financial Affairs, vol. 3.

Evans, P., and Marshall, D., (2002), Economic determinants of the nominal Treasury yield curve, Federal Reserve Bank of Chicago, working paper no. 16.

Evans, P., (1987a), Interest rates and expected future budget deficits in the US, Journal of Political Economy, vol. 95(1).

Evans, P., (1987b), Do budget deficits raise nominal interest rates? Evidence from six countries, Journal of Monetary Economics, vol. 20, p. 281-300.

Fagan, G., Henry, J., and Mestre, R., (2001), An Area-Wide Model (AWM) for the Euro Area, ECB working paper no. 42.

Faini, R., (2006), Fiscal policy and interest rates in Europe, Economic Policy (forthcoming).

Favero, C., (2003), How do European monetary and fiscal authorities behave?, in: Buti, M., (ed.), Monetary and fiscal policies in EMU: Interactions and coordination, Cambridge: Cambridge University Press, p. 217-245.

Favero, C., Giavazzi, F., and Spaventa, L., (1997), High yields: the spread on German interest rates, Economic Journal, vol. 107, p. 956-985.

Feldstein, M., (1986), Budget deficits, tax rules and real interest rates, NBER working paper no. 1970.

Ford, R., and Laxton, D., (1999), World public debt and real interest rates, Oxford Review of Economic Policy, vol. 15(2), p. 77-94.

Friedman, B., (2005), Deficits and debt in the short and long run, NBER working paper no. 11630.

Fry, R., and Pagan, A., (2005), Some issues in using VARs for macro-econometric research, Centre for Applied Macroeconomic Analysis working paper no. 18.

Gale, W., and Orszag, P., (2002), The economic effects of long-term fiscal discipline, Brookings Institution.

Ganelli, G., (2005), The New Open Economy Macroeconomics of government debt, Journal of International Economics, vol. 65(1), p. 167-184.

Giuliodori, M., and Beetsma, R., (2005), What are the spillovers from fiscal shocks in Europe? An empirical analysis, De Economist, vol. 153(2), p. 167-197.

Hansen, L., Roberds, W., and Sargent, T., (1991), Time series implications of present value budget balance and of martingale models of consumption and taxes, in: Hansen, L., and Sargent, T., (eds.), Rational expectations econometrics, Westview Press: Colombia, Boulder, p. 121-162.

Heppke-Falk, K. and Hueffner, F., (2004), Expected budget deficits and interest rate swap spreads – evidence for France, Germany and Italy, Deutsche Bundesbank discussion paper no. 40.

Kitchen, J., (1996), Domestic and international financial market responses to federal deficit announcements, Journal of International Money and Finance, vol. 15, p. 239-254.

Kitchen, J., (2002), A note on interest rates and structural budget deficits, mimeo.

Knot, K., and De Haan, J., (1995), Fiscal policy and interest rates in the European Community, European Journal of Political Economy, vol. 11, p. 171-187.

Knot, K., (1996), Fiscal policy and interest rates in the European Union, Cheltenham: Edward Elgar Publishing.

Landon, S., and Smith, C., (2000), Government debt spillover and creditworthiness in a federation, The Canadian Journal of Economics, vol. 33(3), p. 364-661.

Laubach, T., (2003), New evidence on the interest rate effects of budget deficits and debt, mimeo, Board of Governors of the Federal Reserve System.

Linde, J., (2001), Fiscal policy and interest rates in a small open economy, Finnish Economic Paper, vol. 14(2).

Marcellino, M., (2002), Some stylised facts on non-systematic fiscal policy in the Euro-area, CEPR discussion paper no. 3635.

Miller, S., and Russek, F., (1996), Do federal deficits affect interest rates? Evidence from three econometric methods, Journal of Macroeconomics, vol. 18(3), p. 403-428.

Mountford, A., and Uhlig, H., (2005), What are the effects of fiscal policy shocks?, SFB649 discussion paper no. 39.

Nicoletti, G., (1989), A cross-country analysis of private consumption, inflation and the debt neutrality hypothesis, OECD Economic Studies, no. 11, p. 43-87.

O'Donovan, B., Orr, A., and Rae, D., (1996), A world interest rate model, National Bank of New Zealand, Financial Research Paper no. 7.

Orr, A., Edey, M., and Kennedy, M., (1995), The determinants of real long-term interest rates: 17 country pooled time series evidence, OECD working paper no. 155.

Paesani, P., Strauch, R., and Kremer, M., (2006), Public debt and long-term interest rates: the case of Germany, Italy and the USA, ECB working paper no. 656.

Perotti, R., (2005), Estimating the effects of fiscal policy in OECD countries, CEPR working paper no. 4842.

Prasad, E., and Lumsdaine, R., (2003), Identifying the common component of international economic fluctuations: a new approach, Economic Journal, vol. 113, p. 101-127.

Ramey, V., and Shapiro, M., (1998), Costly capital reallocation and the effects of government spending, Carnegie Rochester Conference on Public Policy, vol. 48, p. 145-194.

Reinhart, V., and Sack, B., (2000), The economic consequences of disappearing government debt, Brookings Papers on Economic Activity, vol. 2, p. 163-209.

Sims, C., (1988), Identifying policy effects, in: Bryant, R., Henderson, D., Holtman, G., Hooper, P., and Symansky, S., (eds.), Empirical macroeconomics for independent economies, The Brookings Institutions, Washington D.C., p. 305-321.

Sims, C., Stock, J., and Watson, M., (1990), Inference in time series models with some unit roots, Econometrica, vol. 58, p. 113-144.

Tanzi, V., and Lutz, M., (1993), Interest rates and government debt: are the linkages global rather than national?, in: Verbon, H., and Van Winden, F., The Political Economy of Government Debt, Amsterdam: Elsevier Science, p. 233-253.

Tavares, J., and Valkanov, R., (2001), The neglected effect of fiscal policy on stock and bond returns, mimeo, UCLA.

Wachtel, P., and Young, J., (1987), Deficit announcements and interest rates, American Economic Review, vol. 77, p. 1007-1012.

4 Budgetary stabilisation and the level of public debt

Niko Gobbin

4.1 Introduction

In this chapter we look into the interaction between the level of government debt and the effects of fiscal policy on private consumption in a number of EU-15 countries. Hence, the chapter somewhat deviates from other chapters in the book: We do not focus on economic spillovers between countries, but remain within the country borders. The questions we address are nonetheless valuable ones to evaluate policy coordination. If the transmission of fiscal policy actions depends on the debt level, a common EU-wide fiscal action will differently affect the individual Member States. Or put differently, to achieve a common goal different actions are needed. In addition, a common fiscal target, such as the Maastricht deficit criterion, might be harder to achieve in a country with a higher or lower initial government debt level. On the other hand, dependence of fiscal transmission on the debt level might also be seen as an additional rationale for the debt convergence criterion.

Existing theory supports the hypothesis that a country's initial debt situation can determine how its agents reacts to fiscal policy changes. In a world that is characterized by some degree of myopia and market imperfections, people will, on aggregate, react in a more Keynesian way if debt levels are low. However, if government debt gets out of control, non-Keynesian behaviour can occur. Empirical support for these hypotheses is weak. The few contributions that present significant results, lack robustness. Existing work also suffers from a large degree of arbitrariness in the analysis. Theory does not provide a practical translation for 'a situation in which government debt gets out of control'. Multiple operational definitions are defendable. This is especially problematic since it has been shown that results are seldom robust to marginal changes in the definition.

In this chapter we apply an alternative estimation method to steer clear of this arbitrary choice. We show that the effects of fiscal policy actions in the EU-15 depend on the initial level of government debt by means of a threshold estimation regression. Private consumption reacts differently to fiscal policy actions once a certain (statistically significant) threshold is crossed. Differently, but, however, not necessarily in more non-Keynesian way. While the overall impact of tax changes and social security expenditure is unambiguously smaller above the threshold, this is not necessarily the case for government consumption and subsidies.

In Sect. 4.2 we look into the relevant theoretical and empirical literature. In Sect. 4.3 we explore the threshold estimation methodology. Sect. 4.4 looks into the data and the regression specification. The estimates are presented in Sect. 4.5. We end with some conclusions.

4.2 A look at fiscal theory and empirics

Traditional Keynesian thinking links a tighter fiscal policy to a reduced aggregate demand. If a government raises taxes or cuts transfer payments, disposable income and private spending are reduced. If a government decreases its consumption or investment, aggregate demand is directly reduced. Multiplier-accelerator mechanisms will reinforce the initial negative impact. This basic Keynesian logic cannot account for the severe fiscal contractions in Ireland and Denmark that coincided with an economic boom in the 1980s (Giavazzi and Pagano, 1990). Many potential explanations for the occurrence of these 'non-Keynesian' effects were formulated, including expectations, wealth and credibility effects and crowding-out. Next it was shown that the strength of these explanations depended on the composition (Alesina and Perotti ,1995; Alesina and Ardagna, 1998; Heylen and Everaert, 2000), the magnitude (Giavazzi and Pagano, 1995; Giavazzi et al., 2000) and the timing of a fiscal consolidation (Alesina and Perotti, 1995; Heylen and Everaert, 2000).

Also the initial debt level has been identified as a potential determinant of the outcome of a fiscal action. Firstly, a high debt rate means high future taxes. When debt increases, so does the tax rate needed to stabilize the debt. Blanchard (1990) postulates that taxes become disruptive if they exceed a certain critical level, known to the public. Thus, the tax rate is a function of the debt level and a rise in this tax rate is non-linear in its effects on output. He concludes that (1) the higher the current tax rate, (2) the larger the potential output loss because of an excessive tax rate and (3) the nearer the debt gets to the critical level, the more a society has to gain from a consolidation. In that 'critical' context the effects of stabilizing the debt will be less negative than those predicted by Keynesian theory. Hence, to be able to predict the effects of a fiscal policy action it is important to know how much 'fiscal space' is left: i.e. how far away the tax rate is from its critical level.

Secondly, the debt rate might also be a good predictor for the timing of the next consolidation. Bertola and Drazen (1993) consider a government that gradually increases its consumption until the government spending-to-GDP ratio reaches a critical level (the so-called 'trigger point'). At that moment the government cuts drastically in its consumption. In this set-up the pre-stabilization situation must deteriorate noticeably to induce an inevitable stabilization. The closer 'unsustainability' comes, the greater the probability of a fiscal contraction in the next period gets. When spending levels are already high, a further unexpected increase advances the necessary expenditure reduction even more, so the present discounted value of future government expenditure (and future taxes) diminishes. As an agent bases his consumption on expected future government spending, he will consume more. An increase in government expenditure may be expansionary if people expect that expenditure will be cut soon. Agents react in a more Keynesian manner when the trigger point is reached and more Ricardian when the debt situation is 'normal' in this set-up. However, when the trigger point is crossed and a consolidation does not occur, then a strong contraction of private consumption will occur. People realize that they made an error in estimating future spending (taxes) and need to correct for it. An anticipated consolidation has no contractionary effects.

The counter-intuitive result that consumers spend more in case of a very profligate government, stems from the assumption that agents are either infinitely lived or value their own well-being no more than that of future generations. Sutherland (1995) assumes a more appealing approach. In his model agents are especially concerned about the present. In normal times, i.e. when debt levels are moderate, consumers expect the next budget consolidation to be far away. They do not adjust their expectation about future taxes in response to a fiscal stimulus as the burden of such a consolidation will likely be put on the next generations. So the current generation will react in a Keynesian way. However, when debt levels are high (a critical level of government debt is reached), every new fiscal expansion brings a consolidation alarmingly near. The bill is then likely to be presented while the current generation is still alive. As the cost of a fiscal consolidation outweighs numerous times the gains of the expansion, any additional fiscal expansion will cause a economic contraction. The link between current fiscal policy and future expected taxes, and the distribution of these expected future taxes across generations will determine whether a fiscal policy is expansionary or contractionary. In the Sutherland model, agents react in a Keynesian manner under 'normal circumstances' and in a non-Keynesian manner in 'crisis situations'.

Perotti (1999) integrates different aspects of the previous models. He first looks at the share of credit constrained people in a society . For those people an unanticipated increase in taxes will always lower their consumption and a positive shock in government expenditure will always increase it. Their consumption is completely determined by disposable income. Hence, they resemble the agents in the Sutherland model. On the other hand, agents who are not credit constrained will not always decrease consumption after an unexpected increase in taxes. If government spending has not changed, the increase in current taxes will be exactly equal to the drop in the present discounted value of expected future taxes (so consumption will not be altered based on this). These agents act in accordance with the Bertola and Drazen model. Finally, Perotti incorporates the Blanchard model. By raising current taxes, current distorting effects of taxation are strengthened. On the other hand, because future taxes are reduced, the future tax distortions are reduced too. The net effect of these two opposite movements will determine the impact on consumption of the unconstrained agents. A surprise increase in government consumption will always depress private consumption as the present discounted value of future taxes increases.

The combined effects of credit constrained and unconstrained agents determines the total effect on private consumption. According to Perotti (1999) the sign of the total effect switches at higher levels of government debt. An expenditure shock will be positive if (1) the debt level is still low, (2) the probability that the same government will still be in office is large and (3) the group of credit constrained people in the society is 'large enough'. A low level of debt also means a low level of future taxes, so slightly higher future taxes will not yet be too distorting. If the same government stays in office, taxes are likely to be lower than if a new government, with new priorities, is installed. These two factors limit the negative response of unconstrained agents' consumption on a fiscal expansion. Hence, the additional consumption by credit constrained people will keep the upper hand.

The percentage of credit constrained agents is crucial in this model. Their increased (decreased) liquidity will produce a Keynesian outcome in case of an expansion (contraction). Only if the 'counter-reaction' of unconstrained people is vigorous, the results will be non-Keynesian.

To summarize: theory suggests that the effects of fiscal policy actions on economic activity are influenced by the level of public debt. The nature of the relationship depends on the degree of 'Ricardianism' in economic life. It seems safe to assume that agents discount the well being of future generations more than their own well being. It is also common knowledge that markets sometimes malfunction. Hence, we obtain the following testable implications from the theory: (i) Controlling for other factors (such as the composition of fiscal policy) economic agents react differently to fiscal policy actions if the debt ratio is very high. (ii) The effects of fiscal policy actions are more Keynesian during low debt times. Non-Keynesian effects are more likely in high debt episodes.

Although theory assigns a significant role to the initial conditions, strong empirical confirmation has yet to be provided. Again most contributions look at episodes of fiscal consolidation. Zaghini (1999) notes that the level of debt before successful consolidations was on average twice as high as before unsuccessful ones in the recent European experiences. Alesina and Ardagna (1998) and Ardagna (1999) detect only a weak (small and statistically insignificant) link between the lagged debt-to-GDP ratio and the probability of a successful consolidation in OECD countries. Heylen and Everaert (2000) reach a similar conclusion.

However, the above studies do not really verify or falsify the theoretical models, as they neither define the critical debt level nor the available fiscal space. Theory predicts that there will occur a regime shift when a certain amount of debt accumulation is reached. Perhaps the importance of the level public debt for the effects of fiscal policy actions cannot be detected, because there are too few observations of these 'critical debt situations' within the sample. One has to face a difficult, but quintessential question: from what level onwards is the accumulated debt problematic?

In recent work different possibilities were explored: (i) Perotti (1999) uses the sum of the present discounted value of future government expenditure and the cyclically adjusted government debt. If the observed value is above the ninetieth percentile of the distribution of the total population, the situation is labelled as problematic. (ii) A second indicator proposed by Perotti (1999) is based on the budget deficit. If the cyclically adjusted deficit as a share of trend GDP has exceeded a certain value in the two previous years, a government is said to be in fiscal distress. (iii) Gobbin and van Aarle (2001) use an indicator based on the Domar conditions on fiscal sustainability. This indicator shows whether economic growth, interest rates, primary deficit and government debt are consistent with achieving a 'steady state level' of debt. (iv) Gobbin and van Aarle (2001) derive an indicator from the Maastricht-criteria concerning fiscal convergence. If a country does not comply with one of these two criteria, it is said to be in fiscal distress.

All of the above indicators make sense, but are not without criticism. Indicators (i), (ii) and (iii) only shift the problem: one still has to choose respectively the percentile, a acceptable value for the deficit or the correct steady state debt level. Moreover, relative measures, such as indicator (i), enforce a number of problematic periods onto the data: in each data set 10% of the observations will be considered as problematic. The fourth criterion is more objective. Countries that did not satisfy the Maastricht-criteria could not join the EMU. So stakes were high. However, it is only applicable to a limited number of countries (EMU-12), for a short period in time.

Höppner and Wesche (2000) use a Markov-switching approach to determine non-conventional fiscal periods in Germany. They can identify two distinct regimes: one in which the effects of fiscal policy are Keynesian and one in which they are rather non-Keynesian. However, the shift between the regimes cannot be explained by a rise in the debt level or a consolidation programme. If the debt situation worsens, the probability of remaining in the Keynesian regime even increases.

Nonetheless, we believe that the approach of Höppner and Wesche is a promising one. They avoid arbitrary choices with respect to the critical debt level. First, they identify different regimes in the data on the basis of a statistical criterion. Secondly, they try to link their findings to the theory. We will use the same strategy and a related methodology: a threshold regression analysis. In the next section we present an overview of the methodology and motivate why we deem it appropriate for our research purposes.

4.3 Threshold regression models

We want to estimate a relationship between the behaviour of economic agents and fiscal policy actions. Since theory indicates that this relationship might be non-linear, we need to allow for a change in the estimated regression coefficients depending on the prevailing regime. A straightforward way to achieve this goal is to interact the fiscal policy variables with a 'critical debt level'-dummy. However, in order to define such a dummy, we must know the critical debt level. Unfortunately this is not the case and we will need to estimate it. This also implies that we should account for a possible estimation error.

The structural equation that we consider has the general form:

$$y_t = \alpha_0 + \alpha_1 Z_t + \gamma_1 I(q_t < t^*)' X_t + \gamma_2 I(q_t > t^*)' X_t + \varepsilon_t \qquad (4.1)$$

A scalar dependent variable (y_t) is regressed on a constant (α_0) an number of exogenous explanatory variables (matrices Z_t and X_t). The error term (ε_t)

is independently and identically distributed (i.i.d.).

The function $I(.)$ is an indicator function: it assumes a value of 1 if the scalar threshold variable q_t satisfies the condition in brackets, else it equals 0. Hence, we sort and divide the data sample on the basis of the value of the threshold variable. The effects of the explanatory variables that belong to X_t differ depending on the state we are in. The effects of the other explanatory variables (Z_t) are independent of the value of the threshold variable. The threshold variable can be one of the explanatory variables, but it doesn't have to be.

As we do not know the precise threshold value (t^*), we need to estimate it. Hansen (2000) proposes to jointly estimate the threshold value and the regression parameters. The threshold value is the value of the threshold variable that minimizes the concentrated sum of squared errors of the regression. So for each possible t^* (i.e. for each possible value of q_t) we re-estimate the equation. Next we select the value of t^* that results in the smallest value for the sum of squared errors. Hansen (2000) advises to restrict the search such that a minimal percentage of observations lies in each of the identified regimes (i.e. t^* should not belong to the n% lowest or n% highest values of q_t).

The threshold regression model is related to the changepoint model (in which the threshold variable is time) and the regression-tree approach. However, contrary to the threshold estimation technique, standard significance tests can still be used in the changepoint model (Hansen, 2000). In the regression-tree approach statistical significance of regimes cannot be tested (Hansen, 2000; Papageorgiou, 2002). The threshold regression model can also be seen as an extension of the Chow test for stability of coefficients across sub-samples. Hu and Schiantarelli (1998) apply a switching regression with an endogenous switching function. In such a model, the regime switch is triggered by multiple variables. Again it is unclear how (if) the significance of the regimes can be tested.

The Threshold Autoregressive (TAR) model is a special case of the threshold regression model. In a TAR model a variable (y_t) is regressed on its own lagged values (y_{t-1}, ... y_{t-p}). The threshold variable q_{t-1} is now a known function of the lags of y: $q_{t-1} = q(y_{t-1}, \dots y_{t-p})$. In the Self-Exciting Threshold Autoregressive model (SETAR) the threshold variable is a lag (y_{t-d}) of the dependent variable. The delay lag d is estimated along with the other parameters. Hence, the estimation problem also includes a search over d next to the estimation of the threshold value and the regression coefficients (Hansen, 1997).

While the threshold regression analysis does not complicate the estimation too much, it does interfere with the standard hypothesis test and inference procedures (Davies, 1987; Hansen, 1996). The basic problem is that under the null hypothesis of 'no threshold', or $\gamma_1 = \gamma_2$, t^* is not identified. We can rewrite (4.1) as

$$y_t = \alpha_0 + \alpha_1 Z_t + \gamma_1 X_t + (\gamma_2 - \gamma_1) I(q_t > t^*)' X_t + \varepsilon_t \qquad (4.2)$$

If $\gamma_1 = \gamma_2$ the fourth term of the function drops out and we can no longer determine t^* by minimizing the concentrated sum of squared errors. This means that: (i) the test of a linear versus a non-linear model has a nonstandard distribution; (ii) we need to derive the asymptotic distribution of the threshold estimate if we want to construct a confidence interval for t^*; (iii) traditional theory might lead to wrong conclusions with respect to the significance of the estimated parameter values (Davies, 1997).

To solve the first problem Hansen (1999, 2000) resorts to bootstrapping methods. First, he conducts a regression under the alternative hypothesis (with a threshold). Secondly, he draws (with replacement) a sample from the error terms of the first regression that is identical in size to the original population. Using these error terms he generates observations for the dependent variable under the null hypothesis (without a threshold). Thirdly, he regresses the generated values on the explanatory variables both under the null and the alternative hypothesis, which allows him to calculate the bootstrap value of the log likelihood ratio (LR) statistic. The procedure is repeated a large number of times. The percentage of draws for which the simulated LR statistic exceeds the actual one is equal to the bootstrap estimate of the asymptotic p-value for the LR statistic under the null hypothesis. The null hypothesis (no threshold effect) is rejected if this p-value is below the desired critical value.

Hansen (1999, 2000) introduces a simplifying condition which enables him to solve the two remaining problems. He conjectures that the difference in regression slopes gets small if the sample size gets large. In other words: the threshold effect is 'not too important'. This allows him to derive the asymptotic distribution of the threshold estimate and of the slope coefficients. Hansen (2000) shows that the dependence of the coefficient estimator on the threshold estimate is not of first-order asymptotic importance. Inference on the coefficient estimates can proceed as if the threshold estimate were the true value of the threshold. But he recommends to use heteroskedasticity-robust standard errors.

The theory of estimation and inference is well developed for linear regression models with exogenous regressors. Caner and Hansen (2004) extend the analysis to threshold models with endogenous variables and an exogenous threshold variable. They show that their estimator is consistent, but they cannot (yet) prove that it is efficient. Hansen (1999) shows that the method can be used in case of non-dynamic panels, although it is unknown if the results extend to unbalanced panels.

4.4 Data description and regression set-up

In the next section we will explore potential non-linearities in the relationship between private household consumption and fiscal policy actions in the EU-15 caused by the initial debt level. We focus on household consumption because that variable closely resembles the choice variable in the theoretical models. Moreover, other components of GDP, e.g., private investment, probably conceal more complicated decisions, which also complicates the empirical analysis.

We use a Keynesian type consumption function. First, we look for a long run relationship between private consumption, disposable income and the long run real interest rate. Next, we will try to explain short run changes in private consumption by means of changes in disposable income, changes in the real interest rate, lagged deviations from the long run equilibrium and changes in a number of fiscal variables (see also the distributed lag model of Blinder and Deaton (1985)). In a Keynesian world, one expects that changes in disposable income positively affect private consumption. The net income effect of fiscal policy changes is incorporated in the changes in disposable income. By including the fiscal policy variables we might pick-up the impact of fiscal policy multipliers. However, the inclusion of these variables also nests the possibility of Ricardian behaviour in the specification: e.g., if the coefficient on governments spending changes is negative, this could be seen as an indication of non-Keynesian effects of fiscal policy actions. Hence, we also include these variables because of their signalling function with respect to changes in the fiscal stance and their impact on households' expectations. Given the above set-up, our analysis should mainly be seen as a test of the Keynesian consumption model. While we might end up rejecting this model, one would need a different set up to test the appropriateness of the Ricardian theory.

We will estimate the following consumption function:

$$\Delta c_{c,t} = \alpha_{0,c} + \gamma_1 (c_c - \beta_{0,c} - \beta_{1,c} y_c - \beta_{2,c} r_c - \delta_c \tau)_{t-1} + \Gamma_2 '(X_{c,t}) \\ + (\Gamma_3 - \Gamma_2) I(q_{ct} > t^*)'(X_{c,t}) + \varepsilon_{c,t} \tag{4.3}$$

with: $X_{c,t} = (\Delta y_{c,t}, \Delta r_{c,t}, \Delta g1_{c,t}, \Delta g2_{c,t}, \Delta t_{c,t}, \Delta pb_{c,t})$, τ, a time trend, and Γ, a coefficient vector.

Household consumption is regressed upon the lagged deviation of the long run equilibrium, changes in disposable income and interest rate and changes in a number of fiscal variables. Next to the primary balance (*pb*), we include separate components of the government budget. Evolutions in the primary balance reflect changes in the *overall* fiscal stance. In the literature their is a near-consenus about the importance of composition effects (e.g., Alesina and Ardagna, 1998). A fiscal consolidation based on tax increases results in different effects on economic activity than a fiscal consolidation based on revenue decreases. Therefore, we include two variables that measure government expenditure (i.e., *g1*: the sum of subsidies and consumption; *g2*: social security payments by the government) and one variable that is related to government revenues (the sum of direct and indirect taxes). All variables are cyclically adjusted and expressed in real per capita terms.

We use both 'government net financial liabilities as a percentage of GDP' and 'government gross financial liabilities as a percentage of GDP' as threshold variable. Net debt, i.e. government liabilities minus government assets, seems (a priori) a better proxy of a country's degree of fiscal distress[1]. This variable can assume negative values, which is the case for most observations for Finland and some observations in Sweden. The gross debt rate has the advantage that it is commonly used (e.g., to evaluate the Maastricht criteria), and hence, is better known to the public. Since expectations are at the heart of the theoretical models, this 'common knowledge' factor might be important. Of course also other indicators of fiscal distress can be considered. One might link government debt to tax revenues instead of GDP, include future pension liabilities or compare the presented discounted value of future revenues to the current debt. Although such adjustments would undoubtedly improve the quality of the fiscal stress indicator, the resulting indicator would be less visible to the big public.

The data panel consists of 10 of the former EU-15 Member States. We exclude Portugal, Greece, Spain and Luxemburg because of data limitations (missing or unreliable series). We also need to exclude Germany due to discontinuities in the data series around the period of re-unification. Hence, the dataset includes Austria, Belgium, Denmark, Finland, France, Ireland, Italy, the Netherlands, Sweden and the UK. We look at the period 1980-2004 and use yearly data.

[1] More information with respect to the data sources and definitions can be found in appendix.

Originally we looked at individual countries, instead of an EU-panel, to account for potential slope heterogeneity across countries. Hogan (2004) notes that there is no reason to expect that the effects of fiscal policy on consumption are the same or even similar in different countries. Given the presence of heterogeneous slope coefficients he believes that estimation by fixed effects is not appropriate. However, estimates on the basis of individual countries turn out to be uninformative, since the variability in the debt level data series is too limited. Hence, we are forced to test for non-linearities in a panel of EU-countries and, by doing so, we implicitly impose a homogenous impact of fiscal policy actions in those countries.

4.5 Results

Step 1: Panel cointegration

The unit root tests (see appendix) show that most data series for consumption, income and the real interest rate are nonstationary. Therefore, we test for panel cointegration. Following Pedroni (2004) we allow for heterogeneity in the cointegrating relation across countries, since there is no a priori motivation of why this relationship should be identical for all countries in the dataset. The tests allow for heterogeneous long-run slope coefficients, fixed effects and trend terms. The following type of regression is considered:

$$c_{it} = \beta_{0,i} + \delta_i \tau + \beta_{1i} y_{it} + \beta_{2i} r_{it} + e_{it} \tag{4.4}$$

Table 4.1 presents cointegration tests based on the within (time) dimension and the between (cross-section) dimension of the panel. The null hypothesis of 'no cointegration' is rejected in four out of five tests. Hence, there is evidence for the existence of a long run relationship between consumption, income and the real interest rate in the data panel. Next we estimate the relationship and calculate the deviations from the long run equilbrium (e_{it}). The lagged (stationary) deviations are included as a variable in the threshold analysis since consumption changes can reflect a delayed adjustment to the long run equilibrium.

Table 4.1. Panel cointegration tests

Within dimension		Between dimension	
Panel v-statistic	3.006***	Group rho-statistic	3.568***
Panel rho-statistic	1.941**	Group pp-statistic	3.042***
Panel pp-statistic	1.002		

*** / ** / * denotes rejection at the 1% / 5% / 10% level of the null hypothesis: 'no cointegration'.

Step 2: Threshold analysis
In this section we examine whether the estimated coefficients of the consumption function (3) statistically differ between low and high debt times. We consider both the net and gross debt rate as potential threshold variable (histograms of these variables are presented in appendix). Following Hansen (1999) we restrict the value of the threshold variable to guarantee that we obtain meaningful estimates for the regime above / below the threshold. For the net debt rate the threshold should lie between 0 and 90%, for the gross debt rate between 30 and 120%.

The results of the threshold analysis are presented in Table 4.2. In the first row we report the estimates for the consumption function without the fiscal variables. Short run changes in consumption are determined by changes in disposable income and the adjustment process towards the long run equilibrium. Changes in the real interest rate are not statistically significant. In the second row we add changes in the primary balance to the list of explanatory variables. The impact of this variable on household consumption is significantly positive (at the 5% level). At first sight, this goes against traditional Keynesian thinking: an improvement of the cyclically adjusted primary balance (i.e., a fiscal tightening), increases household consumption. However, since we already control for changes in disposable income, the overall effect of a fiscal contraction is still likely to be negative. In other words, the government budget multiplier is positive but smaller than one. Next we include different components of the fiscal policy in the regression (row 3). The estimates confirm the hypothesis that composition effects matter: two fiscal components are highly relevant and the primary balance is no longer significant. The sign of $\Delta exp1$ is in line with the existence of strong Keynesian multiplier effects: a higher government expenditure increases private consumption (outside its impact on disposable income). Social security expenditure (*exp2*) does not lead to additional consumption on top of its effect on disposable income. Controlled for the negative impact on disposable income, tax increases positively affect consumption. Hence, the tax multiplier is smaller than one in absolute value.

Next, we allow for sample splitting on the basis of the government's net debt rate. In row 4-a.t. (b.t.) we look only at the observations above (below) the threshold. Following Hansen (2000) we report heteroskedasticity consistent standard errors.

We observe that the reaction of household consumption to changes in disposable income is smaller above the threshold. This observation is in line with non-Keynesian theories. Changes in *exp1* have a larger direct impact above than below the threshold. The same holds for changes in taxes. Hence, while the indirect impact (i.e. through changes in disposable income) of fiscal policy actions is reduced once a certain debt level is reached, the direct impact (i.e. controlled for changes in disposable income) becomes more important. Overall, the effects of taxes increases become less Keynesian above the threshold: consumption reacts less to a reduction of disposable income and the positive, direct effect gets larger. For government consumption changes the picture is mixed: the impact through disposable income is reduced but the direct impact increases. The (direct) impact of changes in *exp2* is only statistically significant and negative below the threshold.

Hence, we end up with a mixed picture. On the one hand, the reduced importance of changes in disposable income, and the changed impact of taxes indicates that crossing the threshold means moving to a more non-Keynesian state of the world. On the other hand, the changes in the impact of government expenditure (both *exp1* and *exp2*) would lead to the opposite conclusion.

Up to here we have been holding back an important piece of information: the precise estimate of the threshold. We obtain the most likely threshold at a net debt level of 10%. At first sight this value seems too low to fit into the theoretical explanations. Moreover, only Denmark, Finland, France and Sweden have some observations below the threshold (see appendix B). This is not due to the fact that we cannot distinguish accurately between different potential values of the threshold. The confidence interval for the threshold estimate lies between 9 and 12%. Hence, while we cannot exclude that the threshold value is in fact equal to 9, 11 or 12%, all values higher than 12% are outside the confidence interval. Secondly, the 'odd' result could be an indication that the threshold is not statistically significant. But this is not confirmed by the bootstrapping procedure described above (p-value of 0.00).

While the obtained threshold estimate seems very low, the finding is not unique in the literature. One should take into account that net debt levels are on average more than 25%-points below gross debt levels. Bhattacharya (1999) identifies a critical (gross) debt level between 30 and 35%. Next, we use the gross debt rate as the threshold variable. The estimates are reported in row 5 of Table 4.2. The overall picture that emerges resembles that of the estimates on the basis of the net debt rate. But now changes in social security expenditure also have a significant, negative effect above the threshold. The threshold value is reached at a gross debt rate of 62% and is highly significant (p-value: 0.00).

Table 4.2. Overview of the estimates

	Δinc	Δr	error(-1)	Δexp1	Δexp2	Δtax	Δpb
(1)	0.57***	-6.64	-0.12***				
	(0.03)	(4.41)	(0.03)				
(2)	0.58***	-5.34	-0.13***				0.02*
	(0.03)	(4.39)	(0.03)				(0.01)
(3)	0.36***	-6.84*	-0.12***	0.69***	0.05	0.03***	0.01
	(0.03)	(3.56)	(0.02)	(0.08)	(0.06)	(0.01)	(0.01)
Threshold variable: net debt rate				10%	C.I.: [9-12] / p-value: 0.00		
(4at)	0.25***	0.75	0.02	0.88***	-0.04	0.03***	
	(0.07)	(0.16)	(0.04)	(0.14)	(0.10)	(0.01)	
(4bt)	0.42***	-11.59	-0.17***	0.59***	-0.25***	0.02**	
	(0.05)	(9.25)	(0.06)	(0.12)	(0.10)	(0.01)	
Threshold variable: gross debt rate				62%	C.I.: [61-62] / p-value: 0.00		
(5at)	0.25***	-10.24	0.05	0.90***	-0.23**	0.03***	
	(0.06)	(8.91)	(0.03)	(0.14)	(0.10)	(0.01)	
(5bt)	0.41***	-0.16	-0.21***	0.50***	-0.35***	0.02	
	(0.04)	(3.48)	(0.04)	(0.10)	(0.09)	(0.01)	
Threshold variable: gross debt rate				62%	C.I.: [61-62] / p-value: 0.00		
(6at)	0.25***		0.06*	0.91***	-0.26**	0.03***	
	(0.07)		(0.03)	(0.14)	(0.11)	(0.01)	
(6bt)	0.42***		-0.21***	0.48***	-0.36***	0.02	
	(0.04)		(0.04)	(0.10)	(0.09)	(0.01)	
Threshold variable: gross debt rate				62%	C.I.: [61-67] / p-value: 0.00		
(7at)	0.27***		0.07**	0.89***	-0.31***	0.03***	
	(0.07)		(0.03)	(0.15)	(0.09)	(0.01)	
(7bt)	0.41***		-0.21***	0.45***		0.02	
	(0.05)		(0.04)	(0.10)		(0.01)	
Threshold variable: gross debt rate				62%	C.I.: [61-63] / p-value: 0.00		
(8at)	0.26***		0.07**	0.89***	-0.31***		
	(0.07)		(0.03)	(0.16)	(0.09)		
(8bt)	0.41***		-0.21***	0.43***		0.03***	
	(0.05)		(0.04)	(0.10)		(0.01)	

1) Standard errors are given in brackets. 2) ***/**/* denotes significance at the 1% / 5% / 10% level. 3) at / bt indicates above / below the estimated threshold.

Fig. 4.1 plots a confidence interval for the threshold estimate. The dotted line (at 10.59) delimits the 'no rejection region' for this estimate. A value below that line indicates that we cannot reject the hypothesis that the estimated threshold statistically differs from the alternative threshold value. Hence, the relevant threshold is located somewhere between 61 and 62%.

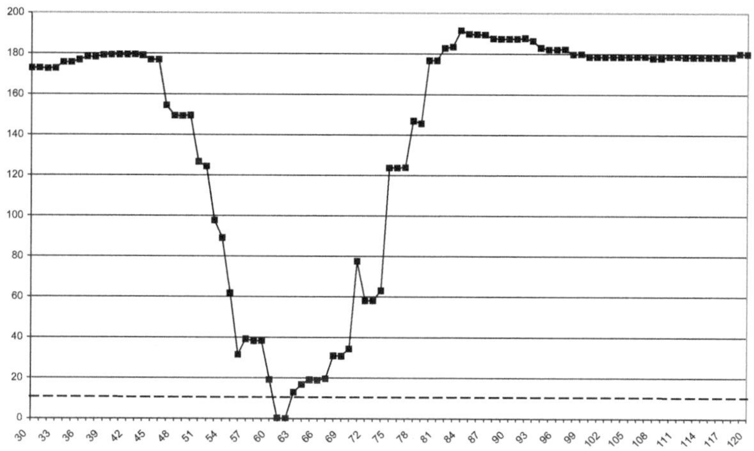

Fig. 4.1. Confidence interval for the threshold estimate – Gross debt (row 5 in Table 4.2)

In row 6 we delete the insignificant long term interest rate from the regression. The results are largely unaffected. Since the statistical difference between the coefficients for social security expenditure is small, we enforce the same coefficient above and below the threshold (row 7). The only difference is that we now find a (more) significant positive coefficient for the deviation from long run equilibrium. Hence, above a certain critical debt level, consumption diverges from its long run equilibrium. Finally, since the confidence intervals for the tax changes coefficients also overlap, we impose an identical coefficient. The results are unaffected.

4.6 Conclusion

In this chapter we provide empirical support for the hypothesis that the effects of fiscal policy actions in the EU-15 depend on the initial level of government debt. Firstly, we identify a threshold that is highly significant and precisely estimated. Secondly, the estimated effects below and above the threshold value of 10% for net debt and 62% for gross debt differ significantly. The threshold mainly affects the impact of changes in disposable income and changes in government consumption and subsidies on consumption. However, we cannot conclude that crossing the threshold debt level means moving from a Keynesian state of the world to a more non-Keynesian one. On the one hand, changes in disposable income matter less for consumption changes above the threshold, which seems to reflect more Ricardian-type behaviour. On the other hand, the coefficient of government consumption increases above the threshold. However, this larger coefficient could also indicate that the reduced impact of government consumption through its effect on disposable income (lower coefficient of disposable income) is compensated by a larger direct impact (controlled for changes in disposable income). Hence, the overall impact of tax changes and social security expenditure is unambiguously smaller above the threshold, while this is not the case for government consumption and subsidies.

Appendix A: Data sources and definitions

Table 4.3 gives an overview of the variables used in the estimates. It sums up the basic series in combination with other (auxiliary) series we have used to adjust the data. The term 'GDP deflator' means that we have transformed nominal series into real data. Each time we mention 'population', we have transformed the data into per capita terms. Finally, 'HP-filter (100)' indicates that we have used a Hodrick-Prescott filter with smoothing parameter 100 to cyclically adjust the data.

Table 4.3. Data sources and definitions

Variable	Definition	Source
C	Cyclically adjusted per capita consumption	
	Private final consumption expenditure (value)	OECD Economic Outlook
	GDP deflator	OECD Economic Outlook
	Population	OECD Economic Outlook
	HP-filter (100)	
Y	Cyclically adjusted per capita household disposable income	
	Household disposable income (value)	OECD Economic Outlook
	HP-filter (100) / GDP deflator / Population	
R	Real long term interest rate	
	Interest rate on long term government bonds	OECD Economic Outlook
	Inflation = change in GDP deflator	
G1	Sum of cyclically adjusted government subsidies and consumption (per capita)	
	Government subsidies (value)	OECD Economic Outlook
	Government final consumption (value)	OECD Economic Outlook
	HP-filter (100) / GDP deflator / Population	
G2	Social security payments by government (per capita)	
	Social security benefits paid by government (val.)	OECD Economic Outlook
	HP-filter (100) / GDP deflator / Population	
T	Government revenue (per capita)	
	Cyclically adjusted indirect taxes (value)	OECD Economic Outlook
	Cyclically adjusted direct taxes households (val.)	OECD Economic Outlook
	Cyclically adjusted direct taxes business (value)	OECD Economic Outlook
	GDP deflator / Population	
CAPB	Cyclically adjusted primary balance (per capita)	OECD Economic Outlook
	Cyclically adjusted primary balance (value)	
	GDP deflator / Population	
DEBTY	Net debt as a percentage of GDP	
	Net financial liabilities as a % of GDP	OECD Economic Outlook
	Gross debt as a percentage of GDP	
	Gross financial liabilities as a % of GDP	OECD Economic Outlook[2]

[2] The series for Italy only starts in 1995. We have extended the series by means of the growth rate of the gross debt – series in the OECD FPBC dataset.

Appendix B: ADF unit root tests

Table 4.4. Unit root tests

	Level			Difference		
Country	C	Y	R	C	Y	R
Austria	0.150	-4.024***	-1.300	-3.250**		-6.632***
Belgium	1.776	-1.770	1.202	-1.801	-2.850*	-5.833***
Denmark	-1.832	-0.681	-1.402	-1.633	-2.864*	-11.821***
Finland	1.941	0.153	-2.456	-3.488**	-2.853*	-6.276***
France	0.517	-0.595	-2.780	-2.590*	-3.100**	-6.112***
Ireland	-0.372	0.059	-0.700	-1.778	-5.011***	-5.561***
Italy	-3.917***	-3.458**	-2.380			-5.901***
The Nether-lands	-0.529	-2.105	-1.316	-3.219**	-1.858	-5.358***
Sweden	2.527	2.713	-3.892***	-0.904	2.469	
The UK	0.974	-1.908	-2.547	-0.942	-3.606***	-3.569***

The optimal lag length for the ADF tests was determined by means of the Schwarz Bayesian information criterion. Null hypothesis: unit root.*** / ** / * denotes rejection at the 1% / 5% / 10% level.

Appendix C

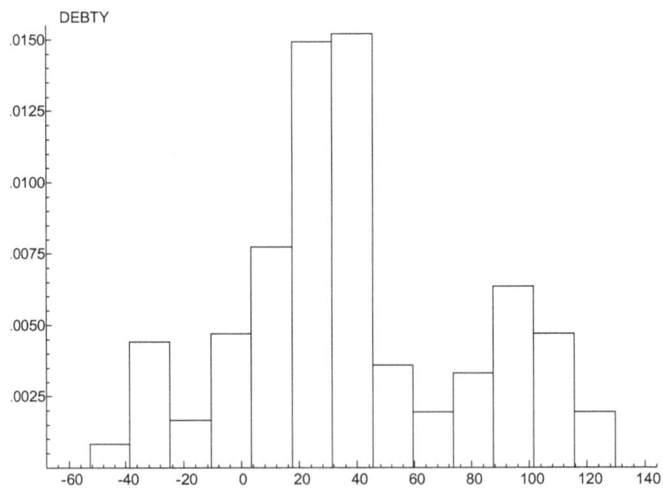

Fig. 4.2. Histogram of the threshold variable: net debt rate

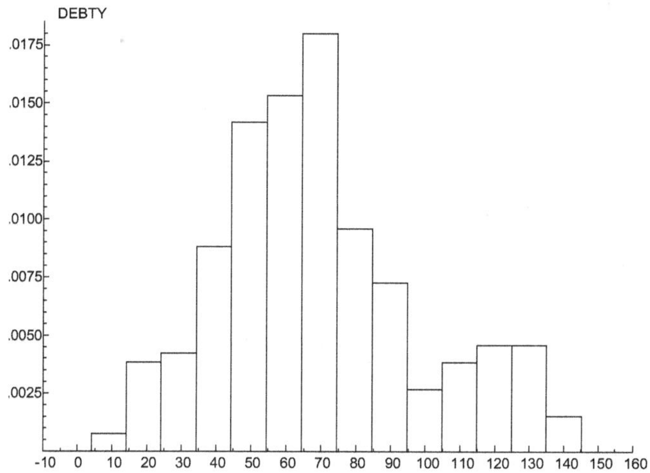

Fig. 4.3. Histogram of the threshold variable: gross debt rate

Appendix D: Years above the threshold

Table 4.5. Years above the estimated threshold

Country	Net debt rate (10%)	Gross debt rate (62%)
Austria	1980-2004	1994-2004
Belgium	1980-2004	1980-2004
Denmark	1981-2000	1982-1999
Finland	/	/
France	1986-2004	1995-2004
Ireland	1980-2004	1980-1997
Italy	1980-2004	1982-2004
The Netherlands	1980-2004	1981-2000
Sweden	1983-1986 / 1993-1998	1982-1987 / 1992-2001 / 2004
The UK	1980-2004	/

References

Alesina, A., Ardagna S. (1998), Tales of fiscal adjustment, Economic Policy, vol. 13, no. 27, p. 487-545.

Ardagna, S. (1999), Fiscal stabilizations: When do they work and why, unpublished manuscript.

Afonso, A., (2001), Non-Keynesian effects of fiscal policy in the EU-15, unpublished manuscript.

Alesina, A., Perotti R. (1995), Fiscal expansions and adjustments in OECD countries, Economic Policy, no. 21, October, p. 207-247.

Bhattacharya, R., (1999), Private sector behavior and non-Keynesian effects of fiscal policy, IMF WP 99/112.

Bertola, G., Drazen A. (1993), Trigger points and budget cuts: explaining the effects of fiscal austerity, American Economic Review, vol. 83, no. 1, March, p. 11-26.

Blanchard, O., (1990), comment on Giavazzi F., and Pagano M., Can severe fiscal contractions be expansionary? Tales of two small European countries, NBER Macroeconomics Annual, p. 111-116.

Blinder, A., Deaton A. (1985), The time series consumption function revisited, Brookings Papers on Economic Activity, no. 2, p. 465-511.

Caner, M., Hansen B.E. (2004), Instrumental variable estimation of a threshold model, Econometric Theory, vol. 20, p. 813-843.

Dalamagas, B. (1993), Fiscal effectiveness and debt illusion in a rational expectations model, Annales d'Economie et de Statistique, no. 31, September, p. 129-146.

Davies, R. (1987), Hypothesis testing when a nuisance parameter is present only under the alternatives, Biometrika, vol. 74, no. 1, p. 33-43.

Giavazzi, F., Pagano M. (1990), Can severe fiscal contractions be expansionary? Tales of two small European countries, NBER Macroeconomics Annual, p. 75-111.

Giavazzi, F., Pagano M. (1995), Non-Keynesian effects of fiscal policy changes: international evidence and the Swedish experience, NBER WP no. 5332.

Giavazzi, F., Japelli T. and Pagano M. (2000), Searching for non-linear effects of fiscal policy: evidence from industrial and developing countries, European Economic Review, vol. 44, p. 1259-1289.

Gobbin, N., van Aarle B. (2001), Fiscal adjustments and their effects during the transition to EMU, Public Choice, vol. 109, no. 3-4, p. 269-299.

Hansen, B.E., (1997), Inference when a nuisance parameter is not identified under the null hypothesis, Econometrica, vol. 64, no. 2, p. 413-430.

Hansen, B.E., (1997), Inference in TAR models, Studies in Nonlinear Dynamics and Econometrics, vol. 2, no. 1, p. 1-14.

Hansen, B.E., (1999), Threshold effects in non-dynamic panels: Estimation, testing, and inference, Journal of Econometrics, vol. 93, p. 345-368.

Hansen, B.E., (2000), Sample Splitting and Threshold Estimation, Econometrica, vol. 68, no. 3, p. 575-603.

Heylen, F., Everaert G. (2000), Success and failure of fiscal consolidation in the OECD: a multivariate analysis, Public Choice, no. 105, p. 103-124.

Hogan, V., (2004), Expansionary Fiscal Contractions? Evidence from panel data, Scandinavian Journal of Economics, vol. 106, no. 4, p. 647-659.

Höppner, F., and Wesche K. (2000), Non-linear effects of fiscal policy in Germany: A Markov-switching approach, Bonn Economic Discussion Papers, no. 2000/9.

Hu, X., and Schiantarelli F. (1998), Investment and capital market imperfections: a switching regression approach using U.S. firm panel data, The Review Of Economics and Statistics, p. 466-497.

Pedroni, P., (2004), Panel cointegration: asymptotic and finite sample properties of pooled time series tests with an application to the PPP hypothesis, Econometric Theory, 20, p. 597-625.

Perotti, R., (1999), Fiscal policy in good times and bad, Quarterly Journal of Economics, November, p. 1399-1436.

Papageorgiou, C., (2002), Trade as a threshold variable for multiple regimes, Economics Letters, vol. 77, p. 85-91.

Sutherland, A., (1995), Fiscal crisis and aggregate demand: can high public debt reverse the effects of fiscal policy, CEPR DP no. 1246.

Zaghini, A., (1999), The economic policy of fiscal consolidation: the European experience, Banca d'Italia, Termi di Discussione, no. 355.

5 Spillovers from economic reform

Klaus Weyerstrass and Johannes Jaenicke

5.1 Introduction

In March 2000, the heads of the European Union countries proclaimed the aim of making Europe the "most competitive and dynamic knowledge-based economy in the world, capable of sustaining economic growth with more and better jobs and greater social cohesion" by 2010. To achieve this overall goal, a set of economic and social reforms called the "Lisbon Strategy" or the "Lisbon Agenda" to be undertaken was defined. Several objectives, grouped in five dimensions (employment, innovation and research, structural economic reforms, social cohesion, environment) were set up. It was agreed upon that the European Commission should annually prepare progress reports in order to evaluate the progress the Member States have made in achieving the Lisbon goals. In its mid-term review in 2005, the European Commission concluded that the implementation of reforms in line with the Lisbon Strategy had in many areas been too slow. In particular, the growth performance of the past five years had been disappointing, particularly as compared to other regions of the world economy such as the US and certain Asian economies. Therefore, the Lisbon Strategy was revised, focussing on growth and the creation of employment (European Commission, 2005 and 2006).

One of the key objectives, both of the original and the revised Lisbon Strategy, concerns the enhancing of the EU growth potential. Among the measures aiming at raising potential growth, supply side reforms play a prominent role. This chapter analyses the benefits of structural reforms on factor and product markets and identifies possible spillovers arising from these reforms. According to the existing literature (e.g. Griffith and Harrison, 2004) the main way in which (de-)regulation and reforms influence the macroeconomic outcome is via the level of economic rents available in the market. This in turn affects price levels, the allocation of inputs and outputs as well as incentives to engage in efficiency-enhancing activities and innovation. The level of economic rents is usually measured by the mark-up or price-cost margin, i.e. the deviation of prices from marginal costs.

Following the approach in, e.g., Griffith and Harrison (2004), for a panel of nine Euro Area countries (Austria, Belgium, Finland, France, Netherlands, Germany[1], Ireland, Italy, Spain)[2], the influence of product and factor market regulation on the macroeconomic performance is measured by a two-stage procedure. Firstly, the link between the mark-up and the macroeconomic performance is investigated. As indicators of the economic performance, total factor productivity growth, labour productivity growth, employment, and unemployment are included in the analysis. Secondly, the influence of product and factor market institutions on the mark-up of prices over costs is estimated. The ultimate effects of product market regulations and reforms on macroeconomic outcomes, as mediated via the level of rents, can be evaluated by combining the estimation results from the first and second stages.[3]

When estimating the mark-ups, the United Kingdom and the United States are included as benchmarks so as to estimate the potential for decreasing the mark-up in the Euro Area by implementing structural reforms. In particular in the 1990s, the US economy, which is characterised by more liberal markets, exhibited a significantly lower mark-up and a better macroeconomic performance than the Euro Area. The UK, while being an EU member, has in some respects more liberal markets than most of the continental EU countries. In the last decade, the UK has experienced higher GDP growth and a better labour market performance than many Euro Area countries, in particular the larger ones.

In the following sections, the determinants of the mark-up and the influence of the mark-up on the macroeconomic performance will be analysed. This requires, in a first step, the determination of the mark-up ratios.

5.2 Determination of mark-up ratios

Following Roeger (1995)[4], the starting point of the calculation is the definition of the Lerner index B (5.1), from which the relative mark-up μ of the

[1] West Germany until 1990, the unified Germany from 1991 onwards.

[2] For Greece, Portugal and Luxemburg, not all relevant data were available.

[3] Alternatively, it would have been possible to find significant direct links from institutional variables to macroeconomic performance indicators.

[4] This method has been widely applied in the literature, see, e.g., Martins et al. (1996) and Badinger (2004).

price P over marginal costs MC can be derived (5.2):

$$B = \frac{P - MC}{P} = 1 - \frac{1}{\mu} \tag{5.1}$$

with $$MC = \frac{W\Delta L + R\Delta K}{\Delta Q - \theta Q}$$ and,

$$\mu = \frac{1}{1 - B} \tag{5.2}$$

in which B denotes the Lerner index, MC, marginal cost, W, the wage rate, L, the number of employees (or working hours), R, the user cost of capital, K, the capital stock, Q, real output, P, the output price, θ, technical progress and, μ, the mark-up.

Under perfect competition, the output price is equal to marginal costs, i.e. $\mu = 1$, and the share of labour and capital, respectively, in total value added equals the elasticity of output with respect to these inputs. With constant returns to scale[5], output q develops according to the following expression (lower case letters denote natural logarithms):

$$\Delta q = \mu\alpha\Delta l - (1 - \mu\alpha)\Delta k + \Delta\theta \tag{5.3}$$

From (5.3) the Solow residual SR, i.e. the growth rate of output not accounted for by increases in labour and capital, can be derived:

$$\begin{aligned} SR &= \Delta q - \alpha\Delta l - (1-\alpha)\Delta k = (\mu - 1)\alpha(\Delta l - \Delta k) - \Delta\theta \\ &= B(\Delta q - \Delta k) + (1 - B)\Delta\theta \end{aligned} \tag{5.4}$$

where α denotes the production elasticity of labour, and $(1-\alpha)$ is the production elasticity of the capital input, assuming constant returns to scale. Equation (5.4) illustrates that under perfect competition, i.e. $\mu = 1$, or $B = 0$, the Solow residual equals technical progress. Roeger (1995) showed that a similar expression can be derived for the nominal or price-based Solow residual (SRP):

[5] Martins et al. (1996) showed that the presence of increasing (decreasing) returns to scale induces a downward (upward) bias in the estimation of the mark-up ratio. In this case the estimated mark-up by means of the Roeger equation will be too low (high). The presence of sunk costs could also generate a downward bias. If a fraction of the capital stock is sunk, this has to be subtracted from the total capital stock leading to lower marginal cost and a higher mark-up ratio.

$$SRP = \alpha\Delta w + (1-\alpha)\Delta r - \Delta p = -B(\Delta p - \Delta r) + (1-B)\Delta\theta) \tag{5.5}$$

By subtracting (5.5) from (5.4), the following equation for the estimation of the mark-up ratio can be derived:

$$\Delta y_t = B\Delta x_t + \varepsilon_t \tag{5.6}$$

in which $\Delta y = (\Delta q + \Delta p) - \alpha(\Delta l + \Delta w) - (1-\alpha)(\Delta k + \Delta r)$ and $\Delta x = (\Delta q + \Delta p) - (\Delta k + \Delta r)$. The dependent variable Δy is the nominal Solow residual, and the explanatory variable Δx is the nominal output-capital ratio. ε denotes the residuals of the equation, and t is the time period.

The following variables[6] have been used for the econometric estimations of the mark-ups: The dependent variable Δy, i.e. the nominal Solow residual, has been calculated by subtracting the labour and the capital inputs from output. Each variable has been entered into the calculation at current prices. Output is given by GDP. Total compensation of employees has been used as the nominal labour input. Under perfect competition, the production factors are paid for according to their respective production elasticities. Though market imperfections cause deviations from the ideal of perfect competition, weighting labour input by the share of compensation of employees in total income seems a reasonable approximation to reality. Assuming constant returns to scale, capital input has been weighted by the share of capital income in total income, i.e. one minus the share of labour income. Capital input has been calculated by multiplying the capital stock in the business sector by the user costs of capital. Ideally, the user costs of capital would consist of the interest rate, the depreciation rate and an average company tax rate. Since consistent data on the latter two variables is not available for all the countries in the sample, the user costs of capital have been approximated by the long-term interest rate.[7] Consistent capital stock data for the considered countries is only available for the business sector, but not for the entire economy.

The explanatory variable, i.e. the nominal output-capital ratio Δx, is defined as GDP at current prices, divided by the nominal capital input. As above, the capital input has been calculated by multiplying the capital stock in the business sector by the nominal long-term interest rate, the latter again approximating the user costs of capital.

---

[6] All data originate from the OECD Economic Outlook and have been extracted from the online database of the Austrian Institute of Economic Research WIFO.

[7] Thus, in the estimations the user costs of capital are too small, implying that the mark-up ratios are probably biased upwards.

The following table shows the estimated Lerner index and the mark-up ratios for the panel of nine Euro Area countries (EUR-9) as well as for the UK and the US. The estimations have been carried out for the period 1970 to 2004. In order to identify the development over time, the total period has been split into two sub-periods: the period 1970 to 1992, i.e. before completion of the Single Market Programme of the European Union, and the period 1993 to 2004. The table also shows the rates of change of the mark-up ratios between the two sub-samples. According to the estimation results, in the most recent sub-period prices in the Euro Area on average exceed marginal costs by about 50 percent, compared to 46 percent in the UK and 39 percent in the US.

Table 5.1. Lerner indices and mark-up ratios

	1970 - 2004		1970 - 1992		1993 - 2004		change between 1st and 2nd sub-period	
	Lerner index	Mark-up	Lerner index	Mark-up	Lerner index	Mark-up	Lerner index	Mark-up
EUR-9 (Panel)	0.34	1.52	0.35	1.53	0.34	1.51	-2,9%	-1.3%
UK	0.32	1.48	0.33	1.48	0.31	1.46	-6,1%	-1.4%
USA	0.29	1.40	0.29	1.41	0.28	1.39	-3,4%	-1.4%
EUR-9 /UK (%)	5.9%	2.6%	5.7%	3.3%	8.8%	3.3%		
EUR-9 /US (%)	14.7%	7.9%	17.1%	7.8%	17.6%	7.9%		

In the period after completing the Single Market Programme, the Lerner index and the mark-up ratio declined in the Euro Area and, more pronouncedly, in the United Kingdom. Thus, the liberalisation and the intensification of trade in the EU seem to have fostered competition, bringing prices closer to marginal costs. Nevertheless, according to the above estimates, the mark-up ratio in the Euro Area still exceeds the US level by 7.9 percent and the UK mark-up by 3.3 percent. Thus, existing regulations and barriers to international trade in goods and services should be removed as mentioned in the new Lisbon Strategy. In this respect, the Directive on Services in the Internal Market should foster competition in the European Union, contributing to reducing the gap in mark-up ratios to the US economy.

The estimated values of the mark-up ratios are broadly in line with results reported in the literature. Based on a literature review, Bayoumi et al. (2004) assume for their simulations that the average price mark-up in the Euro Area is around 10 percent above the US level (1.35 in the Euro Area as compared to 1.23 in the US). Thus, the estimates in the table above are somewhat higher, but the relation between the Euro Area and the US is comparable. For the period 1970 to 1992, Martins et al. (1996) estimate mark-up ratios in the manufacturing industries of a number of OECD countries. Their estimates are about 20 percent above our results, but again the relation between US and Euro Area levels is comparable. Furthermore, the fact that Martins et al. focus on manufacturing while the results shown in the table above cover the entire economy may cause a bias. Griffith and Harrison (2004) estimate mark-up ratios for 13 EU countries (EU 15 excluding Luxembourg and Greece) over the period 1980 to 2002. They measure the mark-up as the ratio of value added to the sum of labour and capital costs. Their mark-up ratios are comparable in size to our results. Regarding the development of the mark-up ratios in individual countries over time, the authors conclude that Austria, Germany, Belgium, France, the Netherlands, Portugal and the UK experienced declining mark-up ratios since the 1990s. In contrast, for Finland, Italy and Sweden they find mark-ups rising over the 1990s. Summing up, while the levels of our mark-up ratios seem to be at the upper bound of values found in the literature, the relation between the Euro Area and the US is broadly in line with findings in earlier studies.

As a complement to the summary results of Table 5.1, the following figures show the trajectories of the mark-up ratios in the nine Euro Area countries in the panel over the period 1971 to 2004. For comparison, the evolution of the mark-ups in the UK and the US is also displayed. For this analysis, time series of the mark-up ratios for the countries under consideration were needed. The mark-up ratios shown in the table above have been estimated for two sub-periods. For the subsequent analyses, rolling regressions have been performed for each country in the panel. The estimations were based on equation (5.6) above. The first regression was run for the ten-year period 1961 to 1970, and the value of the mark-up was assigned to the final year of this period. In each of the subsequent regression runs, the starting and the terminal points were moved forward by one year, and the result was again assigned to the final year of the respective period. This procedure resulted in time series for the mark-up ratios from 1970 to 2004.[8] In order to remove outliers in the time series and to derive smoother time paths for the following figures, moving four-year averages have been

[8] Due to data availability, the mark-up time series for Finland and Ireland start in 1977.

calculated. The first values shown in the graphs cover the period 1971 to 1974.

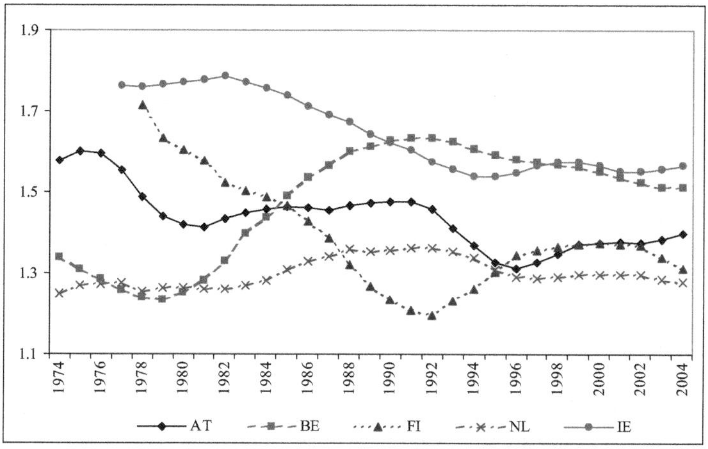

AT - Austria, BE - Belgium, FI - Finland, NL - Netherlands, IE – Ireland

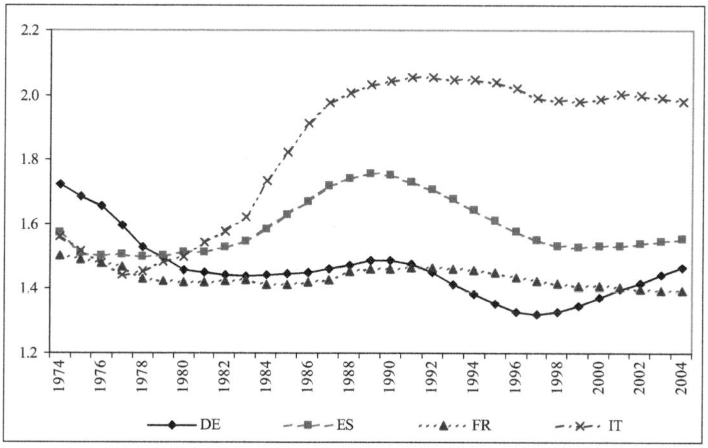

DE - Germany, ES - Spain, FR - France, IT - Italy

Fig. 5.1. Evolution of mark-up in selected Euro Area countries

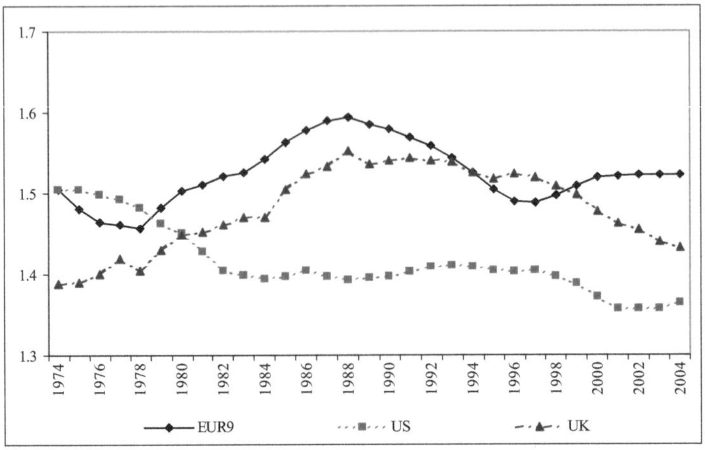

Fig. 5.2. Evolution of mark-up in the Euro Area, the US and the UK. EUR-9 - panel of the nine Euro Area countries of the previous figures, US - United States, `UK - United Kingdom

In Ireland and France, the mark-up ratios exhibit clearly negative trends over the entire period. In Belgium, Italy and, albeit to a much lesser extent, in Spain, the mark-up first declined, then rose remarkably around the middle of the period, before decreasing again towards the end of the period. In the Netherlands, the mark-up has remained virtually constant and low as compared to the other Euro Area countries. For Finland, we find a significant decrease of the mark-up until the beginning of the 1990s. Afterwards, it rose again somewhat, but remained at the lower end of the spectrum. In Austria and Germany, the mark-up ratio increased somewhat in the most recent period, after having been on a decreasing trend until the middle of the 1990s. The German pattern might be related to the restructuring of Eastern German industry after unification. Despite the increase in the most recent years, the mark-up in Germany has remained relatively low. As can be clearly seen, the mark-up in the US has been below European levels since the beginning of the 1980s, and the downward trend has been more distinct as compared to the Euro Area. The UK exhibits increasing mark-up ratios until the beginning of the 1990s and a downward trend afterwards. In the continental European countries, the decrease in the mark-up ratios began in the second half of the 1980s.

The following sections analyse the influence of the mark-up on the macroeconomic performance as well as the link between product and factor market institutions on the one hand and the mark-up ratios on the other hand.

5.3 Mark-up and macroeconomic performance

In this section, the influence of the mark-up ratio on important macroeconomic indicators is analysed by means of panel estimations[9]. Macroeconomic indicators comprise total factor productivity growth, labour productivity growth, employment and unemployment. The subsequent estimations have been performed for the panel of nine Euro Area countries. The starting point is 1976 (1975 in some cases), i.e. after the recession caused by the first oil price shock. The termination points of the estimations depend on data availability. While at the time of performing the analyses, macroeconomic variables are available until 2004, the time series of product and factor market indicators end in 2002, in some cases in 1999.

Previous studies conclude that structural reforms such as the Single Market Programme could increase the long-run level of total factor productivity in the EU by 0.5 to 1 percent (European Commission, 2004). Simulating a 10 percentage point cut in the mark-up brought about by product market reforms, the IMF (2003) concludes that in the long-run, GDP could increase by 4.3 percent. Also based on model simulations, Bayoumi et al. (2004) estimate that reducing the mark-up in the Euro Area to the US level would raise GDP in the long run by 8.6 percent.

5.3.1 Total factor productivity growth

The analysis of the link between the mark-up of prices over marginal costs and the macroeconomic performance begins with total factor productivity (TFP) growth. TFP can be viewed as an indicator for technical progress. It is therefore an important determinant of economic growth. According to IMF estimates, GDP per capita in the Euro Area grew in the period 1995 to 2003 by 1.7 percent per annum, compared to 2.4 percent in the United States. This gap between the two areas can to a large extent be traced back to a divergent development of total factor productivity. In the period under consideration, TFP growth reached 0.8 percent per annum on average in the Euro Area, far behind the 1.4 percent per annum recorded in the United States (Estevao, 2004). Not only does the TFP growth rate in the Euro Area lag behind the US level, total factor productivity growth in most of the Euro Area countries has also declined over time. According to our calculations, TFP growth in the aggregate of the nine Euro Area countries under consideration decreased from nearly 5 percent per annum in the 1970s to less than two percent per year in the period 1995 to 2004. In the four

[9] The estimations have been performed with the software package EViews 4.1.

largest Euro Area economies (Germany, France, Italy, and Spain), TFP growth fell from more than 5 percent per annum in the 1970s to only 1¼ percent annually in the most recent decade.

One important source of the rather unsatisfactory growth performance of the Euro Area, in particular compared to the United States may be found in the less competitive environment, visible in higher mark-up ratios. TFP growth can be interpreted as an indicator of dynamic efficiency. The level of competition, reflected in the mark-up ratio, influences dynamic efficiency through incentives to engage in innovation activities (Griffith and Harrison, 2004). However, from a theoretical point of view it is not unambiguously clear that lower economic rents positively affect dynamic efficiency. This is because a higher degree of competition reduces the gains from innovation. Early publications on endogenous growth and industrial organisation suggested that increased product market competition negatively influences innovation and thus TFP growth as more competition diminishes possible rents to be accrued by innovators. These results rest upon the assumption that only outsiders engage in innovation activities. Thus, in these models, rents prior to innovation are zero, and the total extra profit to be earned by innovation is equal to post-innovation rents. Therefore, incentives to innovate are positively correlated with rents. Under these assumptions, product market reforms that reduce rents decrease innovation and thus dynamic efficiency.

More recent endogenous growth models extend the basic Schumpeterian model by allowing not only outsiders but also incumbent firms to innovate. If insiders also innovate, pre-innovation rents are not zero, but positive. In this case, fostering competition may reduce pre-innovation rents by a larger degree than post-innovation rents. Thus, mark-up reducing reforms may have a positive influence on dynamic efficiency, i.e. raise TFP growth.

As these theoretical considerations have shown, the link between the degree of competition and dynamic efficiency may either be positive or negative. Thus, in this section the relationship between the mark-up ratios in the EUR-9 and TFP growth are investigated empirically.

The calculation of TFP growth has been based on the growth accounting framework, assuming a Cobb-Douglas production function with constant returns to scale. TFP growth can be identified as that part of real GDP growth, which is not explained by increasing inputs of the production factors. Labour, capital and technical progress, i.e. TFP, have been taken into consideration as input factors. Capital input has been approximated by the capital stock in the business sector, deflated by the GDP deflator. As mentioned above, consistent OECD data on capital stocks are only available for the business sector, but not for the entire economy. For reasons of consistency, employment has been approximated by the number of employees in the business sector only.

Total income is given by the sum of "compensation of employees" and "income from property and other", the latter approximating capital income. Thus, labour input has been derived by multiplying the number of employees by the share of compensation of employees in total income, while capital input is given by the real capital stock, multiplied by the share of income from property and other in total income. The residual GDP growth not accounted for by labour and capital input, i.e. the Solow residual, can be identified as TFP growth.

The estimation has been performed with fixed country effects and with the lagged endogenous variable.[10] Using random effects resulted in an insignificant coefficient of the mark-up. Random effects would only work without the lagged endogenous variable, but in this case there would be problems with serial correlations of the residuals. The results of the fixed effects model in the table below show that the influence of the mark-up ratio of prices over marginal costs on TFP growth is significantly negative. According to the estimates presented and taking into account the average values of the mark-ups in the countries under consideration, a reduction of the mark-up in the Euro Area by around 10 percent (which, according to the estimates presented in Sect. 5.2, is about the gap to the US level) would raise average TFP growth in the Euro Area by 0.57 percentage points (pp). Looking at the Member States, the effect ranges from 0.5 pp in Finland and the Netherlands to 0.75 pp in Italy.

---

[10] Including a lagged endogenous variable in a fixed-effects model may result in biased and inconsistent estimates However this bias is small if the cross-section dimension is small in relation to the time dimension of the panel. This is clearly the case here.

Table 5.2. Effects of mark-up on TFP growth rate

Dependent variable: TFP growth rate, GTFP

Variable	Coefficient	t-statistic (absolute value)
$GTFP_{-1}$	0.240**	4.033
MARKUP	-3.448**	3.169

Fixed Effects	
Austria	6.797
Belgium	6.464
Germany	6.230
Spain	6.925
Finland	7.583
France	6.966
Ireland	8.953
Italy	9.006
Netherlands	6.306

Sample	1976 – 2004		
Observations	257		
R^2	0.234	F-statistic	8.816
Durbin-Watson	1.897		

** denotes significance at the 1 percent level.

5.3.2 Employment

In addition to total factor productivity, employment can be expected to be influenced by the degree of competition as captured by the mark-up ratio. Blanchard and Giavazzi (2001) consider a model with a product market characterised by monopolistic competition. The elasticity of demand is assumed to depend negatively on the degree of product market regulation. This negative relationship can be explained by the notion that the demand elasticity is an increasing function of the number of firms. The latter in turn depends negatively on the costs of entry. Thus, removing barriers to entry increases the number of firms, which raises the elasticity of demand and thus lowers the level of economic rents in the economy. In this context, firms choose labour to maximise the present discounted value of future cash flows. Changing employment causes adjustment costs. The authors assume that these adjustment costs can be affected by product market regulation. The model generates predictions about the relationship between product market regulations, the mark-up (or the level of rents) and the level of employment. Deregulation, by reducing the mark-up, leads to a higher demand for labour.

Another reason for a negative relationship between the mark-up and employment is that economies of scale should disappear as a result of emerging new technologies (Coppens and Vivet, 2004). If sunk costs are low and entry and exit barriers are reduced, the number of firms increases, entailing a positive impact on job creation. Employment is also supported by the fact that lower profit margins are accompanied by lower real wage claims and thus by reduced structural unemployment. More competition in product markets tends to lead to lower wage mark-ups. Thus, the price mark-up and the wage mark-up are generally positively related, and reforms diminishing the former also lead to declines of the latter.

For the panel of nine Euro Area countries, the following table shows that employment is indeed negatively influenced by the mark-up.[11] The low Durbin Watson statistic in combination with the high coefficient of determination points to some problems with the statistical properties of the regression. However, using the growth rate instead of the level of employment or including the lagged dependent variable resulted in an insignificant coefficient of the mark-up. The regression has been performed with fixed country effects. A random effects estimation led to almost exactly the same results. Based on the Hausman test, the specification with fixed effects was preferred.

Bringing the mark-up in the countries of the Euro Area to US levels would raise employment in the Euro Area by about 2.7 percent. In 2005, about 137 million people in the Euro Area were in paid employment. The simulated cut of the mark-up by 10 percent could therefore raise employment to about 141 million.

[11] Here, the logarithm has been used in order to account for the different orders of magnitude of the variables.

Table 5.3. Effects of mark-up on employment

Dependent variable: logarithm of employment, ln (EMP)

Variable	Coefficient	t-statistic (absolute value)
ln (MARKUP)	-0.251**	2.853
Fixed Effects		
Austria	15.260	
Belgium	15.272	
Germany	17.377	
Spain	16.492	
Finland	14.722	
France	17.023	
Ireland	14.199	
Italy	17.000	
Netherlands	15.794	

Sample 1976 - 2004
Observations 259
R^2 0.991 F-statistic 3019.5
Durbin-Watson 0.067
** denotes significance at the 1 percent level.

5.3.3 Unemployment rate

An increase in employment brought about by enhanced competition and thus a decrease in the mark-up of prices over costs would also reduce unemployment. But the decline of unemployment is not symmetric to the increase in employment. When employment rises, more people engage in actively seeking employment as they see improving opportunities on the labour market. Therefore, the decline in unemployment is typically less pronounced than the increase in employment. Thus, a separate panel estimation has been performed for the relationship between the unemployment rate and the mark-up. Again, the model includes fixed country effects. A random effects estimation produced almost the same results; the Hausman test suggests that the fixed effects model is superior. The low Durbin Watson statistic points to problems with serial correlation. However, this phenomenon cannot be alleviated by including the lagged unemployment rate. Furthermore, in the latter case the mark-up becomes insignificant.

Table 5.4. Effects of mark-up on unemployment rate

Dependent variable: unemployment rate, UR

Variable	Coefficient	t-statistic (absolute value)
MARKUP	3.306*	2.214
Fixed Effects		
Austria	-1.393	
Belgium	3.607	
Germany	1.755	
Spain	8.154	
Finland	3.817	
France	4.020	
Ireland	5.491	
Italy	2.767	
Netherlands	1.444	

Sample 1975 - 2004
Observations 266
R^2 0.493 F-statistic 29.615
Durbin-Watson 0.154
*denotes significance at the 5 percent level.

Taking the estimation results into account, cutting the mark-up in the Euro Area by 10 percent would result in a decline in the average unemployment rate by about 0.5 percentage points. Among the member countries, the effect ranges from 0.4 percentage points in Finland to 0.65 percentage points in Italy.

In 2006, the average Euro Area unemployment rate amounted to 7.9 percent. According to the estimation results, a cut of the mark-up by 10 percent could thus reduce the unemployment rate to about 7.4 percent.

5.3.4 Labour productivity growth

Besides total factor productivity and employment, labour productivity is an important macroeconomic indicator. If real wages increase in line with labour productivity growth, unit labour costs remain constant. Thus, rising labour productivity growth widens the scope for wage increases without endangering price stability. According to IMF estimates, labour productivity growth in the Euro Area lags considerably behind the US (Estevao, 2004). Between 1995 and 2003, output per employee expanded by 1.2 percent per annum in the Euro Area and by 2.1 percent annually in the US. In addition, while in the US labour productivity growth accelerated in the second half of the 1990s, in the Euro Area it declined markedly.

Lack of competition in the goods and labour markets, leading to higher mark-ups of prices over costs may be a reason for the less favourable productivity performance in the Euro Area as compared to the United States. Griffith and Harrison (2004) find a *positive* relationship between the mark-up and the *level* of labour productivity, but a *negative* influence on the *growth rate*. The authors explain the positive influence of economic rents on the productivity *level* with recourse to the job creation effect of lower mark-ups. If new workers entering the workforce are less productive than incumbents, then the overall productivity *level* declines. The same effect can be observed if new jobs are created in less productive sectors. This notion seems realistic because the more productive workers and firms have already been in place at higher mark-up levels. However, the link between economic rents and the *growth rate* of labour productivity may still be negative. If the productivity of newly created jobs is lower than that of existing jobs, then a rise in employment as a result of lower mark-ups will be associated with a reduction in labour productivity *growth*, but only while employment is growing. Once employment has reached its new - higher - level, the *growth rate* of labour productivity may rise again, even though the *level* of labour productivity may remain lower for some time.

In this section, the influence of the mark-up on the *growth rate* of labour productivity is investigated. The latter is defined as real GDP per employee. For the estimation, the cyclicality of labour productivity growth has been removed by taking the growth rate of trend rather than actual labour productivity. The trend has been determined by applying the Hodrick-Prescott filter. The following table shows the estimation results. Based on the Hausman test, the estimation has been performed with fixed country effects. As in the employment equation, the low Durbin Watson statistic cannot be improved upon by including the lagged dependent variable. In addition, the latter would result in an insignificant mark-up ratio.

Table 5.5. Effects of mark-up on labour productivity growth

Dependent variable: trend labour productivity growth rate, GTRENDPROD

Variable	Coefficient	t-statistic (absolute value)
MARKUP	-1.015**	3.041
Fixed Effects		
Austria	3.515	
Belgium	3.307	
Germany	2.479	
Spain	3.211	
Finland	3.698	
France	3.116	
Ireland	5.025	
Italy	3.685	
Netherlands	2.466	

Sample 1976 – 2004
Observations 259
R^2 0.547 F-statistic 35.556
Durbin-Watson 0.039
** denotes significance at the 1 percent level.

As can be seen, the negative influence of the mark-up on the development of trend labour productivity is highly significant. According to the above results of the panel estimation, a reduction of the mark-up in the Euro Area by 10 percent would raise the growth rate of trend labour productivity by 0.15 percentage points (pp). The effect would lie in the range of 0.13 pp in the Netherlands to 0.2 pp in Italy.

5.4 The influence of regulation on the mark-up

After having analysed the influence of the mark-up on the macroeconomic performance, this section looks at the link between institutions and the mark-up ratios. The institutional framework is an important determinant of the degree of competition. The latter in turn determines the scope for setting prices significantly above marginal costs and thus exploiting economic rents. According to previous studies, institutional reforms could lead to mark-up reductions in the European Union of between 0.5 and 0.9 percentage points (European Commission, 2004).

A highly regulated labour market allows employers' and employees' associations to share economic rents. Labour market regulations protecting workers or providing generous benefits to unemployed persons tend to increase the reservation wage, thus leading to higher wage claims. As a result, wages tend to be higher and employment would be lower than under more intensive competition; the deviation of prices from marginal costs widens (Nunziata, 2001). In a more competitive environment, the scope for such behaviour would be smaller. Thus, both the duration of receiving unemployment benefits and the benefit replacement rate should positively influence the mark-up. In contrast, a higher degree of wage bargaining coordination would allow account to be taken of economy-wide developments in the wage negotiations. Thus, a higher degree of coordination would reduce the wage pressure and thus the mark-up (see, e.g., Nunziata, 2001). On the other hand, not only a high but also a low level of wage bargaining coordination may lead to wage restraint as in this case firm-specific developments can be taken into account. Thus, both a highly centralised and a largely decentralised wage bargaining process seem to dominate the intermediate case, where the advantages of both systems cannot be fully exploited and wages tend to be too high (Calmfors and Driffill, 1988). In line with these considerations, labour market institutions used in the subsequent regression comprise the unemployment benefit replacement rate (BRR), the benefit duration index (BD), and an index measuring the degree of wage bargaining coordination (CO). The benefit replacement rate is defined as the unemployment benefit in the first year as a percentage of average earnings before tax. The benefit duration index is a weighted average of the ratio between the unemployment benefit in the second and first years and the ratio between the unemployment benefit in the fourth and first years. The wage bargaining coordination index lies in the range of 1 to 3, increasing in the degree of coordination in the wage bargaining process on the employers' as well as on the trade unions' side. Details on the definition and construction of these indicators can be found in Nickell and Nunziata (2001) and in Nickell (2003).

In addition to labour market institutions, an index increasing with openness to international trade (TRADE) has been included in the estimation. This index has been taken from the Fraser Institute database (Gwartney and Lawson, 2004). Including this indicator rests upon the notion that a high degree of actual or potential international competition reduces the scope for companies to set prices above marginal costs, and therefore a negative influence on the mark-up is to be expected.

Other labour market indicators that are published by Nickell and Nunziata (2001), such as union density, an indicator measuring the degree of employment protection, or the tax wedge on labour income, proved to be insignificant or had an economically implausible sign.

The following table shows the estimation results. The regression was run with fixed country effects. If random effects were used, the benefit duration index and the trade variable become insignificant. Including the lagged mark-up also resulted in insignificant coefficients. As was to be expected, both higher benefit replacement rates and longer unemployment benefit durations lead to larger mark-up ratios. On the other hand, more openness to international trade and thus international competition reduces the mark-up. The respective coefficient is almost significant at the 1 percent level. In addition, a higher degree of coordination in the wage bargaining process negatively influences the mark-up. The hump shaped hypothesis, i.e. the notion that both lower and higher degrees of wage bargaining coordination are superior to an intermediate solution could not be confirmed.

Table 5.6. Effects of institutions on mark-up

Dependent variable: MARKUP

Variable	Coefficient	t-statistic (absolute value)
BRR	0.486**	5.085
BD	0.376**	3.209
CO	-0.084**	2.965
TRADE	-0.047*	2.397
Fixed Effects		
Austria	1.521	
Belgium	1.562	
Germany	1.605	
Spain	1.719	
Finland	1.435	
France	1.486	
Ireland	1.855	
Italy	2.277	
Netherlands	1.360	

Sample 1976 – 1999
Observations 214
R^2 0.688 F-statistic 40.110
Durbin-Watson 0.416
*, ** denotes significance at the 5, 1 percent level.

In 1999, the last year for which data on labour market institutions are available in Nickell (2003), the benefit replacement rate BRR in the nine

Euro Area countries considered in the estimation amounted to 0.52 on average. This value compares to 0.29 in the United States and just 0.17 in the United Kingdom. Thus, not only compared to the US, but also with respect to the UK, unemployment benefits are more generous in the Euro Area. Simulations show that a reduction of the benefit replacement rate in the Euro Area by 25 percent would result in a decline of the mark-up ratio by 4.3 percent on average. In 1999, the average value of the benefit duration index BD took the value 0.56 in the Euro Area, compared to 0.22 in the US. A 25 percent reduction of the benefit duration variable would lead to a decline of the average Euro Area mark-up by 3.7 percent. Both the wage bargaining coordination and the openness to international trade are already comparatively high in the Euro Area. Nevertheless, in some areas barriers to international trade still exist in the EU. In 2002, the last year for which data on this variable are available, the freedom to international trade index in the EU countries under consideration on average amounted to 8.3. Increasing the openness to international trade, resulting in a rise of the index by one point to 9.3 would lead to a decline in the mark-up by 1.8 percent on average. The largest effect would occur in Finland, where the mark-up would decrease by 6 percent.

As an alternative to using detailed variables measuring the labour market regulation, an overall index could be applied. Such a summary index is contained in the database of the Fraser Institute. This indicator (LREG) takes values between 1 and 10, rising with the degree of economic freedom, i.e. the index decreases with increasing labour market regulation. It consists of the following five sub-indices (Gwartney and Lawson, 2004):

i. Impact of minimum wage: the minimum wage, set by law, has little impact on wages because it is too low or not obeyed.
ii. Hiring and firing practices: hiring and firing practices of companies are determined by private contract.
iii. Share of labour force whose wages are set by centralised collective bargaining.
iv. Unemployment benefits: the system of unemployment benefits preserves the incentive to work.
v. Use of conscripts to obtain military personnel.

In the nine Euro Area countries under consideration, the index had an average value of 4.3 in 2002, compared to 7.3 in the US. Thus, labour markets in the Euro Area are more regulated than in the United States. In the UK, the indicator amounts to 6.7. Thus, the UK labour market is more flexible than the labour markets in the Euro Area countries, but it is significantly more regulated than its US counterpart. Although over time the indicator has risen in the Euro Area countries, in the UK and in the US it increased to a larger extent. In the latter two countries, the share of the labour force whose wages are set by centralised wage bargaining has declined, and the unemployment benefit system has become less generous. As a result of the former development, economic conditions of individual companies can better be taken into account in wage negotiations, while the latter effect reduces the reservation wage. Both effects diminish the scope for workers to exploit economic rents, thus decreasing wage pressure.

Using this summary labour market regulation indicator instead of the more detailed variables taken in the previous regression resulted in significant coefficients with the economically correct sign only if country-specific time trends were included.[12] Other variables on product and factor market regulation that are also published by the Fraser Institute, such as openness to international trade, ease of starting a new business, overall business regulation, size of government or the overall freedom of the world index are either available for too short a time span or resulted in coefficients that were insignificant or had an economically implausible sign.

The following table shows the estimation results. Again, the low Durbin Watson statistic points to problems with serial correlation. However, including the lagged dependent variable cannot alleviate this problem. If the lagged mark-up but not the time trends are included, the labour market regulation variable becomes insignificant. Overall, the estimation results show that the above specification with more detailed labour market regulation indicators is superior.

Taking, nevertheless, these estimation results into account, decreasing the labour market regulation in the nine Euro Area countries in the panel to the US level would result in a decline in the average Euro Area mark-up by about 14 percent or 0.2 percentage points. Among the Member States the reduction ranges from 7 percent (0.11 percentage points) in Ireland to about 24 percent (0.33 percentage points) in Germany.

[12] All other estimations discussed in this chapter have been performed without country-specific time trends.

Table 5.7. Effects of labour market regulation on mark-up

Dependent variable: MARKUP

Variable	Coefficient	t-statistic (absolute value)
LREG	-0.069**	3.587
Country-specific time trends		
Austria	-0.007**	3.624
Belgium	0.017**	7.079
Germany	-0.006**	3.097
Spain	-0.005*	2.154
Finland	-0.006**	2.656
France	-0.001	0.420
Ireland	-0.014**	5.841
Italy	0.022**	10.390
Netherlands	0.008**	2.993
Fixed Effects		
Austria	1.950	
Belgium	1.275	
Germany	1.842	
Spain	1.727	
Finland	1.802	
France	1.681	
Ireland	2.494	
Italy	1.511	
Netherlands	1.306	
Sample 1975 – 2002		
Observations	248	
R^2 0.809	F-statistic	59.167
Durbin-Watson	0.583	

*, ** denotes significance at the 5, 1 percent level.

5.5 Conclusion

The empirical investigations have shown that there is room for improving the macroeconomic performance in the Euro Area. One means of achieving higher GDP growth rates, generating employment and reducing unemployment would be the intensification of competition as envisaged in the Lisbon Strategy.

In the following table, the results of the preceding panel analyses are summarised. Here, the effects of structural reforms on the macroeconomic performance are shown for the aggregate Euro Area. The following table shows the effects of labour market deregulation on the mark-up.

Table 5.8. Effects of deregulation on the mark-up

	Reduction of benefit replacement rate by 25 percent	Reduction of benefit duration index by 25 percent	Increasing the openness to international trade index by 1 point (12 percent)
Mark-up	4.3 percent decline	3.7 percent decline	1.8 percent decline

According to these results, making the unemployment benefit system in the Euro Area less generous could be expected to result in a decline of the average Euro Area mark-up ratio by around 4 percent. More freedom of trade leads to a lower mark-up and therefore to lower economic rents.

The following table summarises the influence of the mark-up on the macroeconomic performance. In particular, the effects of a 10 percent cut in the average Euro Area mark-up on TFP growth, labour productivity growth, employment, and unemployment are depicted.

Table 5.9. Macroeconomic effects of a 10 percent cut in the Euro Area mark-up

Indicator	**Effect**
TFP growth rate	0.57 percentage points increase
Labour productivity growth rate	0.15 percentage points increase
Employment	2.7 percent increase
Unemployment rate	0.5 percentage points decline

As the table shows, a 10 percent reduction of the Euro Area mark-up, bringing prices closer to marginal costs, would boost total factor productivity growth by 0.57 percentage points. Labour productivity growth would increase by 0.15 percentage points. In addition, a positive employment effect can be expected: employment would rise by 2.7 percent, and the unemployment rate would be half a percentage point lower.

Appendix: Data sources and definitions

Table 5.10. Variables used in Chapter 5

Acronym	Definition	Description	Source	Maximum time span	Minimum time span
UR	Unemployment rate	Unemployment rate	Nickell and Nunziata, 2001; EUROSTAT	1960 - 2004	1975 - 2004
EMP	Employment	Total employment	OECD, Economic Outlook	1960 - 2004	1969 - 2004
MARK UP	Mark-up	Mark-up of prices over costs	own calculations	1970 - 2004	1977 - 2004
PROD	Labour productivity	Real GDP over employees	own calculations	1960 - 2004	1969 – 2004
GTREN DPROD	Trend labour productivity	Growth rate of Hodrick-Prescott filtered labour productivity (PROD)	own calculations	1961 - 2004	1970 - 2004
GTFP	TFP growth (Solow residual)	Annual growth rate of total factor productivity	own calculations	1961 - 2004	1977 - 2004
BRR	Benefit replacement rate	Benefit in the first year of unemployment, as a percentage of earnings before tax	Nickell and Nunziata, 2001; Nickell 2003	1960 - 1999	1975 - 1999
BD	Benefit duration	Index; weighted average between ratio of BRR in 2nd year to BRR in 1st year and ratio of BRR in 4th year to BRR in 1st year	Nickell and Nunziata, 2001; Nickell 2003	1960 - 1999	1975 - 1999
CO	Bargaining coordination	Index {1,3}, increasing in degree of coordination in the bargaining process on the employers' and the unions' side	Nickell and Nunziata, 2001; Nickell 2003	1960 - 1998	1975 - 1998
LREG	Labour market regulation	Index {1;10}, decreasing in regulation	Fraser Institute	1970 - 2002	1975 - 2002
TRADE	Freedom to trade	Index {1;10}, decreasing in regulation	Fraser Institute	1970 - 2002	1970 - 2002

References

Badinger, H. (2004), Do we really know that the EU's Single Market Programme has fostered competition? Testing for a decrease in markup ratios in EU industries. Europainstitut, Wirtschaftsuniversität Wien, Working Paper 55.

Bayoumi, T., D. Laxton, and P. Pesenti (2004), Benefits and spillovers of greater competition in Europe: A macroeconomic assessment, NBER Working Paper 10416.

Blanchard, O. and F. Giavazzi (2001), Macroeconomic effects of regulation and deregulation in goods and labour markets, NBER Working Paper 8120.

Calmfors, L. and J. Driffill (1988), Centralization of wage bargaining; Economic Policy 2, p.14-61.

Coppens, F. and D. Vivet (2004), Liberalisation of network industries: Is the electricity sector an exception to the rule?, National Bank of Belgium, Working Paper 200409.

Estevao, M. (2004), Why is Productivity Growth in the Euro Area so sluggish? IMF Working Paper WP/04/200.

European Commission (2004), The EU Economy: 2004 Review, European Economy no. 6.

European Commission (2005), Communication to the Spring European Council: Working together for growth and jobs. A new start for the Lisbon Strategy, Brussels.

European Commission (2006), Communication to the Spring European Council: Time to move up a gear. The new partnership for growth and jobs, Brussels.

Griffith, R. and R. Harrison (2004), The link between product market reform and macro-economic performance, European Commission, Economic Papers no.209.

Gwartney, J. and R. Lawson (2004), Economic Freedom of the World: 2004 Annual Report, Fraser Institute, Vancouver, http://www.freetheworld.com.

IMF (2003), Unemployment and labour market institutions: why reforms pay off; April World Economic Outlook.

Martins, J.O., S. Scarpetta and D. Pilat (1996), Mark-up Ratios in Manufacturing Industries. Estimates for 14 OECD Countries. OECD Economics Department Working Paper no. 162.

Nickell, S. (2003), Labour Market Institutions and Unemployment in OECD Countries, CESifo DICE Report 2/2003, p.13-26.

Nickell, S. and L. Nunziata (2001), Labour market institutions database, vers. 2.00, LSE, Centre of Economic Performance; http://cep.lse.ac.uk/pubs/download/data0502.zip

Nunziata, L. (2001), Institutions and Wage Determination: a Multi-Country Approach, University of Oxford, Nuffield College, Working Paper 2001-W29.

Roeger, W. (1995), Can imperfect Competition explain the Difference between Primal and Dual Productivity Measures? Estimates for US manufacturing. Journal of Political Economy, vol. 103, no. 2., p.316-330.

6 Macroeconomic and welfare effects of structural and budgetary policies: spillovers in the MSG3 model

Reinhard Neck and Gottfried Haber

6.1 Introduction

In this chapter, we aim at analysing and evaluating the macroeconomic effects of structural policy measures and of policies of budgetary consolidation. For the former, we build upon the results obtained in Chapter 5 regarding the spillovers from economic reforms that close the efficiency gap between the Euro Area and the US. For the latter, we start from the fact that at present, several Euro Area (and other EU) countries have difficulties in fulfilling the deficit and debt criteria of the Stability and Growth Pact and try to consolidate their budgets. In Chapters 3 and 4, empirical estimates of the spillovers from budgetary policies that increase the surplus of the public budget were provided. Here we will use the MSG3 Model, the most recent version of the McKibbin-Sachs Global Model, to simulate policies which we consider to be feasible (see the Appendix to this chapter, for more information on this model). First, we consider structural and budgetary policies separately, and then we combine both of them. Both isolated (non-coordinated) policy actions of one country only and coordinated (joint) Euro Area policies will be investigated. We will concentrate on isolated policies by Germany and Italy only; effects for France are between these two, and spillovers for a small economy are negligible. In order to arrive at policy recommendations, we will also provide some tentative welfare calculations comparing different scenarios.

6.2 Effects of structural policies

One of the main results of Chapter 5 was an estimate of the effects of deregulation policies in the Euro Area on the mark-up in the Euro Area, which amounted to somewhere between 6 and 14 percent decline. Taking the mean of a 10 percent decline of the mark-up in the Euro Area, the effect of this on the total factor productivity growth rate was estimated as an increase by 0.57 percentage points, with some variation between the different countries (Germany 0.57, France 0.54, Italy 0.75, Austria 0.54 percentage points). We will use these estimates in the following as inputs into the MSG3 Model. Total factor productivity is an exogenous variable in this model that can easily be shocked. The other variables possibly affected by the deregulation reforms (labour productivity, employment, unemployment) are mostly endogenous variables that will be changed through the channels of the model by changes of total factor productivity. Estimates of the effects on these variables resulting from the MSG3 Model need not coincide with those from the econometric estimations obtained in Chapter 5 because the effects in the MSG3 Model incorporate all kinds of feedbacks from other national variables and from international spillover effects. Indeed, as we shall see, the effects vary within the MSG3 simulations depending on the assumptions made about the implementation of the structural policies under consideration.

Another problem arises from the fact that the econometric estimations of Chapter 5 indicate an effect of cutting the *level* of the mark-up (a one-time though once-for-all change) on total factor productivity *growth.* The latter may mean a one-time effect on the growth of total factor productivity (TFP) or a permanent increase in the growth rate, which would imply cumulative increases of TFP forever. We consider the latter interpretation as by far too optimistic. To be on the safe side, it seems more realistic to assume that TFP will gradually increase over a period of 5 years to a level higher by 0.57 percent (for the Euro Area as a whole; the values for the individual countries are given above) than the baseline and grow from this higher level with the baseline growth rate later on. These simulations amount to an increase of TFP by 0.11 percent in the first period, by 0.23 percent in the second, by 0.34 percent in the third, by 0.46 percent in the fourth and by 0.57 percent in the fifth and all following periods as compared to the baseline solution (numbers for the Euro Area; numbers for individual countries differ slightly in accordance with the different long-run values given above). Alternatives like continued TFP growth by an additional 0.114 percentage points (the mean additional growth over the first five periods) for each period to follow forever or an additional growth rate of 0.57 percentage points forever were tried to be simulated, too, but we arrived at completely unrealistic effects in an unstable model solution, hence these attempts were discarded. Results from an unstable solution of the model (because the model is formulated in level terms) are not reliable, and it is highly questionable that one-time (though permanently upheld) structural reforms will result not only in ever-lasting but even in ever-increasing gains to the economies affected. Even if this were true, it is not clear whether we can rely on the results from a local linearisation solution procedure under such a severe structural change, quite apart from the Lucas critique counter-argument. For these reasons, we consider results from a TFP shift scenario as described above as much more reliable estimates of the macroeconomic effects of structural policy reforms.

For all simulations in this section, we assume the policy rule of monetary targeting for Euro Area monetary policy. The reason for this will be argued in more detail in Sect. 6.5. Figs. 6.1 and 6.2 provide the values of selected endogenous variables resulting from the simulations. Responses are shown for two countries, namely Germany and Italy, assuming that only one of these countries implements the deregulation policy leading to the TFP growth according to the estimates, with the other Euro Area countries going on with "business as usual" (no economic reforms). Effects in the other countries are purely international spillover effects. These simulations can be regarded as non-coordinated structural policies. On the other hand, we also show in Fig. 6.3 the effects of a coordinated Euro Area economic reform, assuming that all Euro Area countries implement the policies leading to the lower mark-up and the higher TFP. The values for other variables as well as results for other countries and regions of the model are available on request. In the following, we show the time paths of a few key variables originating from each shock. All numbers are deviations from the baseline values of the MSG3 Model. In each case, we present (row-wise) the variables real GDP, current account, budget deficit (general government), public debt (general government), labour (employment), rate of inflation, short-term and long-term nominal rates of interest. Countries are denoted by the following symbols: Germany – square, France – triangle, Italy – asterisk, Austria – circle.

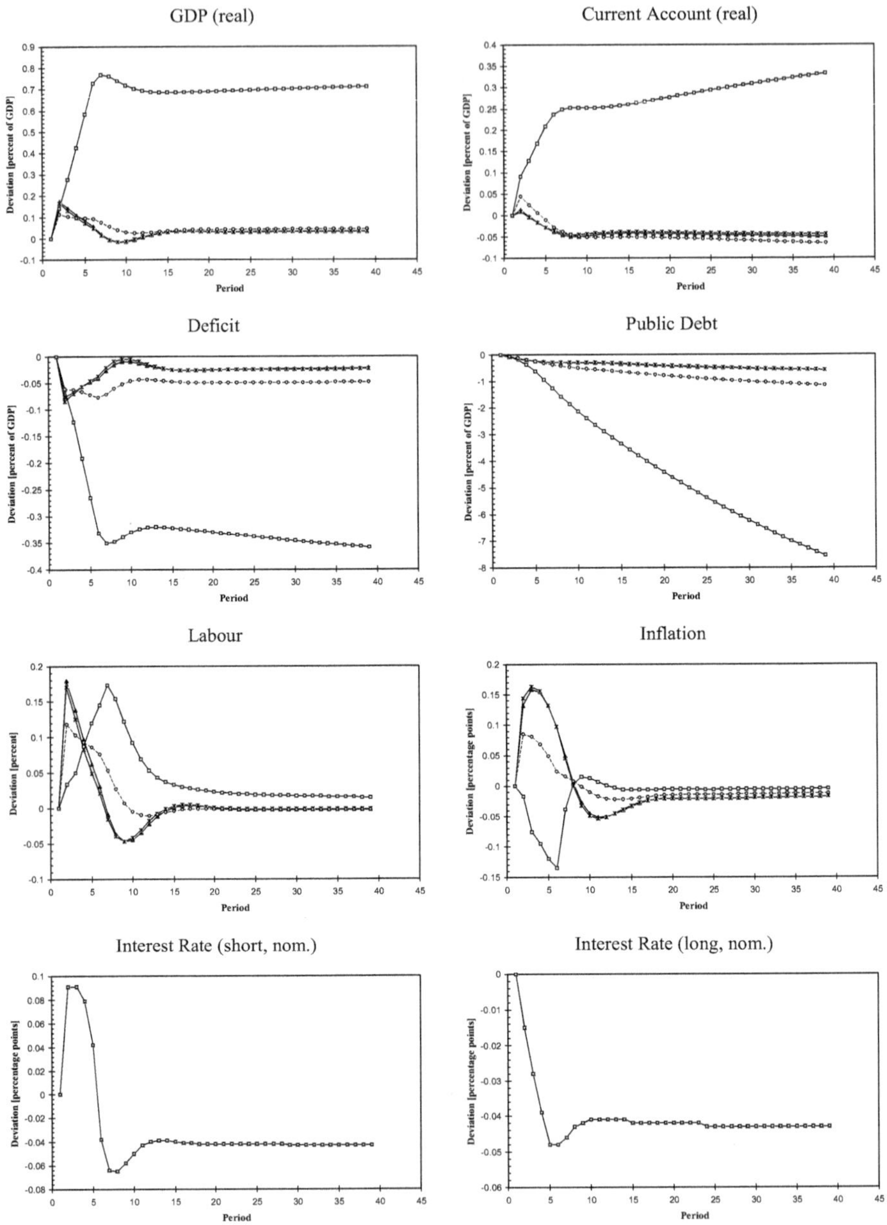

Fig. 6.1. Structural policy, Germany

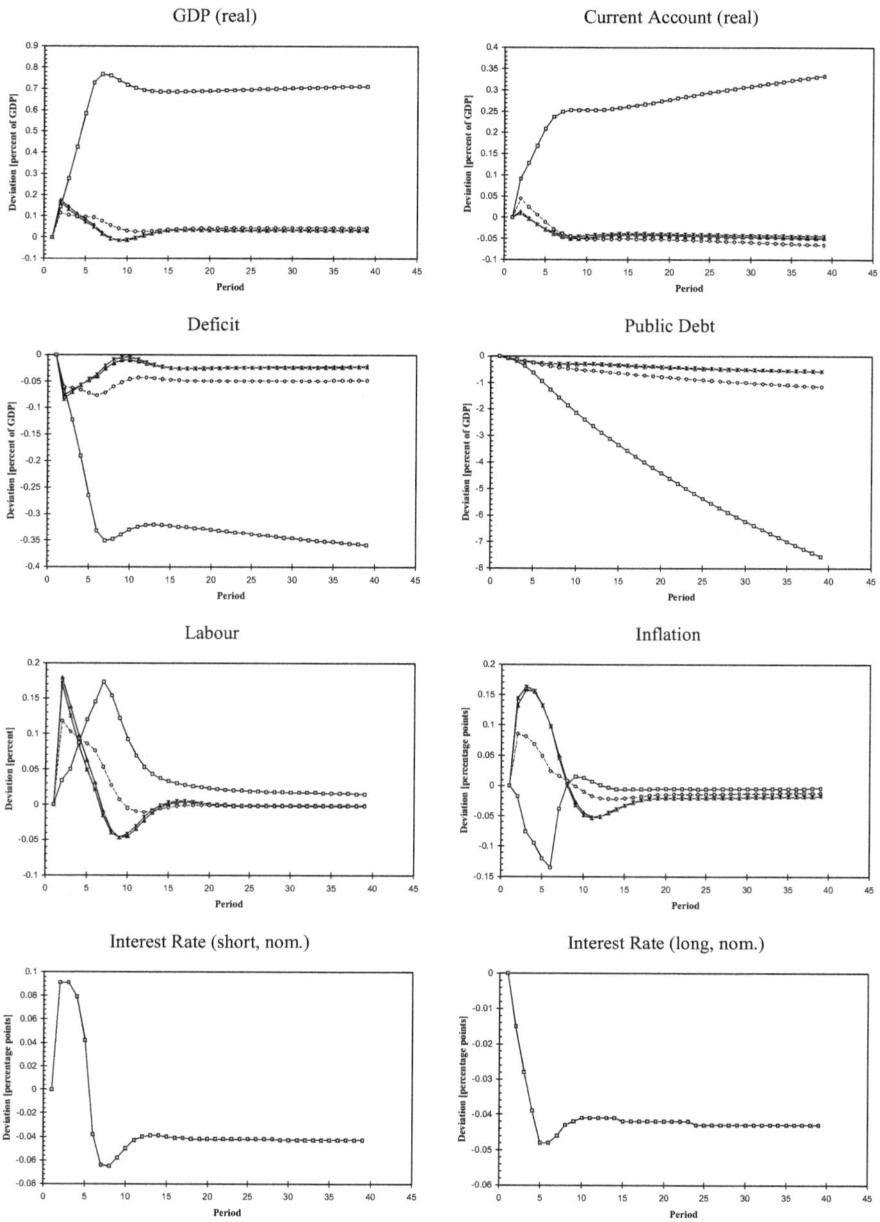

Fig. 6.2. Structural policy, Italy

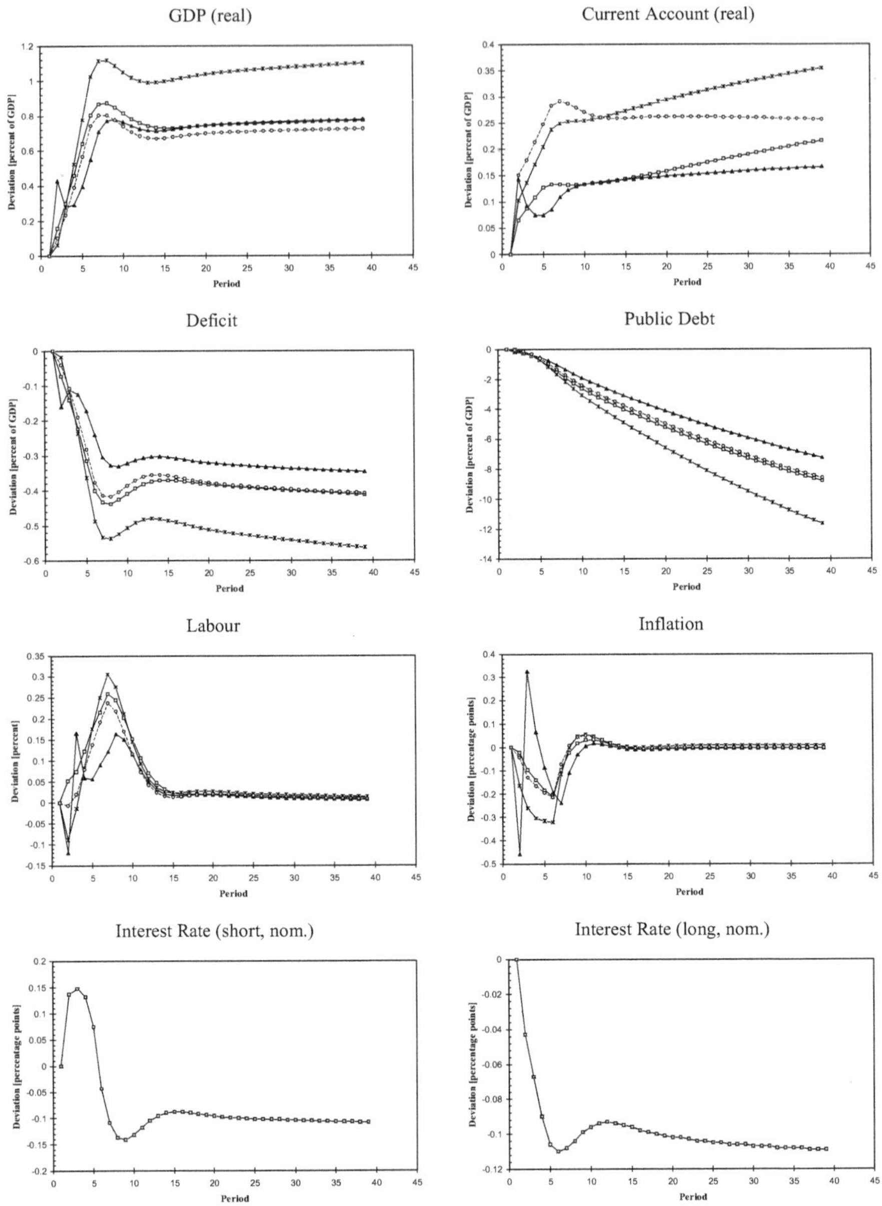

Fig. 6.3. Structural policy, Euro Area (coordinated policy)

The results of these simulations can be summarised as follows: Under the TFP shock to a single country, real GDP of the country directly affected rises over 6 years and stays then at the higher level forever. Effects are stronger for Italy (GDP above baseline by 1 percent of baseline GDP) than for Germany (GDP above baseline by 0.7 percent). The current account improves permanently, the public-sector deficit remains below baseline values, causing public debt to fall indefinitely (in Italy, it is lower than baseline by 10 percent of baseline GDP after 40 years, in Germany by 8 percent). Employment rises slightly (with a minimal permanent effect), inflation falls temporarily. Euro Area countries not directly affected exhibit only temporary positive spillovers effects to GDP, small permanent negative ones to the current account and positive ones to the public deficit and public debt. Interest rates rise in the short run and fall below baseline in the long run. Spillovers effects are stronger for Germany than for Italy due to the size of the economy affected directly. The shock to the entire Euro Area brings about positive effects for all Euro Area countries. Interestingly, also the effects on Germany and Italy are stronger than in the case where only one of these countries is affected. Hence, there are positive spillovers effects from a coordinated structural policy in the Euro Area. For example, GDP remains at higher levels in Germany and Italy than in the case of isolated structural reforms, and the rates of interest remain below baseline by 0.1 percentage points, causing public deficits to improve more and public debt to fall by 6 to 12 percent of baseline GDP after 40 years. These effects are due to positive spillovers from the respective other countries (including the rest of the Euro Area). For example, if labour market regulations or price distortions due to imperfect competition are reduced in, say, the Netherlands, this will support similar measures in Germany by increasing competition also in this country as Dutch products compete with German ones, inducing further positive supply effects. Hence, there are truly international feedback effects in addition to direct effects from structural policy changes.

These results allow a fairly positive evaluation of the effects of structural policies on the Euro Area economies. Output will rise to levels permanently above those that would occur without these reforms, the public deficit will be lower without additional budgetary policy measures, allowing public debt to decrease over a long time horizon. Spillovers effects are not too strong, but there is some gain from coordinated policies that implement the structural reforms in all Euro Area countries as compared to scenarios where these policies are implemented in one or some countries only. A cautious estimate of a coordinated Euro Area structural reform scenario implies a level of GDP that is permanently higher by 1 percent than without these reforms, virtually without negative effects on other politically relevant variables and with considerable positive effects on public finances (permanently lower budget deficit, hence cumulatively lower public debt).

6.3 Budgetary consolidation policies

In this section, we analyse some possibilities of policies for budgetary consolidation and their macroeconomic effects, using the MSG3 Model. It is well known that several Euro Area countries have difficulties in meeting the public deficit (3 percent of GDP) and debt (60 percent of GDP) criteria of the Stability and Growth Pact and the requirement to obtain a balanced budget or even a budgetary surplus over the business cycle and have therefore to consolidate their budgets. On the other hand, Keynesian macroeconomic theory predicts that reducing government expenditures or raising taxes in a not fully employed economy will increase unemployment and reduce economic growth; hence there may be undesirable side-effects of budgetary consolidation policies. Here we consider two instruments to reduce the public-sector deficit (and, by this, public-sector debt): decreases of public consumption and increases of lump-sum taxes (or, equivalently, decreases of lump-sum transfers). The use of lump-sum taxes is the easiest way to model a tax change within the MSG3 Model as this is a purely exogenous variable in the MSG3 Model. Simulating such a change shows the endogenous reactions of other variables that may, in reality, also be influenced by political actions, such as income or consumption taxes or taxes on particular goods (energy taxes can be changed in the MSG3 Model). A more elaborate and realistic analysis would simulate changes of these taxes, too, which would involve re-calibrating the model for each simulation as for these simulations, parameters (tax rates) instead of exogenous variables would have to be changed. Lack of space prevents such an analysis here; it should be borne in mind that raising (reducing) lump-sum instead of distortionary taxes underestimates welfare losses (gains).

Due to adverse absorption and supply-side effects, reducing public investment is not to be recommended as a means of reducing public deficits and debt and is therefore not taken into account here (although it is often used in actual political processes because it can be relatively easily changed). In addition to the two instruments mentioned, we also consider a third strategy that aims at diminishing the size of the public sector by reducing both public consumption and (lump-sum) taxes. In order to fulfil the aim of consolidating the budget, in this case public consumption has to be decreased more than taxes, of course.

As for other policies, the time pattern of the policy actions will determine the outcome in terms of macroeconomic target variables to a large extent. In principle, it is possible to reduce public expenditures (or raise taxes) by some amount or relative to GDP over a long period in order to bring public debt down to low values. Such a policy experiment (aiming at diminishing the size of the public sector) is analysed in Haber et al. (2006), resulting in unexpectedly strong long-run non-Keynesian effects. However, it may be more realistic to consider a shorter time horizon for budgetary consolidation. Here we consider a policy change over 12 years, which may be regarded as corresponding approximately to the length of a full business cycle or a sequence of three election periods. During the first four years, the budget deficit is gradually diminished. Then it is kept at lower values for another four years. Finally, during the last four years, the budget deficit is gradually brought back to the baseline values. This policy assumption amounts to a temporary budgetary adjustment. As the baseline solution is a stable adjustment path towards a steady state of the model, it results also in a permanent fiscal consolidation at a lower level of the debt-to-GDP ratio, which seems to depict an already ambitious but nevertheless not completely unrealistic program of a government or an agreement of governments aiming at reversing the growth trend of public debt that dominated most European countries' public finances since the first oil price shock in the 1970s.

In particular, for the first two simulations conducted with the MSG3 Model, we assumed public consumption to decline, and lump-sum taxes to rise, respectively, by 0.5, 1, 1.5, 2, 2, 2, 2, 2, 2, 1.5, 1 and 0.5 percent of baseline GDP during the 12 years of the budget consolidation episode. Afterwards, these variables stay at their baseline values forever. For the third simulation (simultaneous decrease of expenditures and taxes), we assumed reductions of the two variables in proportion 3:1, i.e., public consumption was decreased by 0.75, 1.5, 2.25, 3, 3, 3, 3, 3, 3, 2.25, 1.5 and 0.75 percent of baseline GDP, with lump-sum taxes declining at the same time by 0.25, 0.5, 0.75, 1, 1, 1, 1, 1, 1, 0.75, 0.5 and 0.25 percent of baseline GDP during the 12-years budget consolidation period. The three policy experiments are comparable as all of them intend to reduce the budget deficit by about 2 percent of GDP over six years, with a gradual phasing-in and phasing-out. Obviously, a lot of other time profiles are conceivable, but for the purpose of evaluating the three strategies and their macroeconomic consequences, we confine ourselves to these scenarios.

As in Sect. 6.2, isolated (non-coordinated) policy actions of one country only and coordinated Euro Area policies will be investigated. Again, we concentrate on isolated policies by Germany and Italy only. Moreover, we assume again the policy rule of monetary targeting for Euro Area monetary policy for similar reasons as before. The following diagrams show the values of the same endogenous variables resulting from the three types of simulations as in Sect. 6.2. Responses are shown for Germany and Italy, assuming that only one of these countries implements the budgetary consolidation policy, with the other Euro Area countries going on with "business as usual" (no change of budgetary policies). Effects in the other countries are hence again purely international spillovers effects. These simulations are interpreted as budgetary policies without coordination. On the other hand, we also show the effects of a coordinated Euro Area budgetary consolidation, assuming that all Euro Area countries implement the same budgetary policy strategies. As before, countries are denoted by the following symbols: Germany – square, France – triangle, Italy – asterisk, Austria – circle.

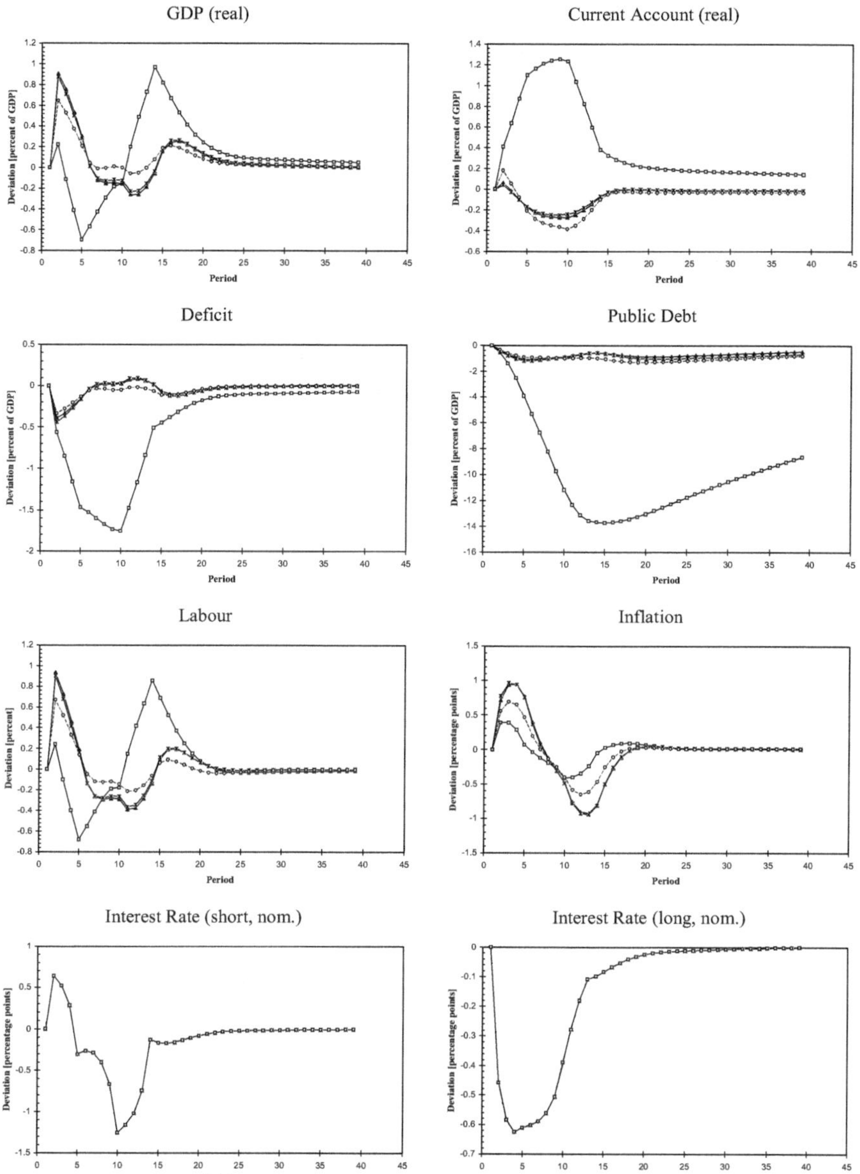

Fig. 6.4. Budget consolidation, public consumption decrease, Germany

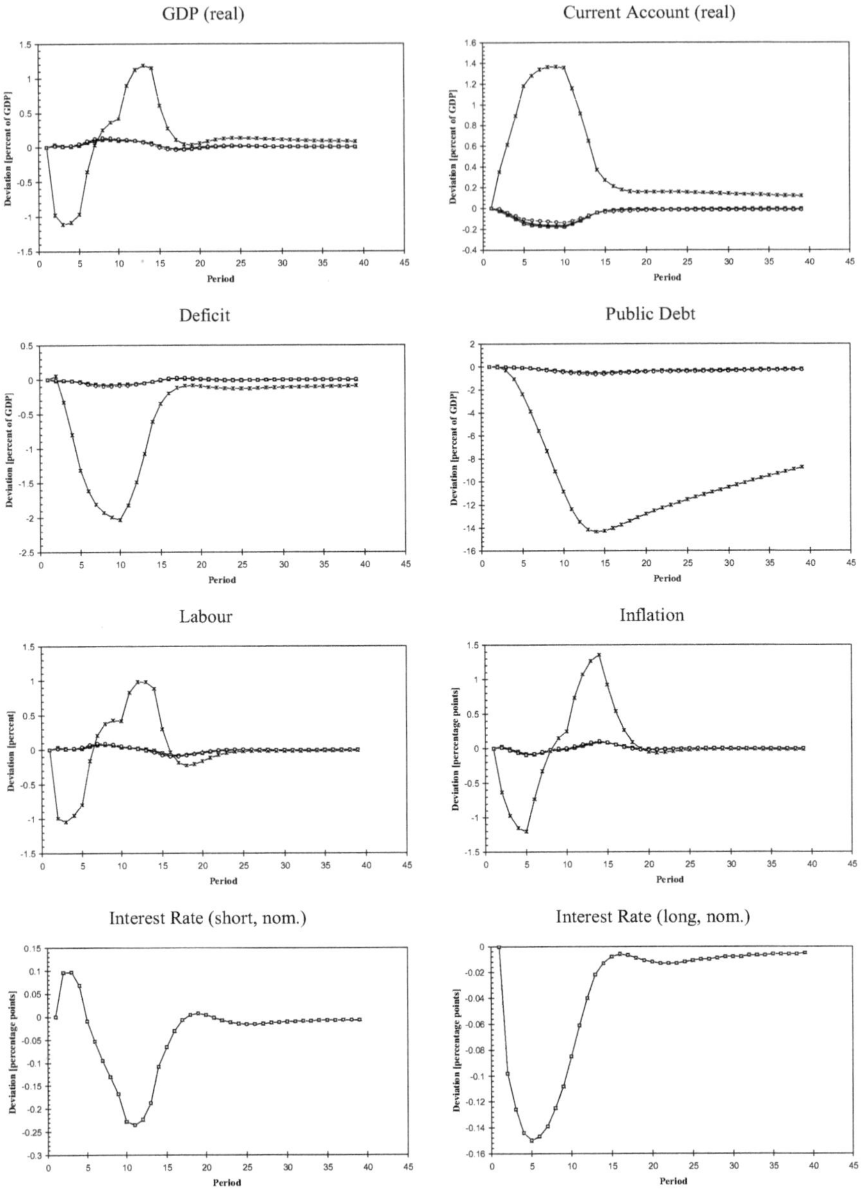

Fig. 6.5. Budget consolidation, public consumption decrease, Italy

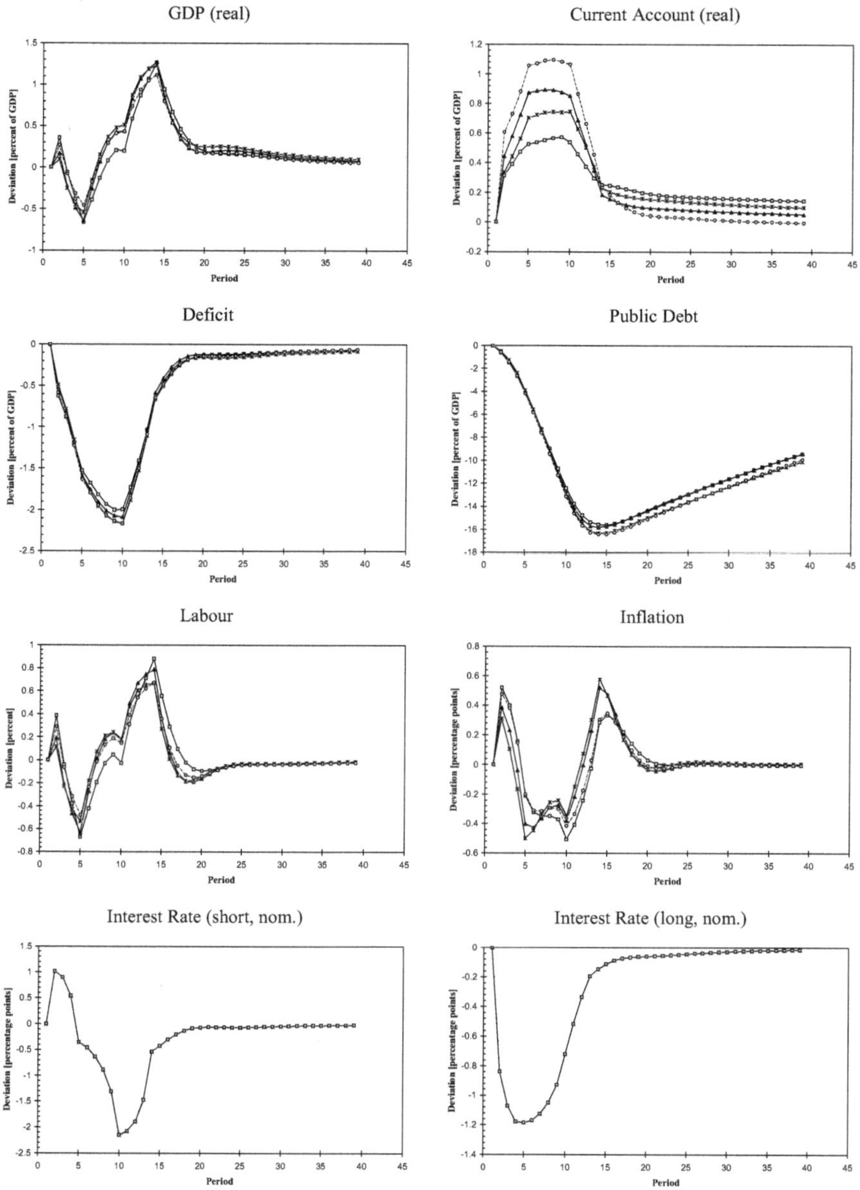

Fig. 6.6. Budget consolidation, public consumption decrease, Euro Area

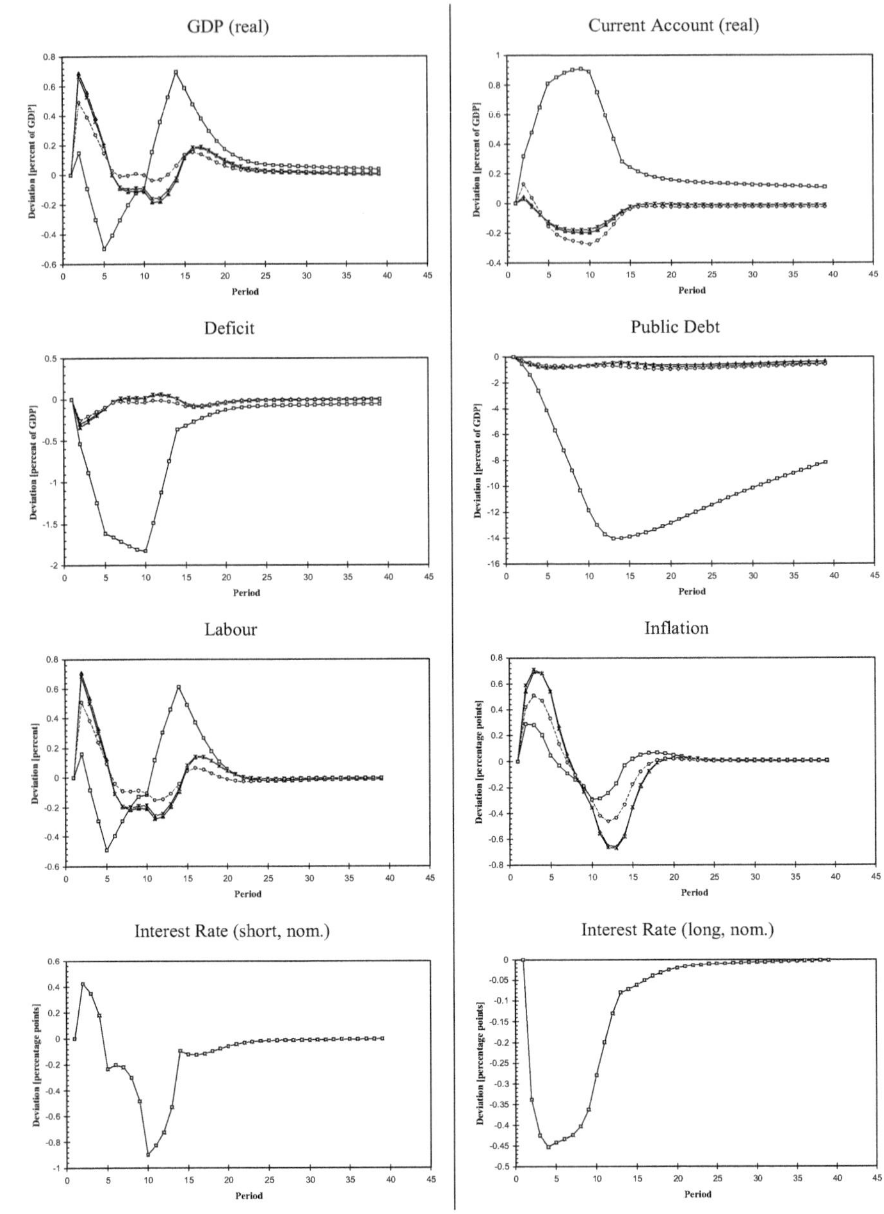

Fig. 6.7. Budget consolidation, tax increase, Germany

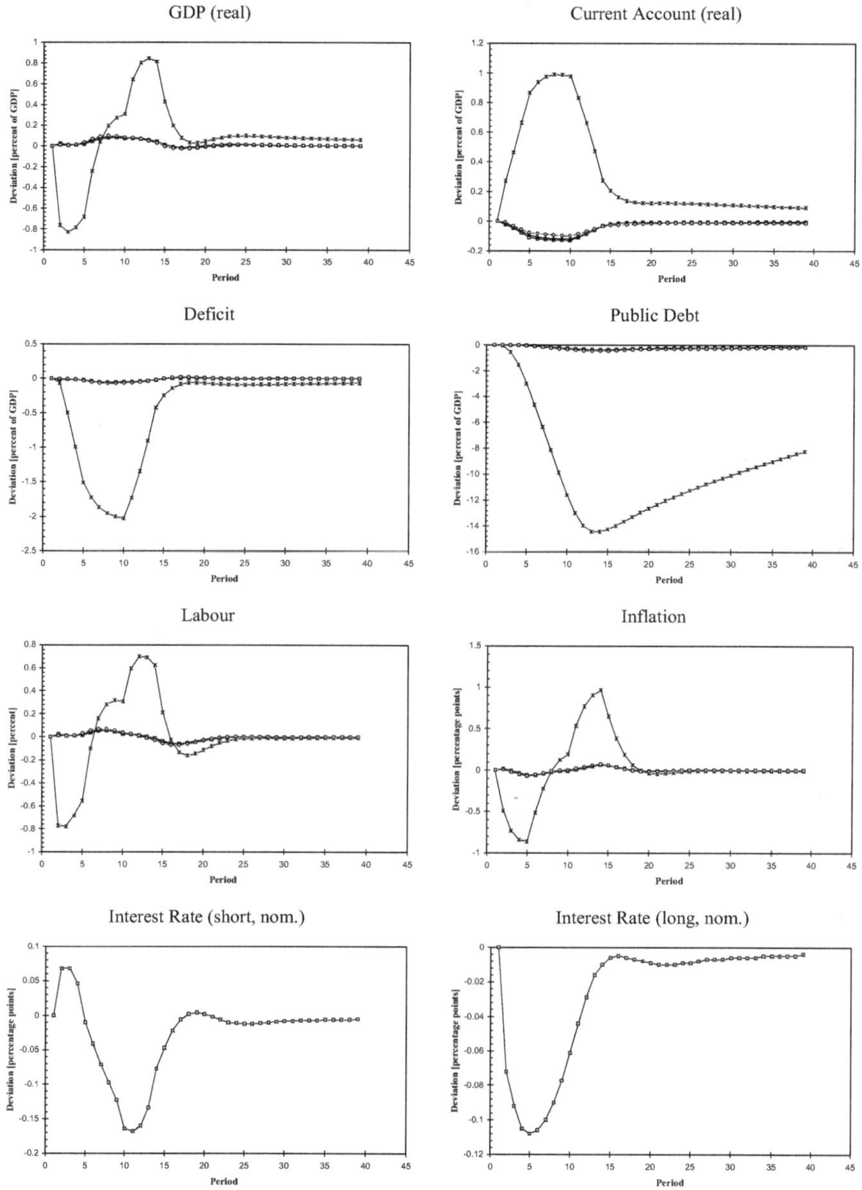

Fig. 6.8. Budget consolidation, tax increase, Italy

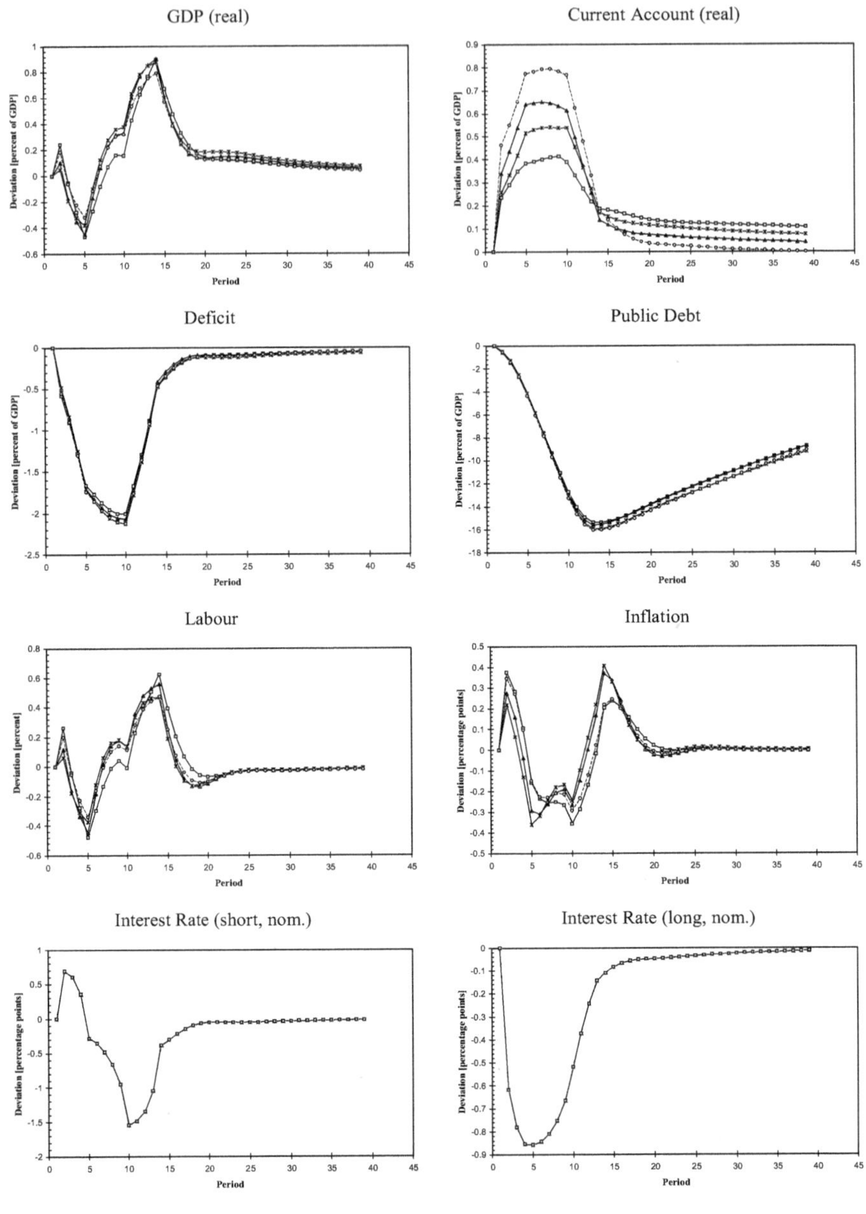

Fig. 6.9. Budget consolidation, tax increase, Euro Area

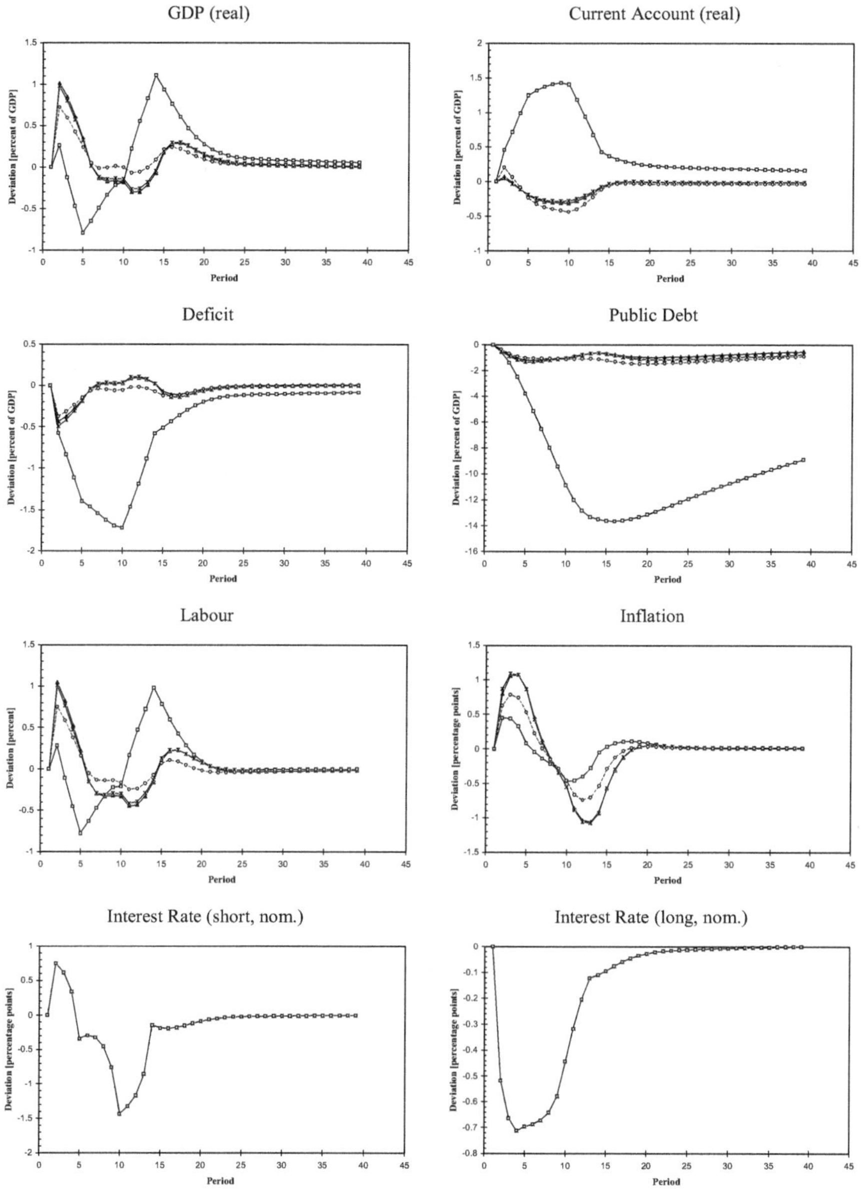

Fig. 6.10. Budget consolidation, public consumption and tax decrease, Germany

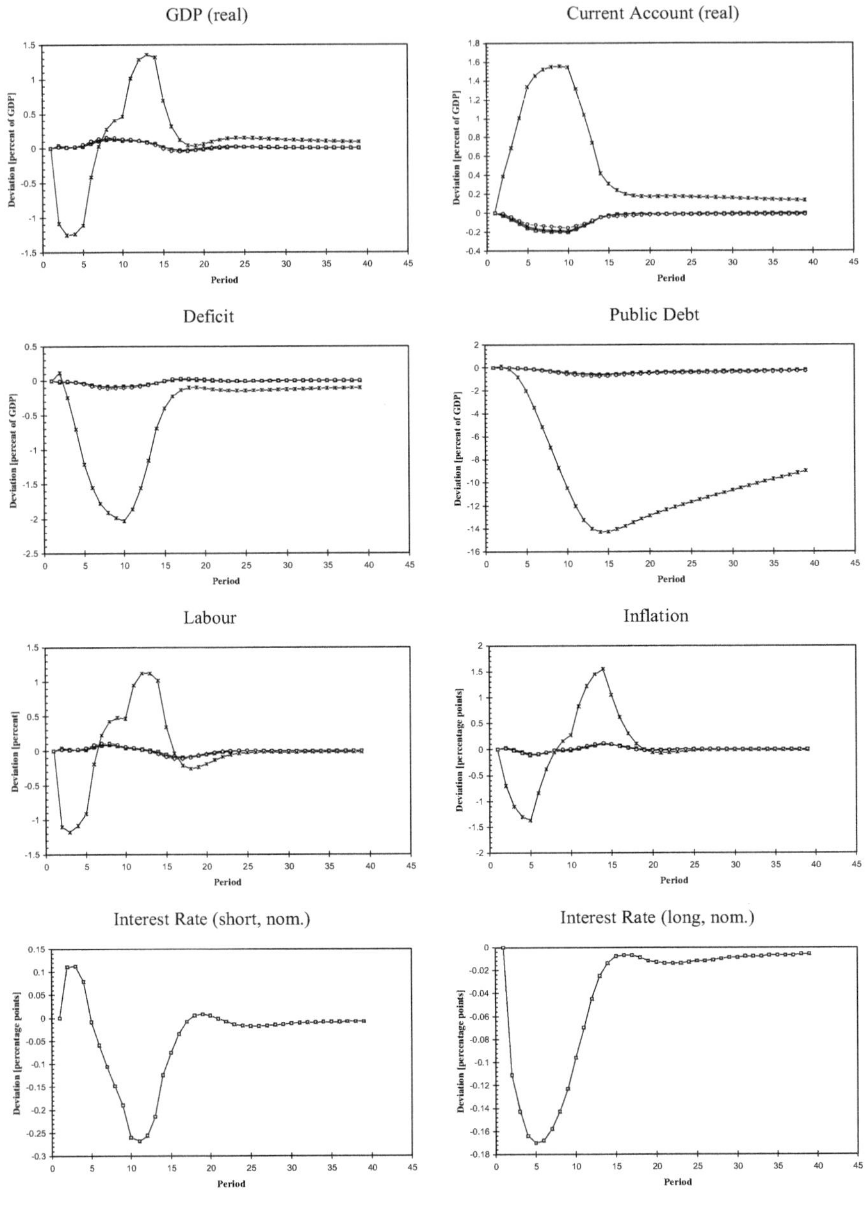

Fig. 6.11. Budget consolidation, public consumption and tax decrease, Italy

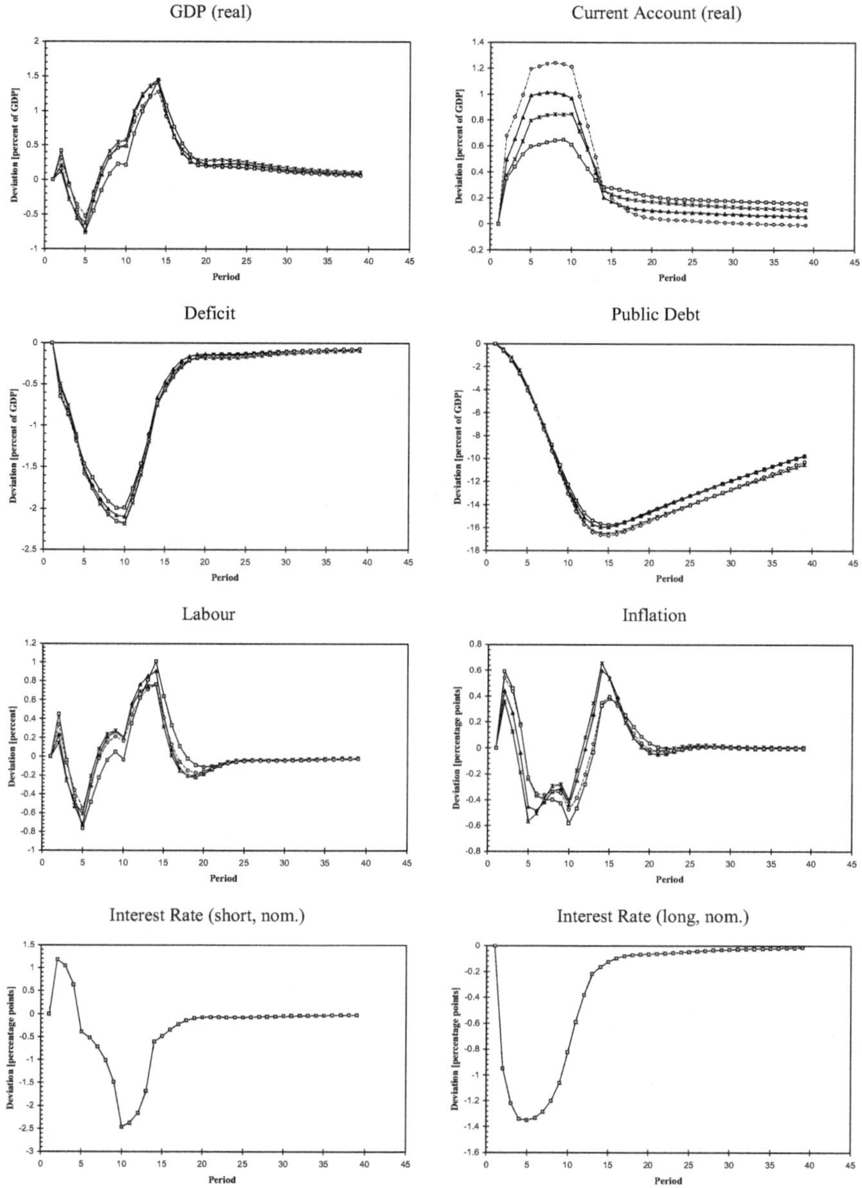

Fig. 6.12. Budget consolidation, public consumption and tax decrease, Euro Area

The results of these simulations can be briefly summarised as follows: In the country/region directly affected by the budgetary consolidation policies, all simulations are characterised by a Keynesian reaction of lower than baseline real GDP and employment in the short run and a non-Keynesian reaction of higher than baseline real GDP and employment in the medium run. The former effect is the familiar result of a reduction of (public or private) demand. It occurs in the MSG3 Model due to its short-run Keynesian features, which were introduced into the model mainly for reasons of better empirical fit: wages are sticky in the short run, and private consumption depends not only on wealth but also on current disposable income. The first feature can be justified by several theoretical arguments (incomplete information of workers, efficiency wages, insider-outsider theory, etc.), the latter by liquidity constraints of consumers (in the MSG3 Model, one half of private consumption depends on private wealth, the other one on current disposable income, which gave the best results when calibrating the model). Therefore non-Keynesian short-run effects, which have been analysed by some authors, cannot be observed here.

The medium-run non-Keynesian effect, which in most cases exceeds the short-run Keynesian effect, is mainly due to the reduction of the public deficit and hence public debt, resulting in lower rates of interest and higher private wealth; it is also partly due to the increase in competitiveness as shown by the improved current account. As the budgetary consolidation policy is modelled as temporary (although over a fairly long time horizon of 12 years), in the long run the economies return to the baseline path rather quickly after these 12 years. Only public debt remains permanently well below baseline values (by more than 10 percent of GDP after 40 years in the case where the budget consolidation policy is most effective; see Fig. 6.12), inducing a (very modest) long-run increase of real GDP over its baseline values. By contrast, in Haber et al. (2006) we have shown that a permanent reduction of public consumption and hence the budget deficit can lead to substantial permanent gains in output.

Although the general behaviour of the variables of the countries directly affected by the policy shock is the same in all simulations considered here, there are some differences in detail. Comparing the three methods of reducing the budget deficit, we can see that lowering public consumption and taxes simultaneously gives the strongest effects, followed by decreasing public consumption only, while lump-sum (net) tax increases result in the weakest reactions. These differences are not dramatic, however. For example, in the case of budgetary consolidation for the entire Euro Area, the maximum reduction of the short-term and the long-term rate of interest is 2.5 and 1.4 percentage points, respectively, when both public consumption and taxes are reduced; 2.4 and 1.2 percentage points, respectively, when only public consumption is reduced; and 1.6 and 0.88 percentage points, respectively, when lump-sum taxes are increased. Again, it has to be stressed that these simulations are biased against tax reductions due to the use of lump-sum instead of actual (distortionary) taxes; if the latter were reduced, consolidating the budget by reducing the size of the public sector through simultaneous expenditure and (smaller) tax reductions would appear even more favourable.

There are some differences between spillovers effects when only one country undergoes the budgetary consolidation. When Germany is the only country to consolidate, the effects on its own GDP, employment, current account, public deficit and debt and rate of interest are weaker than in the case of Italy consolidating its budget. On the other hand, budgetary consolidation in Germany induces much stronger spillovers effects on the other Euro Area economies and the common Euro Area interest rates than budgetary consolidation in Italy, where the spillovers effects are negligible. Spillovers effects to GDP, employment and current account of other Euro Area countries are anti-symmetric, i.e., they have the opposite signs than those of the respective own-country effects, reflecting shifts of demand due to both absorption and relative price effects. When Germany consolidates, the effects on its own inflation rate are weaker than those on the inflation rates of the other Euro Area economies, which is due to the strong first-period spillovers effect from German to other Euro Area countries' GDP and employment.

A more interesting distinction can be made between the simulations where only one country implements the budgetary consolidation policy and those where the entire Euro Area consolidates. In the case of a coordinated budgetary consolidation for the entire Euro Area, there are gains from coordination: negative short-run Keynesian effects on GDP and employment are weaker, deficit and debt reduction are stronger and hence medium-run positive non-Keynesian effects on GDP and employment are also stronger than if one country only consolidates; this is true also for the respective country (both Germany and Italy in our simulations). Moreover, inflation oscillates less in the coordinated than in the non-coordinated scenarios. As for the simulations of structural policies and their effects on TFP, it turns out that coordinated policy-making brings about a "coordination dividend" for the participating countries. The reason is the same as for structural policies: If one country pursues an isolated policy, either of structural reforms or of budgetary consolidation (or both), this will affect this particular country and, via trade and financial flows, to some extent other Euro Area countries. But if all Euro Area countries implement a coordinated policy of the same type, the spillovers effects will reinforce the direct effects. The above-mentioned anti-symmetric effects are eliminated and even reversed, because now the entire Euro Area is affected in the same (desirable) way. Moreover, there may be some effect of increased credibility of such a coordinated policy, which is not really reflected in the simulations as all policies are assumed to be credible; hence our results may even underestimate the advantages of a coordinated policy of the type proposed here.

6.4 Structural reform and budgetary consolidation

Next, we investigate macroeconomic results of combining the structural policies analysed in Sect. 6.2 and budget consolidation policies analysed in Sect. 6.3 with the MSG3 Model. There are many possibilities of combining these two instruments within the Euro Area, depending on which country/region implements which policy. Results of all possible combinations of structural policy (the "TFP level shift" version from Sect. 6.2) with each of the three versions of budgetary consolidation policies (reduction of public consumption, increase in (net) lump-sum taxes, and simultaneous decrease of public consumption and of lump-sum taxes) for the countries Germany and Italy and for the Euro Area as a whole will be documented elsewhere. We concentrate on Germany and Italy for the same reason why we have omitted results for France, Austria and the rest of the Euro Area (REA) in the previous sections: The results for France are in between those for Germany and Italy, those for Austria lack virtually all international spillovers effects (due to the small size of this country's economy), and those for the REA block would be completely artificial and not policy-relevant, as this block consists of several small- and medium-sized economies with fairly different economic and geographical characteristics (which result in close to Euro Area average reactions if shocked together, thereby neglecting the differences between such countries as, for instance, Ireland, Spain, Finland and Greece). Again, we assume the policy rule of monetary targeting for Euro Area monetary policy. Still, we are left with 27 simulations whose main results are shown in the following diagrams for the values of the same endogenous variables as in Sects. 6.2 and 6.3. As before, countries are denoted by the following symbols: Germany – square, France – triangle, Italy – asterisk, Austria – circle. Here, we summarise only the most relevant results.

In the short-run, policy combinations result in nearly additive combinations of the effects of the single policies combined. For instance, with respect to GDP and employment, the negative short-run effect of budgetary consolidation combines with the positive effect of structural policy to give ambiguous results in the first periods, whereas for public deficit and debt, inflation and interest rates, the favourable effects of both policies reinforce each others. The long-run effects are probably more revealing, given the EU political objective of boosting economic growth during the next decade and beyond, hence we concentrate on them here.

We can distinguish between five main cases, each of which will be illustrated by the results of one simulation representative of a group containing several others.

1. One Euro Area country only implements both the structural policy and a budgetary consolidation policy. Take, for example, Germany. The results are shown in Fig. 6.13. Here budgetary consolidation is achieved by reducing public consumption; if instead taxes are raised, long-run effects are slightly weaker; if both public consumption and taxes are reduced, long-run effects are slightly stronger. It can be seen that the combination of structural and budgetary consolidation policies, even when confined to one single Euro Area country without any policy change in other countries, suffices to make higher GDP, higher current account surplus, lower public budget deficit and lower public debt sustainable in the long run. Germany obtains real GDP permanently increased above baseline values by 0.8 percent, current account by 0.5 percentage points of GDP, deficit reduced by 0.5 percent of GDP and public debt by 15 percent of GDP. If instead of Germany, Italy is the country to conduct these combined policies, the own-country effects are even higher with 1 percent for GDP, –0.7 percent for the public deficit, and –19 percent for public debt. There are also some permanent international spillovers effects to the other Euro Area economies: In the case of Germany, the other countries' current account deteriorates by about 0.1 percent of GDP, the public deficit is reduced by 0.1 percent of GDP, public debt is reduced by about 1 percent of GDP, and the common Euro Area interest rates are reduced by 0.1 percentage points. These international spillovers effects are much smaller for Italy even though the primary effects of this country's policies are stronger than those for Germany (e.g., the rates of interest are only 0.03 percentage points below baseline values in the long run), showing that the size of long-run international spillovers effects depends primarily upon the economic size of a country and its international trade and financial flows with the other Euro Area countries and less on the effectiveness of its policies on its own economy.

2. One Euro Area country only implements structural policy, another one a budgetary consolidation policy. Fig. 6.14 shows such a scenario with Italy reducing its public consumption and Germany conducting the structural policy. In these cases, permanent effects on GDP are achieved only in the country implementing the structural reform. The output effects in the country enacting the budgetary consolidation are temporary only. Negative international spillovers effects on the current account are permanent for the countries not affected by either policy. There is also a weak permanent effect on the rates of interest (about 0.05 percentage points if Germany implements the structural reform, even less if another country does so instead). This results in a small permanent decrease of the public deficit and of public debt below baseline for both countries in which policy changes take place and still smaller ones in the other Euro Area countries.

3. One Euro Area country only implements structural policy, the entire Euro Area implements a budgetary consolidation policy. Fig. 6.15 shows this scenario under the assumption that it is Germany that does the structural reform. This combination of policies is sufficient to generate long-run effects on GDP and the budgetary variables, although these are rather small. The country that carries out both kinds of policies is clearly better off than the others, both in the short and in the long run: it enjoys higher GDP, higher current account surplus, lower public budget deficit and public debt and less volatile inflation. The Euro Area interest rates remain below baseline by approximately 0.1 percentage points in the long run. If Italy instead of Germany is the country implementing structural policies, its own-country effects are stronger but the international spillovers effects in the Euro Area are considerably smaller than those from German structural policy reforms.

4. One Euro Area country only implements a budgetary consolidation policy, the entire Euro Area implements structural policy. Fig. 6.16 shows the resulting scenario with Germany being the budget consolidating country. Now there are permanent favourable effects on GDP in all countries, especially Germany and Italy. Interestingly, the stronger impulse from Italian structural reforms makes its long-run GDP rise more above its baseline GDP (in terms of its own GDP) than that of Germany in spite of the latter's combined policies. Public deficits remain below baseline by 0.5 percent of GDP in all countries, public debt is also lower than in the baseline path (most so, of course, in Germany), and the rates of interest are below by 0.15 percentage points. If Italy instead of Germany is the country consolidating its budget, its macroeconomic variables fluctuate more than those of Germany in the simulation where Germany consolidates, the long-run effects on Italy's GDP are still stronger, and the spillovers effects to other countries are considerably weaker.

5. All Euro Area countries implement both the structural policy and a budgetary consolidation policy. This is the ultimate coordinated scenario for the Euro Area (although it must be noted that also scenarios assuming common Euro Area policies in one area only would require a considerable amount of cooperation to become true in reality). Fig. 6.17 gives the results, again assuming that budgetary consolidation is done by reducing public consumption. As in the other four types of scenarios, increasing net lump-sum taxes gives slightly weaker, reducing public consumption and taxes slightly stronger effects, but the qualitative pattern of all macroeconomic variables remains the same, and there are only minor quantitative differences between the three kinds of budgetary consolidation policies. Fig. 6.17 shows that in the Euro Area common policy scenario, real GDP remains above baseline by at least 1 percent for all countries in the long run; for Italy, the corresponding number is even 1.4 percent. Permanent improvements also apply to the current account, the public deficit and public debt in all Euro Area countries. The short-run interest rate is below baseline by 0.5 percent, the long-run by 0.2 percent.

The most important lessons from these simulations are the following: In the long run, the effects of structural policy reforms that increase TFP permanently (even if they raise only its level) dominate and can bring about a permanent improvement of key macroeconomic target variables such as output and public finances. In the medium run, budgetary policies are stronger, but as we have assumed that the budget consolidation will be done over a limited time period, it exerts nearly no permanent effects (except on public debt) unless supported by structural reforms. International spillovers effects within the Euro Area are relatively small (except those from the biggest economy, Germany) and can be advantageous (mostly through the channel of the common interest rate) or disadvantageous (especially if they affect the competitiveness of some countries at the expense of other ones within the Euro Area). As many other studies on international macroeconomic policy-making have shown, we can confirm that cooperative policies brought about by policy coordination are superior to non-cooperative policies, and using two (or more) instruments is superior to relying on one instrument only. Our results show that the most effective way of achieving permanently higher output and lower public debt without undesirable side-effects is via a Euro Area wide coordinated design of both structural and budgetary consolidation policies. How such coordination can be achieved is a political question which goes beyond the scope of the present study.

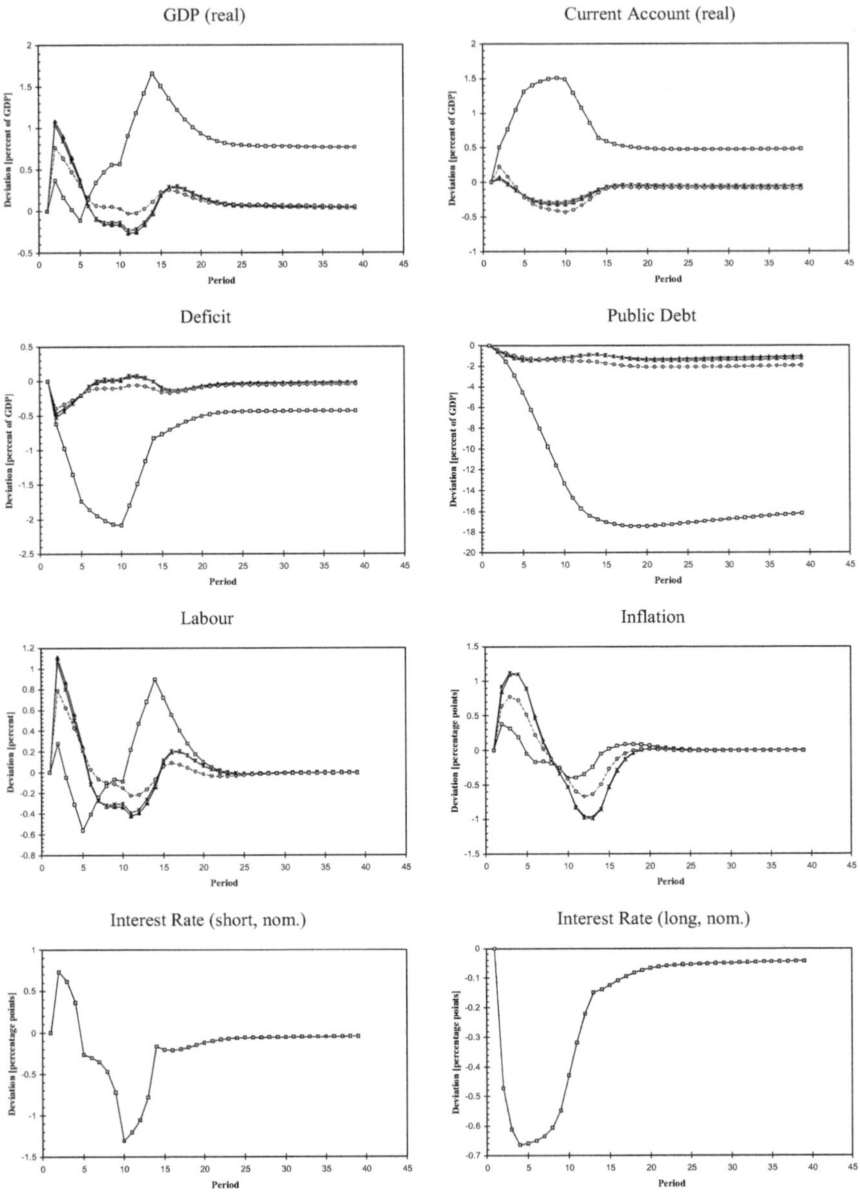

Fig. 6.13. Public consumption decrease and structural policy in Germany

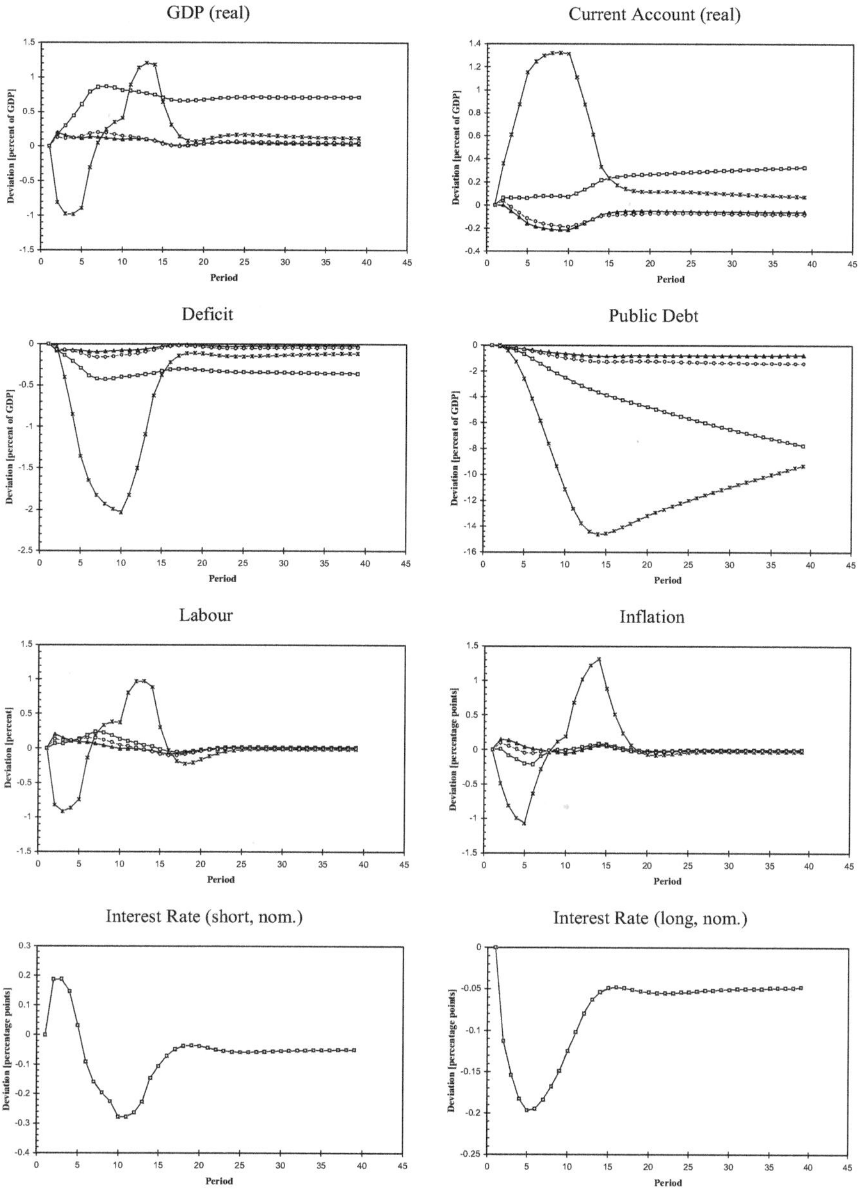

Fig. 6.14. Public consumption decrease in Italy, structural policy in Germany

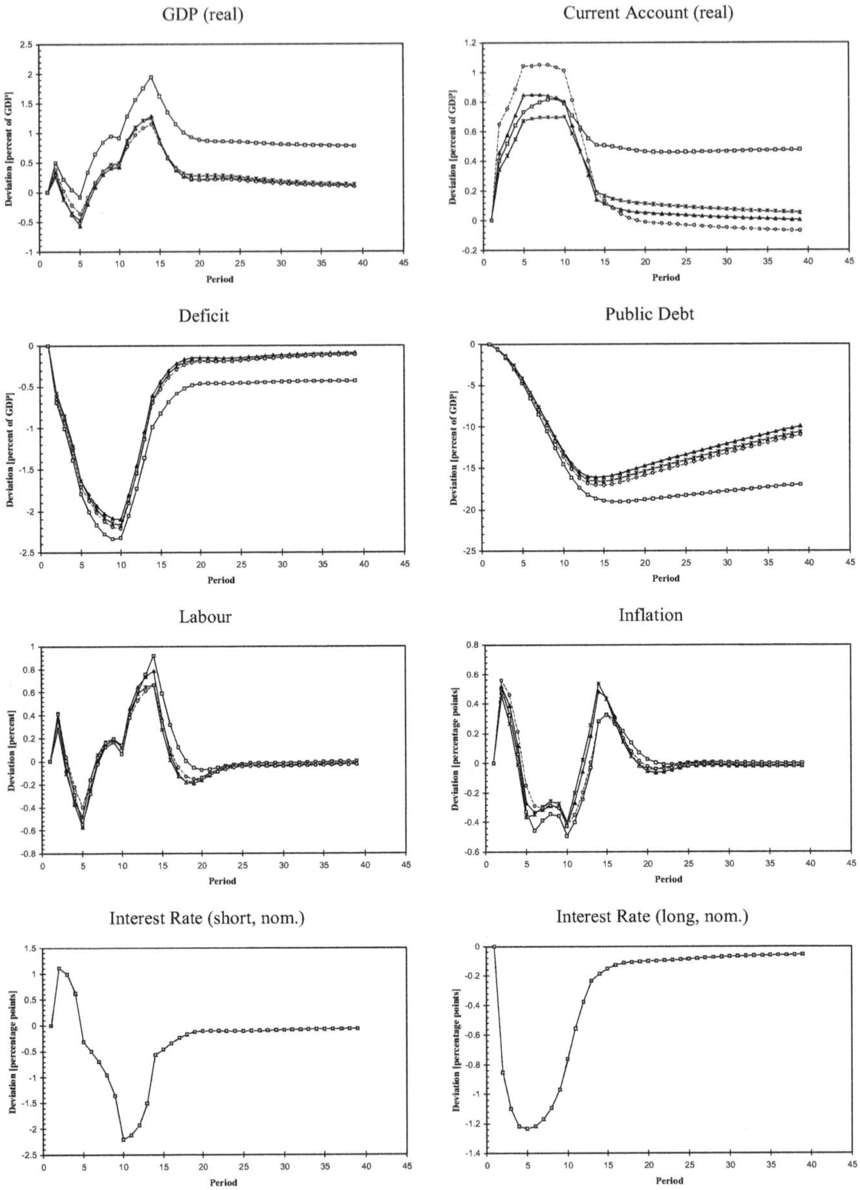

Fig. 6.15. Public consumption decrease in Euro Area, structural policy in Germany

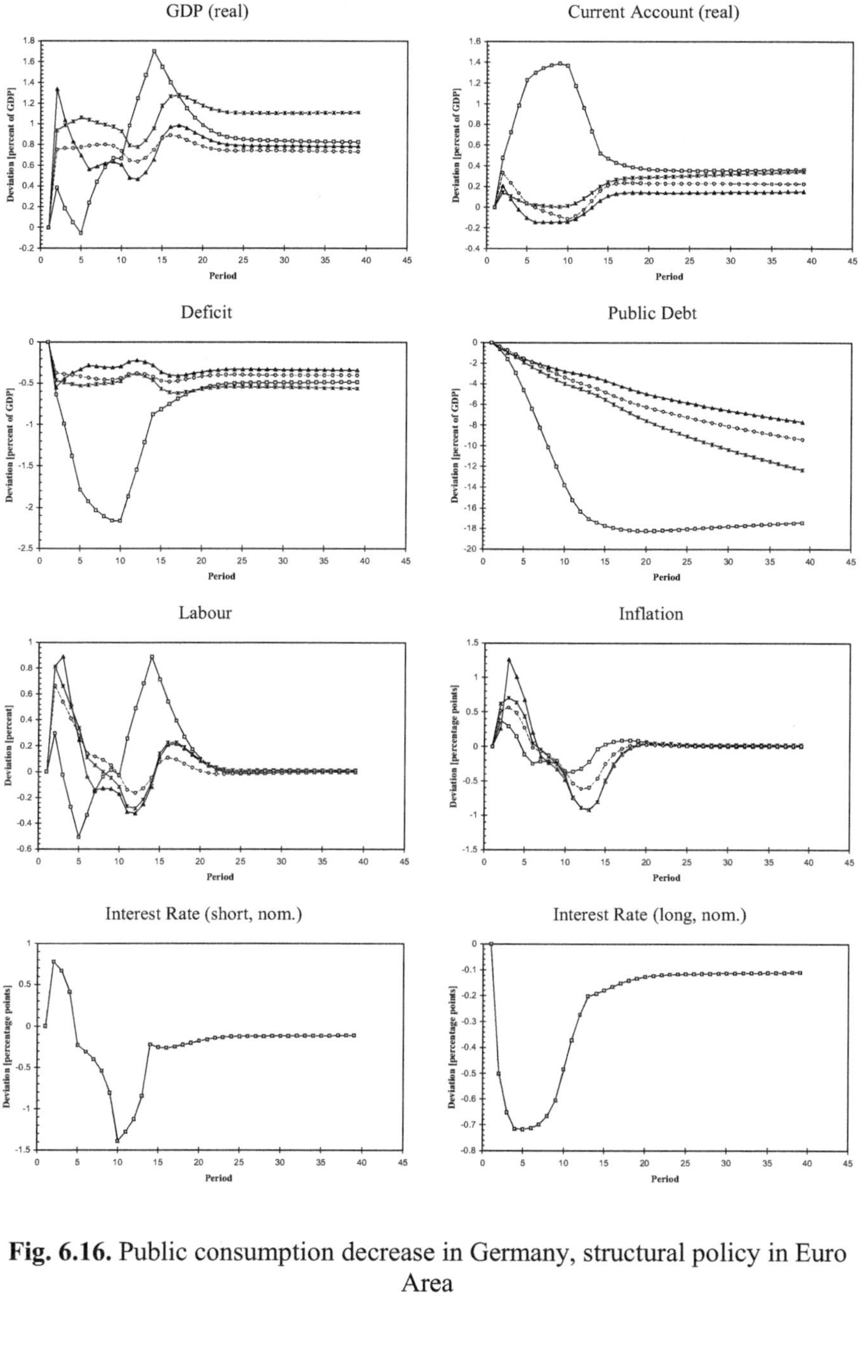

Fig. 6.16. Public consumption decrease in Germany, structural policy in Euro Area

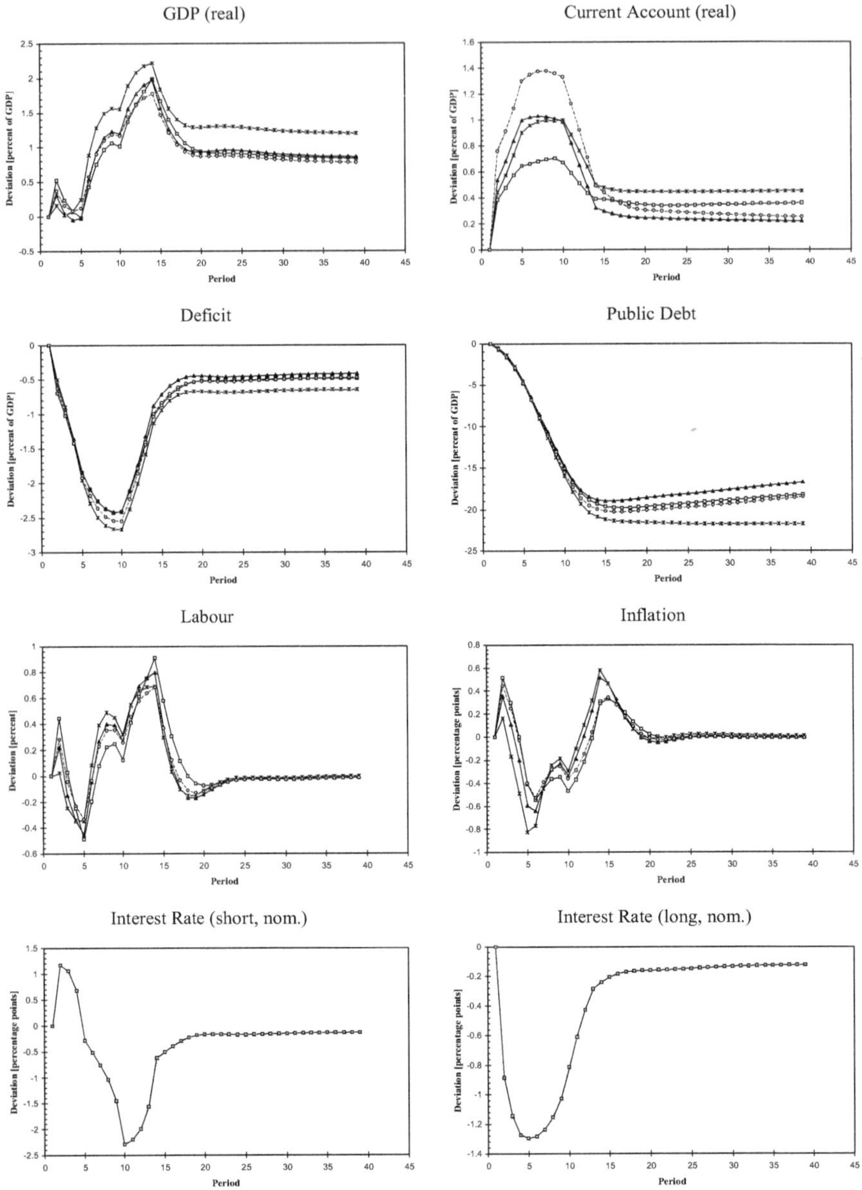

Fig. 6.17. Public consumption decrease and structural policy in Euro Area

6.5 Sensitivity analysis: monetary versus inflation targeting

As can be seen from the diagrams in Sect. 6.2, under the assumption of monetary targeting (i.e., the ECB sets its money supply for the Euro Area as in the baseline solution) in no case do inflation rates of any Euro Area country exceed 0.4 percentage points above the baseline solution. In fact, inflation and the price level are *lower* in all but a few periods for all countries of the Euro Area. The reason for this is the fact that the TFP shock is a positive supply shock that raises output and lowers price level variables. It would be highly counterproductive if the ECB would, by following a monetary policy rule of inflation targeting, annihilate these effects by a mostly restrictive policy activism to *raise* the price level and the rate of inflation, and we think such a policy of the ECB would be unrealistic either. Hence, we assume monetary targeting (or an "inactive" monetary policy) here. Moreover, we know from previous experiments with the MSG Model that under a (positive or negative) supply shock, "inactive" monetary policy (which is equivalent to monetary targeting in the framework of the MSG Model) gives results that are superior to those obtained under an "active" monetary policy (rules like inflation targeting, Taylor rules, nominal income targeting, exchange rate targeting, etc.); see, e. g., Neck et al. (2004).

The situation is less clear for demand shocks such as those emanating from the budgetary consolidation, where previous work with the MSG Model did not reveal one particular monetary policy rule as dominant. Therefore we re-ran several of the experiments of the previous subsections under the assumptions of monetary policy following a rule of inflation targeting (keeping Euro Area inflation at baseline values) and alternatively a rule comparable to a Taylor rule (a strict Taylor rule cannot be implemented in the MSG Model because money supply instead of an interest rate is the monetary policy instrument in that model). We report here only the results of three simulations with inflation targeting as monetary policy rule for the ECB. Monetary policy of the ECB following a modified Taylor rule (with a non-negligible weight on Euro Area real GDP) always resulted in an unstable model solution. The reason for this is simple: both structural and budgetary consolidation policies as assumed here result in *higher* GDP in the medium and long run without negative effects on price level and inflation rates. In this case, monetary authorities following a mechanical Taylor rule would implement restrictive policies to reduce real GDP to its baseline values. It is obvious that such policies were severely misguided and would not be attempted by any reasonable monetary policy-maker.

Hence we look only at simulations with inflation targeting instead of monetary targeting as policy rule for the ECB. Inflation targeting is introduced into the model by implementing dynamic optimisation for the ECB. The ECB is regarded as an active player, adjusting money supply in order to keep the average Euro Area inflation rates in each period at the baseline values (which are close to the 2 percent European inflation target). As inflation is assumed to be the only objective of the ECB under the monetary policy rule of inflation targeting and there is one instrument (money supply), the well-known Tinbergen results concerning the number of instruments and the number of objectives ensure that the inflation target will be strictly met in all periods. Note that this does not imply zero deviations of the national/regional inflation rates in all member countries and regions of the Euro Area, as the ECB cannot effectively account for differences in regional output and demand. At least for an asymmetric shock, there will be deviations from the baseline in both directions (positive and negative), but they will always be smaller than under a monetary targeting regime.

We show the results of structural policy (TFP shock) only and of budgetary consolidation by reducing public consumption only, both for the case of Germany implementing such a policy, and the results of combined structural and budgetary consolidation policies for the Euro Area in order to illustrate the varieties of isolated versus combined policies and of national versus coordinated policies. Fig. 6.18 shows the results of structural policies for Germany and should be compared to Fig. 6.1; Fig. 6.19 shows the result of budgetary consolidation by reducing public consumption in Germany and should be compared to Fig. 6.4; and Fig. 6.20 shows the results of combined structural and (expenditure-side) budgetary consolidation policies for the entire Euro Area and should be compared to Fig. 6.17 as the respective monetary targeting-counterpart to the inflation targeting rule considered here.

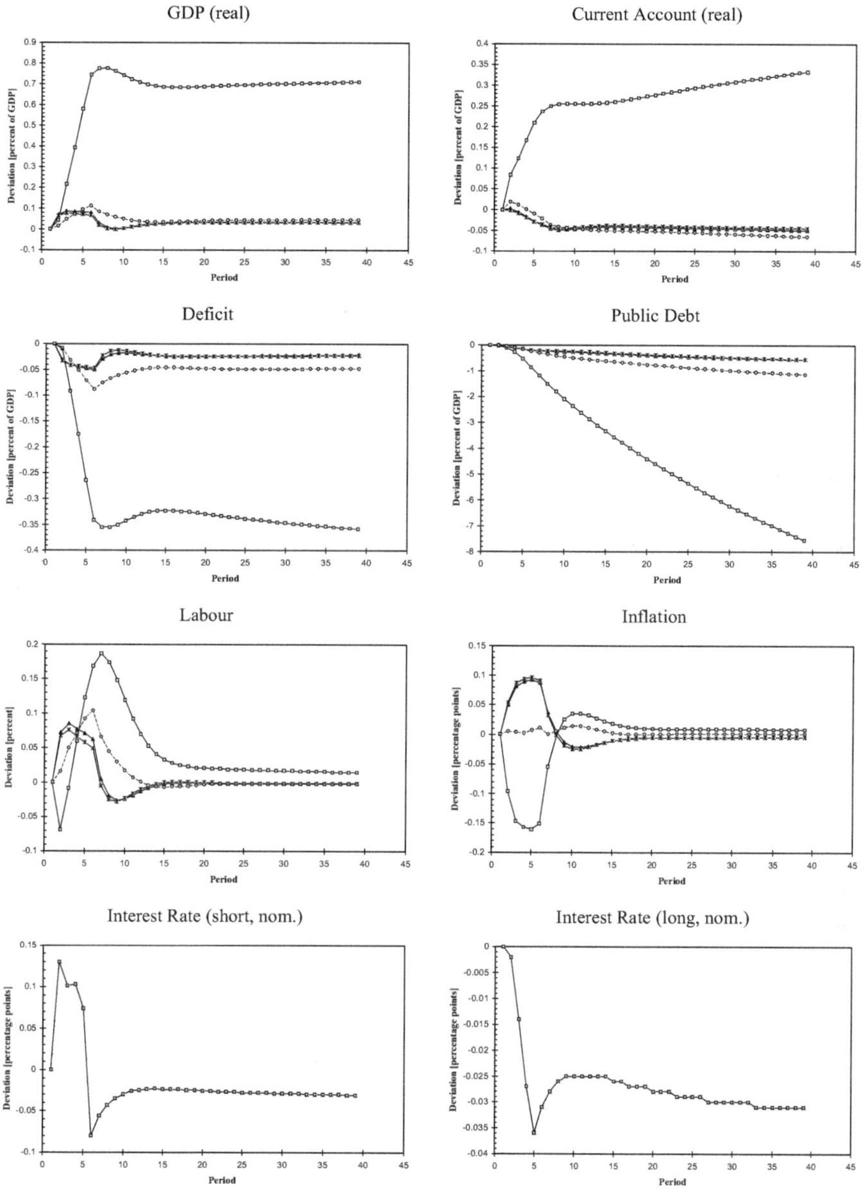

Fig. 6.18. Structural policy, Germany (inflation target)

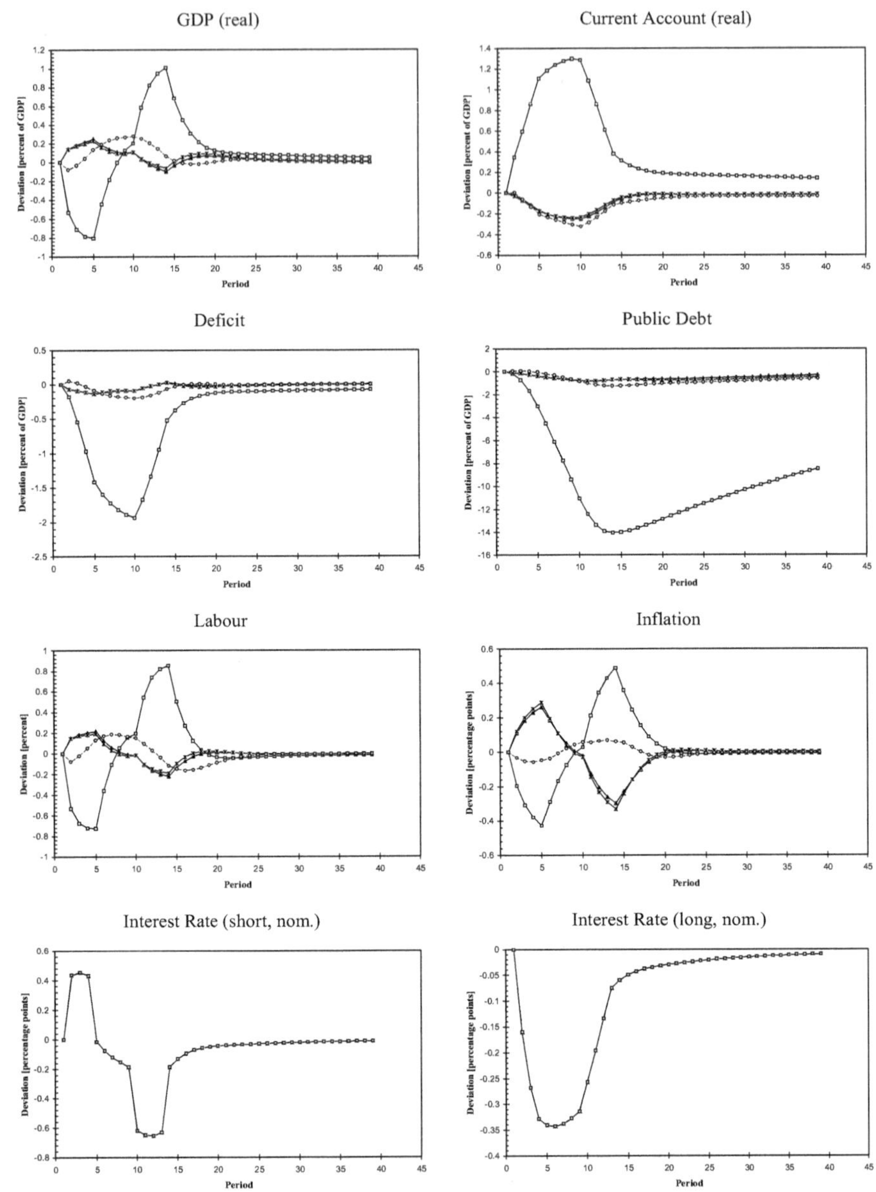

Fig. 6.19. Budget consolidation, public consumption decrease, Germany (inflation target)

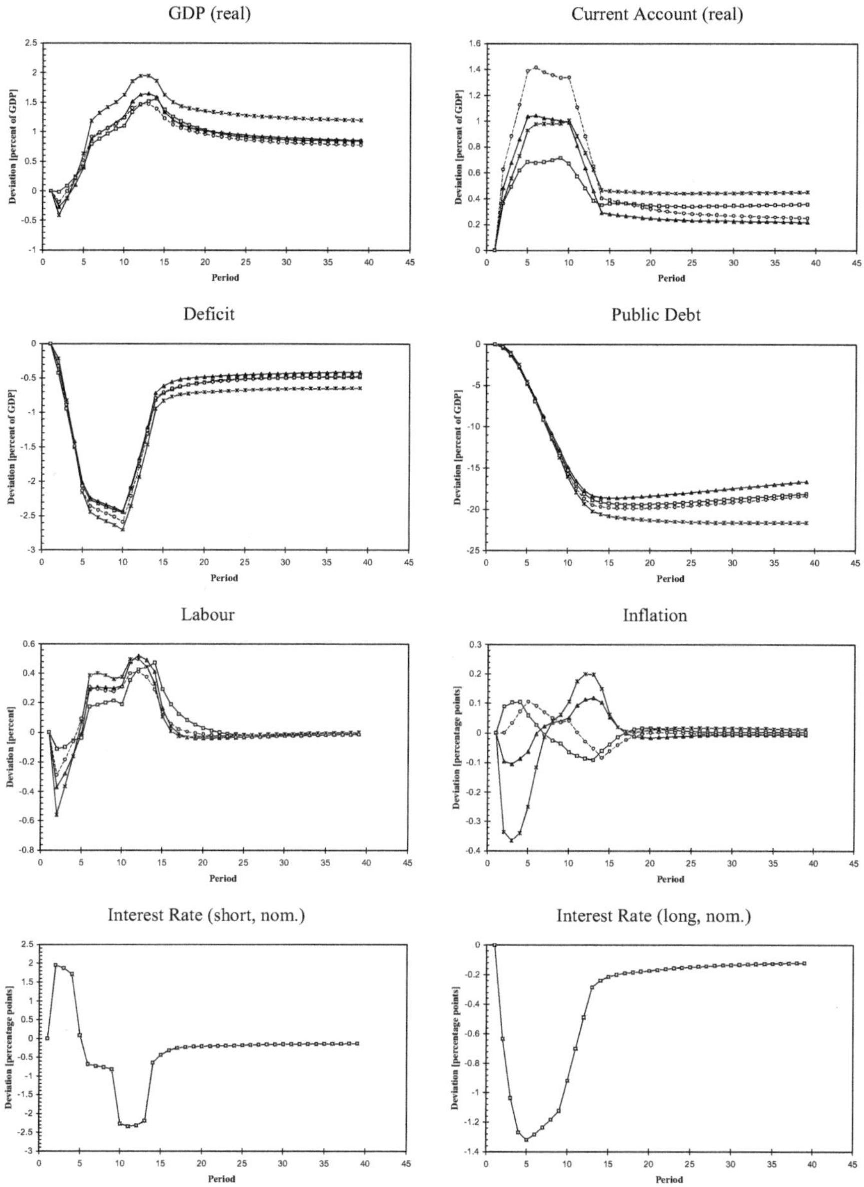

Fig. 6.20. Public consumption decrease and structural policy, Euro Area (inflation target)

Comparing these results to those obtained with the monetary targeting policy rule, the most prominent features are the similarities of the results under the two monetary policy rules for the respective simulations. In the long run, monetary policy is neutral with respect to real variables, and this is reflected by the fact that time paths of virtually all variables are identical between simulations differing only by the monetary policy rule after the adjustment period, which in no case is longer than 15 years (and mostly much shorter). But even in the short run, differences are minor. Compare, for example, Fig. 6.18 and Fig. 6.1 (the structural policy TFP shift in Germany). During the first four years, the short-run and (less so) the long-run rate of interest are higher under inflation than under monetary targeting, resulting in slightly lower increases of GDP in Germany and smaller (positive) GDP spillovers to the other Euro Area countries, lower positive (in the first period for Germany even negative) effects on employment, and a slower decrease of the public budget deficit. The rate of inflation differs less than under monetary targeting and Euro Area inflation effects are annihilated, reducing negative spillovers effects from Germany from a maximum of 0.16 percentage points under monetary targeting to 0.1 percentage points under inflation targeting. In effect, monetary policy during the first few years puts on the brakes slightly to obtain a minimal reduction of Euro Area inflation at the cost of slightly less favourable effects for real GDP, employment and the budget deficit.

Similarly, in the case of budgetary consolidation by reducing public consumption in Germany (Fig. 6.19 and Fig. 6.4), inflation targeting implies a more restrictive monetary policy during the first periods than monetary targeting, which is reflected in a slightly higher short-run interest rate until year the 14th year after the start of the policy shock, slower fall of the long-run interest rate, lower GDP in Germany, especially in the first year, and nearly no spillovers on other Euro Area regions' GDP. Employment, public deficit and current account are virtually the same under both monetary policy rules. The (modest) initial increase of inflation occurring under monetary targeting is prevented by the policy of inflation targeting, as are the amplitude of the inflation rate as well as the differences between inflation rates of different Euro Area countries. Altogether, the effects of the alternative monetary policy rule are minor and short-lived.

The same is true for the case where both structural and budgetary consolidation policies are applied, either in one country only or in several or all Euro Area countries. Look at Fig. 6.20 and Fig. 6.17 to compare the effects of the monetary policy rule on the (most favourable) case of all Euro Area countries implementing both structural and budgetary consolidation policies. Under inflation targeting, short-run interest rates increase by about 2 percentage points under inflation targeting instead of 1 percentage point under monetary targeting in the short run due to a more restrictive monetary policy of the ECB under the former rule. Also long-run interest rates are slightly higher during the first few years. This leads to a small decrease of GDP in the first year, a decrease of employment during the first 5 periods, and virtually no change for public deficit, debt and the current account, all compared to the baseline solution. It is interesting to note that the variability of inflation is reduced from a range of +0.6 to –0.8 percentage points under monetary targeting to a range of +0.2 to –0.4 percentage points under inflation targeting only. Hence there are some short-run costs and some short-run benefits from applying a policy rule of inflation instead of monetary targeting, but both are minor, and we doubt whether the ECB will really react upon such small changes of the inflation rate as resulting from the structural and/or the budgetary consolidation policies.

6.6 Welfare Effects

The results of the previous sections already provide some information about politically relevant effects of different kinds of economic policies in the Euro Area. To assess the welfare effects originating from structural economic reforms and from budgetary consolidation policies, however, we need some numerical measure of "welfare" or political desirability of the results of the policies under consideration (a "performance index").

In order to compare the macroeconomic outcomes of the different policies considered in this chapter, an assessment of the results in terms of welfare gains or losses for each of the simulations that we have performed with the MSG3 Model is required. For this purpose, we define an overall objective function as the sum of the respective welfare loss functions of the Euro Area countries/regions (assuming equal weights for each Euro Area country/region in the model and neglecting possible welfare losses of other countries/regions). The values of this function are calculated for each scenario, given a specific policy shock or combination of policy shocks. Since the objective function is specified as a welfare loss function, lower values would represent better results in terms of welfare, but to make results intuitively more appealing, we use the convention to denote welfare gains by positive and welfare losses by negative numbers.

As the results of the welfare analysis might depend on the specification of the welfare loss function, we provide a sensitivity analysis by showing the results of alternative specifications with different objective variables and different assumptions on the welfare impact of lower inflation rates as compared to the baseline (symmetric vs. asymmetric treatment of inflation deviations from the baseline values).

Generally, the objective function of each Euro Area country/region is specified as an asymmetric quadratic function that includes some or all of the following macroeconomic variables of the respective country/region: the inflation rate, employment, real GDP, and the fiscal surplus. Deviations of these target variables from their reference values are the arguments of the quadratic objective functions, but (with the exception of the inflation rate in some calculations) these deviations are evaluated in an asymmetric way: while overshooting of reference values is rewarded, undershooting is punished (vice versa for the rate of inflation). We assume that future periods are discounted by a discount rate of 4 percent in the objective function, which is in line with estimates of long-term market interest rates and the rate of depreciation of the capital stock.

The reference values in the objective functions are the respective baseline values of the model without any shocks. This makes sense, as the baseline represents a stable adjustment path towards the long-run equilibrium of the model. The inflation objective can be defined symmetrically, thus assigning penalties for deviations in both directions, because deflation could be regarded as no less of an evil than inflation (see the recent Japanese case of sustained deflation and the related economic problems). Alternatively, it can be argued that the objective function already includes output and employment, thus negative effects of sustained deflation would be captured by undesired deviations of those objective variables. Moreover, slightly lower inflation rates than in the baseline scenario might be recognised as desirable in case of a sustained positive supply shock, as long as no strong deflationary effects are observed. Thus welfare scenarios with both symmetric and asymmetric inflation assessment are calculated.

On the other hand, we depart from the traditional symmetric objective function of the theory of economic policy because we know from the previous sections that some policies result in attractive long-run effects, for example, in a permanently higher output or lower public deficit (and hence debt). It would not make sense to evaluate such an outcome in a negative instead of a positive way. Moreover, increases in employment, even if only temporary, are generally regarded as politically desirable and should not be penalised by the (political) objective function. Needless to say, the objective function used is fairly ad-hoc (as is every macroeconomic objective function in the tradition of the theory of quantitative economic policy), but it summarises effects of policies in a convenient and easily computable way.

It should be noted that the numerical values of the alternative specifications of the objective function cannot be compared, as different magnitudes of the results must necessarily arise. While a comparison of the outcomes of different scenarios within each of the following tables is just the core of the welfare analysis, cross-table comparisons (across different specifications of the objective function) should be strictly avoided.

Although we have calculated the values of the objective function for all scenarios discussed in this chapter, and with different discount rates for each scenario, we confine ourselves to showing only a few results; again, more detailed results are available upon request. The following tables give an overview of the welfare effects of some of the previously described simulation exercises for all Euro Area countries/regions of the MSG3 Model, both separately and as a total.

Scenario [1] is the TFP level shock (structural reform policy) for the entire Euro Area (Fig. 6.3), scenario [2] is the decrease of public consumption in the Euro Area (Fig. 6.6), scenario [3] is the simultaneous TFP level shock on Germany and decrease of public consumption in Italy (with no policy change in the rest of the Euro Area; Fig. 6.14), scenario [4] is the simultaneous structural policy (TFP level) and public consumption decrease shock on Germany only (Fig. 6.13), and scenario [5] is the simultaneous structural and budgetary consolidation policy (decline of public consumption) shock on the entire Euro Area (Fig. 6.17).

As the end of economic policy is higher output (or consumption), a natural (and rather straightforward) approach to assess the welfare effects of different kinds of economic policy scenarios is to include only real GDP in the objective function. The results are shown in Table 6.1 (positive values are welfare gains).

Table 6.1. Welfare effects (GDP target)

	Scenario [1]	Scenario [2]	Scenario [3]	Scenario [4]	Scenario [5]
Germany	9.65	3.09	8.92	14.28	20.29
Austria	8.20	3.28	0.23	1.43	18.93
Italy	17.26	4.15	0.59	2.29	34.69
France	8.59	3.66	0.18	2.45	21.61
Rest of Euro Area	8.95	2.58	0.12	1.49	19.02
Total Euro Area	52.66	16.76	10.03	21.95	114.54

Positive figures denote welfare gains, negative figures welfare losses

As suggested by the simulations in the previous chapters and by economic theory, for the coordinated structural reforms within the Euro Area (scenario [1]), positive welfare effects can be observed in all of the Euro Area countries. The welfare gains are not perfectly equally distributed among the Euro Area Member States, but of similar magnitude for most regions.

Italy exhibits higher GDP gains than the other regions due to the assumption of a stronger structural policy shock in this country.

Next, the coordinated reduction of public consumption also gives gains in terms of economic welfare, but the effects are lower for all regions than the effects originating from structural reform. Of course, the overall magnitude of the welfare effects depends on the magnitude of the "shocks", but the scenarios developed in the previous chapters were identified as being empirically realistic, so it can be argued that the long-run benefits of coordinated structural reforms will exceed the gains from coordinated budgetary consolidation efforts. Note that the consolidation might produce minor short-run welfare losses, but the overall results are determined by the positive long-run non-Keynesian effects of lower public debt.

The combined coordinated structural reforms and budgetary consolidation efforts within the Euro Area (scenario [5]) give the best results in terms of the GDP-only specification of the loss function (114.54 for the Euro Area as compared to 52.66 and 16.76, respectively). For all countries, the welfare gains are substantially higher than just the sum of the isolated consolidation and structural reforms scenarios. This is partly due to the economically sensible higher "rewards" of larger (positive) deviations from baseline GDP implied by the quadratic specification of the objective function, but partly also due to positive effects originating from the policy mix.

If two countries enact different policies (structural reforms in Germany, fiscal consolidation in Italy – scenario [3]), the welfare effects on the country with the budgetary consolidation are weak, and the welfare effects for the country with structural reforms are lower than in the coordinated cases. Welfare spillovers effects on other countries are negligible, as scenario [3] shows.

The Germany-only combined structural reforms and fiscal consolidation scenario [4] again gives welfare gains for Germany, which are higher than the sum of the isolated scenarios (14.28 > 9.65 + 3.09). But still the effects are significantly lower for Germany than in the Euro Area coordinated combined policy scenario [5] (20.29 > 14.28).

From the GDP-only specification of the objective function we conclude that structural policies are superior in the long-run and dominate fiscal reforms. Significant advantages of coordination can be confirmed. Fiscal consolidations without structural reforms have a lower overall impact, but can make sense as additional policy measures in combination with structural reforms.

One can argue that economic policy-makers usually have a larger number of targets and hence their preferences should be modelled by a more comprehensive welfare (loss) function. For this reason, and to get some hints on the sensitivity of the welfare results, we include real GDP, employment, and inflation as arguments in the objective function (Table 6.2). For this set of calculations, we chose an asymmetric specification of the inflation objective, meaning that lower inflation will be regarded as a benefit in terms of the objective function.

From the qualitative point of view, the results are very similar to the results in the previous specification, which only includes GDP. Still the coordinated Euro Area structural reforms (scenario [1]) dominate the coordinated Euro Area fiscal reforms (scenario [2]) significantly, both on the individual country levels and on the overall Euro Area level. Combined coordinated policy (scenario [5]) again proves to give better results than isolated policy measures scenarios (41.14 > 18.11 + 6.61, for the Euro Area).

For the Italian fiscal consolidation in combination with the German structural reforms efforts (scenario [3]), now even negative (but very small) effects can be observed (–0.06). Welfare gains for Germany are slightly lower compared to the Euro Area coordinated structural reforms scenario (3.07 < 3.33). Spillovers effects to the other Euro Area countries and regions are very small (but positive). The combined German structural and fiscal reforms scenario (scenario [4]) leads to welfare gains in Germany and moderate positive spillovers effects to the other Euro Area countries. Note that from the point of view of Italy, welfare effects are higher if Italy pursues no active fiscal consolidation in combination with the German structural reforms but Germany also reduces public consumption. These external effects (due to relatively strong spillovers effects from Germany to Italy) might be again a case for international policy coordination.

Table 6.2. Welfare effects (GDP, inflation, and employment targets with asymmetric inflation target)

	Scenario [1]	Scenario [2]	Scenario [3]	Scenario [4]	Scenario [5]
Germany	3.33	1.29	3.07	5.18	7.40
Austria	2.83	1.28	0.10	0.65	6.79
Italy	5.96	1.59	–0.06	0.84	12.37
France	2.96	1.44	0.07	0.98	7.81
Rest of Euro Area	3.04	1.01	0.04	0.51	6.77
Total Euro Area	18.11	6.61	3.22	8.17	41.14

Positive figures denote welfare gains, negative figures welfare losses.

As a next step, we modify the objective function by including the deficit of the public sector, still maintaining an asymmetric inflation target (Table 6.3). There is no consensus among economists whether the public deficit should be present in the objective function. On the one hand, deficits can be regarded as intermediate objectives for sustainable public budgets. As there is an intertemporal budget constraint for the public sector, sustained excessive deficits will eventually lead to higher taxes (or a reduction in public expenditure) in the long-run and might influence output by this mechanism. In this view, public deficits will be indirectly included in the output target. On the other hand, the deficit constraints imposed by the Stability and Growth Pact are binding for the Euro Area Member States and could therefore be seen as one of the important goals of economic policy makers. Irrespective of this discussion, we also look at some results including the deficit target to assess the sensitivity of the results with respect to this variable. The calculations show that most of the main findings of the previous welfare calculations can be confirmed with the deficit present in the objective function. The most striking difference to the previous results is that now fiscal consolidation scenarios yield higher benefits than the structural reforms. This is of course due to the inclusion of the deficit as an explicit target in the objective function. This result is simply implied by the objective function and states that, if the deficit is regarded as an important separate target, fiscal consolidation efforts will be most beneficial.

Table 6.3. Welfare effects (GDP, inflation, employment, and public deficit targets with asymmetric inflation target)

	Scenario [1]	Scenario [2]	Scenario [3]	Scenario [4]	Scenario [5]
Germany	3.12	6.58	2.81	10.90	14.61
Austria	2.69	7.30	0.12	0.62	14.82
Italy	5.49	7.45	5.17	0.80	20.24
France	2.61	6.98	0.07	0.87	14.47
Rest of Euro Area	2.83	6.10	0.05	0.48	13.49
Total Euro Area	16.74	34.41	8.21	13.67	77.62

Positive figures denote welfare gains, negative figures welfare losses.

To assess the implications of switching to a symmetric punishment of inflation deviations, Table 6.4 presents the results of such an exercise. The calculations show again that the main findings of the previous welfare calculations can be confirmed. Generally, positive welfare effects are lower now because deviations of the inflation rate in both directions are regarded as welfare losses. The most interesting differences can be found in scenario [4], the Germany-only structural reforms and fiscal consolidation shock. Spillovers to the large Euro Area countries are now negative; the spillovers to Austria (as a small country with a high level of interdependence with the German economy, mainly due to foreign trade flows) are close to zero. Obviously, this result provides an argument against non-coordinated policies.

Table 6.4. Welfare effects (GDP, inflation, employment, and public deficit targets with symmetric inflation target)

	Scenario [1]	Scenario [2]	Scenario [3]	Scenario [4]	Scenario [5]
Germany	3.07	6.21	2.76	10.68	14.10
Austria	2.64	7.02	0.11	0.04	14.44
Italy	5.31	7.11	3.60	–0.53	19.43
France	2.46	6.65	0.06	–0.42	13.95
Rest of Euro Area	2.79	5.71	0.04	–0.50	12.97
Total Euro Area	16.27	32.69	6.57	9.27	74.88

Positive figures denote welfare gains, negative figures welfare losses.

The results of the welfare assessment of different scenarios show that coordinated Euro Area wide structural reforms are likely to be very successful in terms of improving economic welfare. If deficits also matter as final objectives (which is denied by many economists), fiscal reforms also produce good welfare results. If deficits are only intermediate objectives, structural reforms outperform fiscal reforms significantly, but overall economic performance can still be improved by implementing both structural and fiscal reforms.

It can be concluded that coordinated Euro Area wide structural reforms will always give good results and should be implemented in any case. Coordinated fiscal consolidation efforts will be suitable supportive policy measures (or even useful stand-alone strategies, if the fiscal deficit itself is regard as an objective). In any case, coordination pays off for the participating economies and avoids negative external effects or free rider problems, which can be identified in some asymmetric scenarios with different policies in different countries.

Appendix: The MSG3 Macroeconomic Global Model

The MSG3 Model is a dynamic, intertemporal, general-equilibrium model of a multi-region world economy. Based on microeconomic foundations by assuming that economic agents maximise intertemporal objective functions, the model exhibits a mixture of classical and Keynesian properties: partly rational expectations in combination with various rigidities allow for deviations from fully optimising behaviour. In particular, nominal wages are assumed to adjust slowly in the major industrial economies. Nevertheless, the model solves for a full intertemporal equilibrium. McKibbin and Sachs (1991) describe the original version of the model in full detail.

The MSG3 model is a two-sector version of the twelve-sector G-Cubed multi-country of McKibbin and Wilcoxen (1998). In many ways the aggregation gives a model similar to the McKibbin and Sachs (1991) MSG2 model except that there is substantial estimation of key parameters in the MSG3 model. The two sectors of production are energy and non-energy. There is also a third capital goods producing sector. MSG3 is therefore very similar in sectoral and country coverage to the MSG2 model but includes many of the features of the newer G-Cubed model. Overall, the model is designed to provide a bridge between computable general equilibrium models and macroeconomic models by integrating the more desirable features of both approaches. Details on this integration and how the G-cubed bridges the gap between CGE and traditional macro-econometric models can be found in McKibbin and Wilcoxen (1998). Additional resources are available on the website of the MSG model at: http://www.msgpl.com.au/.

The main features of the new MSG3 model relative to the previous MSG2 model are:

- A better mapping of the energy flows in the economy based on country specific input-output data from the G-Cubed database.

- Estimated production technologies based on the G-Cubed twelve-sector aggregation are aggregated to the two-sector level, which gives a better depiction of the aggregate production substitution possibilities than in the MSG2 model which assumed a Cobb-Douglas specification.

- Explicit treatment of capital goods in the household and firm sectors. Because the MSG3 model is based on G-Cubed, we also have two additional sectors which create capital goods for investment by firms and capital goods for investment by households. This structural depiction of economies enables a closer examination of the impact of computers and other capital goods investment on overall economic activity globally.

- There are no residual country blocks in the MSG3 model but detailed structural models for all regions captured by the model.

The MSG3 model has been constructed to contribute to the current policy debate on macroeconomic policy design in different economies. It is a world model with substantial regional disaggregation and some sectoral detail. In addition, countries and regions are linked both temporally and intertemporally through trade and financial markets. Like the MSG2 and G-Cubed models, the MSG3 model contains a strong foundation for analysis of both short run macroeconomic policy analysis as well as long run growth consideration of alternative macroeconomic policies. Intertemporal budget constraints on households, governments and nations (the latter through accumulations of foreign debt) are imposed. To accommodate these constraints, forward looking behaviour is incorporated in consumption and investment decisions.

The long run of the world economy is driven by a neoclassical growth model, with exogenous technical progress and population growth. Keynesian rigidities in the goods and labour markets in the short run and optimal decisions, conditional on expected future paths of the world economy, drive the short run of the model. Thus, the model captures long-run effects of shocks and short-run dynamics towards these long-run outcomes based on historical experience, with expectations formation providing a link between the long-run outcome and the short-run adjustment.

As the MSG3 Model is a fully specified dynamic general-equilibrium model, it incorporates both the demand and the supply sides of the major industrial economies. Stock-flow relations are carefully observed, and intertemporal budget constraints are imposed. Asset prices are determined by intertemporal arbitrage conditions and rational expectations. For the long-run behaviour of the model, stock equilibrium rather than flow equilibrium is important. Asset prices stabilize in real terms once the desired ratios of asset stocks to GDP are reached. The short run of the model behaves similarly as the basic Mundell-Fleming model under flexible exchange rates and high capital mobility; however, the future paths of the world economy are important in the short run because of the forward-looking behaviour in asset and goods markets. The assumptions of rational expectations in financial markets and of partially forward-looking behaviour in real spending decisions allow for the incorporation of the effects of anticipated policy changes.

The supply side of the model is specified in an internally consistent manner. Factor input decisions are based in part on intertemporal profit maximization by firms. Labour and intermediate inputs are determined to maximise short-run profits, given a stock of capital that is fixed within each period and adjusted according to a Tobin's q-model of investment, where Tobin's q evolves according to a rational-expectations forecast of future after-tax profitability.

The version of the MSG3 Model used in this chapter, called MSG3v54o, consists of models of the following countries and regions: the United States, Japan, Canada, Australia, the United Kingdom, Germany, France, Italy, Austria, the rest of the Euro Area (REA), the rest of the OECD (ROECD), China, Central and Eastern European economies (CEEC), non-oil developing countries, oil-exporting countries, and Russia. Although the basic theoretical structure for all industrial regions is the same, institutional differences are taken into account, especially in modelling labour markets.

For the simulations and optimisations regarding Euro Area policy problems described in this chapter, the MSG3 Model was modified to implement the European System of Central Banks (ESCB) for the EA. Money supply in all current EA countries (twelve in reality, five in the model) is no longer available as an instrument; instead, monetary policy is conducted by the ECB, which acts independently of the instruments and goals of national fiscal policies. Therefore we assume a single monetary authority in the EA (the ECB) and several national fiscal policy-makers in the EA.

The MSG3 Model was fitted to empirical data by a mix of calibration techniques for CGE models and econometric time-series estimates. Behavioural parameters taken from econometric studies and data for macro aggregates were combined with steady-state relations in the model to generate other data. The reference year, for which actual data is replicated, is regarded as representing a point on the stable adjustment path towards the steady state of the model; hence not all steady-state relations are assumed to hold for that year. The model is solved in linearised form around the base year of 2002.

References

Haber, G., Neck, R., and McKibbin, W.J. (2006), Less government – more wealth? On the macroeconomics of a smaller public sector in Europe, International Advances in Economic Research, vol.12, p.1–15.

McKibbin, W.J., and Sachs, J.D. (1991), Global linkages, Brookings Institution, Washington, DC.

McKibbin, W.J., and Wilcoxen, P. (1998), The theoretical and empirical structure of the G-cubed model, Brookings Discussion Paper in International Economics no. 118.

Neck, R., Haber, G., and McKibbin, W.J. (2004), European monetary and fiscal policies after the EU enlargement, Empirica, vol.31, p.229–245.

7 Have Europe's labour markets become more flexible? An exercise in measuring the relative flexibility of wages across countries and time

Andrew Hughes Hallett, Christian Richter and Xiaoshan Chen

7.1 Introduction

Wage and price flexibility, and the structural and institutional reforms required to induce this kind of flexibility, have now become the leading economic issue in Europe. This is not a new development. It has long been argued that structural reforms were a necessary condition for a successful monetary union (Delors, 1989). Nor has this gone unrecognised within Europe itself. The Lisbon Agenda, agreed in 2000, was introduced precisely to create greater market flexibility.

Yet not much has happened. Few reforms have been carried out, and anecdotal evidence suggests that there is little wage and price flexibility in either the Euro Area as a whole or in its larger or more influential members. The sluggishness of the German, French and Italian economies, and their difficulty in generating growth and jobs over the past three years, stand witness to that. It is almost as if they thought that once inside the relatively closed European economy, they did not have to worry about reform and flexibility; the competitive pressures of the outside world (including the new Member States in Central and Eastern Europe) would be shielded from them. Yet since the Euro Area economies appear to have less flexible markets than their American or Asian counter-parts, policies to restore economic performance to US and Asian levels have become more and more focused on the need to generate higher productivity, lower costs and (above all) flexibility in the labour markets.

This view is typically derived from the analytic and empirical evidence of a negative link between economic performance and (real) wage rigidity across many countries (Bruno, 1986)[1]. The same link has been found in the labour and the product markets in Europe (Koedijk and Kremers, 1996), and in the transition economies (Kaminski et al., 1996), where performance is measured in rates of growth and employment; and where deregulation/flexibility is reflected in competition policy, merger codes and the liberalisation of employment and wage bargaining practices. For the non-members and some of the periphery economies, this rapidly becomes a question of whether they would ever want to join, or remain in, a union of economies less flexible than themselves.[2]

The purpose of this paper is to consider how one might set about measuring the degree of wage flexibility in an economy. Despite the concern about wage flexibility, there are no serious estimates in the literature, no accepted methodology for making such estimates, and little more than anecdotal evidence of the "greater than", "less than" kind. We therefore investigate the degree of wage flexibility in a sample of European countries, in particular at the business cycle frequency. We then examine, first, whether flexibility differs across countries (is it lower in the core economies like France, Germany, Italy? and higher in the smaller economies like Finland, Austria or Ireland?). Second, we ask if it is really higher in countries outside the Euro? And, third, whether the degree of wage flexibility has been increasing over time, especially after the increased market pressures with the coming of the Euro. Or has joining the Euro reduced the incentive and perceived need for the kind of reforms that would produce greater labour market flexibility, similar to the "reform fatigue" which appeared in the attempts at fiscal consolidation after 2000? If the latter were true, it would go a long way to explain why labour market reforms are often discussed and advocated in Europe – but so seldom undertaken. The fate of Harz IV in Germany, the new labour laws in France, and pension reform in Italy are just three of the most obvious examples of that pattern of behaviour.

---

[1] The link is usually made with real wage rigidity, but in an era of low inflation (and in the Euro Area in particular with its common monetary policy) real wage rigidity will be approximately synonymous with nominal wage rigidity. Since the latter is more transparent and easier to measure accurately, we investigate the flexibility of nominal wages in this paper.

[2] See Hughes Hallett (2003), Hughes Hallett (2003), Hughes Hallett et al. (2005).

7.2 Methodology: The analytic background and estimation technique

While there is little disagreement that monetary union and structural reforms are linked, those links are clearly not well understood. For example, the Delors Committee (1989) stressed the importance of parallelism in the monetary and economic spheres in such a union, but took the view that economic structures were exogenous and could only be changed through policy reform. Policy reforms, rather than market structures, are therefore seen as necessary to ensure that economic developments are flexible across Member States. Others, for example Frankel and Rose (1998), argued that these structures themselves will be endogenous. If so, the need for reform is less obvious. The necessary flexibility might materialise anyway, simply as a consequence of unification. In that spirit, Andersen et al (2000) have found that monetary integration in Europe is changing labour market structures and inducing some wage convergence, but only on a very small scale. In fact, Saint-Paul (2004a, b) argues that, due to political constraints and special interests, these changes in behaviour are really only visible in Ireland. In addition, Hughes Hallett and Piscitelli (2002) have shown that convergence through greater market flexibility may not happen in volatile economies; or where there are differences in industrial structure; or where a lot of integration has already taken place.

By contrast, two papers by Calmfors (1998; 2001) make the point that although money-wage flexibility is likely to be larger inside a union such as the Euro Area, labour market reforms are less likely to be implemented if the motive for that union was to solve a time-inconsistency problem. If true, this would suggest that we will find "reform fatigue" after 1998, and declining flexibility. But Sibert (1999) and Sibert and Sutherland (2000) argue that asymmetric shocks will modify that conclusion since countries will find it more necessary to develop measures against such shocks to replace their ability to adjust by changing exchange rates. But that would mean that, given an economy with less than average distortions, the partners will face an incentive either to reform themselves; or to encourage the flexible economy to converge on their less flexible market practices. In a world of political and financial costs to reform, and where there are special interests to reform and the use of fiscal policy is limited, it is clear which way the argument will go and it will not be in the direction of altruistic reforms.

Our Estimation Technique

We identify wage flexibility as the ability to vary the growth in wages with different frequencies of intervention – and at the business cycle in particular. Many studies have attempted to capture the variability of a particular variable at different frequencies, that is the weight of the different cycle lengths in its evolution, and the natural way to do it would be to use spectral analysis since that decomposes the overall variability in a series into the components due to each of the cycles present in the data. The appendix to this paper sets out how we can best do that in the presence of structural breaks and comparatively short spans of data.

Most cyclical analysis in economics has been concerned with assessing the correlations between national business cycles, and has therefore used simple correlation techniques which average across all the cyclical components (frequencies) once the raw data has been detrended to provide the underlying variations. The results of that approach have been very mixed. For example, Mankiw et al. (1992), Dowrick and Nguyen (1989), Barro and Sala-I-Martin (1991; 1992), Quah (1993) find evidence of convergence for a sample of OECD countries at similar level of development over the years 1960-1985, but reject it for a wider sample of 75 economies whose development varies rather more. In contrast, Chauvet and Potter (2001) report that the US business cycle was in line with the G7 from the mid 70s, but then diverged thereafter. Stock and Watson (2002; 2005) likewise find divergence in individual cases caused by structural breaks, but convergence on average at the world level.

As far as the Euro Area is concerned, Frankel and Rose (1998) and Prasad (1999) argue that if exchange rates are pegged and trade links intensify, business cycles are likely to converge. But Inklaar and de Haan (2000) and Baxter and Kouparitsas (2005) find no evidence of a corresponding convergence among the OECD economies (see also: Doyle and Faust, 2003; Kalemli-Ozcan et al., 2001; Peersman and Smets, 2005). All these results suggest a time-varying approach is going to be necessary if we are to analyse any cyclical properties in economics[3]. Indeed new evidence suggests that the NAIRU is not constant, therefore calling for time-varying estimators such as the Kalman Filter (Driver, 2006; Grant, 2002). We therefore go back to the more direct approach of spectral analysis, and show how this can be adapted to produce time varying spectra in which the flexibility of wages is displayed at each frequency or cycle length.

A second point is that the correlation studies cited above also make it clear that variance decompositions will be sensitive to: a) the choice of correlation measure; b) the choice of cyclical measure (classical

[3] It appears that cyclical properties may also change with the degree of industrial specialisation which is increasing with trade and financial links (Kalemli-Ozcan et al, 2003).

or growth cycles); and c) the detrending measure (linear, Hodrick-Prescott filter, band pass etc.). This sensitivity is a problem emphasised by Canova (1998). The advantages of using our time-frequency analysis are: (i) It does not depend on any particular detrending technique, so we are free of the lack of robustness found in many studies. (ii) Our methods also do not have an "end-point problem" – no future information is used, implied or required as in band-pass or trend projection methods. (iii) There is no arbitrary selection of a smoothing parameter, such as in the HP algorithm, equivalent to an arbitrary band-pass selection (Artis et al., 2004).

However, any spectral analysis technique is tied to a model based on a weighted sum of sine and cosine functions. That is not very restrictive. Any periodic function may be approximated arbitrarily well over its entire range, and not just around a particular point, by its Fourier expansion (a weighted sum of sine and cosine terms) – and that includes non-differentiable functions, discontinuities and step functions. Hence, once we have time-varying weights (the time-frequency approach) we can get almost any cyclical shape we want. For example, to get long expansions, but short recessions, we need only a regular business cycle plus a longer cycle whose weight increases above trend but decreases below trend (i.e. varies with the level of activity). This is important because many observers have commented on how the shape of economic cycles has changed over time in terms of amplitude, duration and slope (Harding and Pagan, 2001; Peersman and Smets, 2005; Stock and Watson, 2002). A time-varying spectral approach is necessary to provide the flexibility to capture these features. Similarly it is necessary to accommodate, and reveal the possibility of structural breaks which must be expected with the operation and breakdown of the EMS, the coming of the Euro, the changes in monetary institutions, and the increasing integration and volatility of financial markets.

7.3 The empirical evidence on wage flexibility

To illustrate the degree of wage flexibility, and how it may have changed in the recent past, we have applied our time-frequency estimation techniques to the wage data of twelve countries in and outside the Euro Area. We start with data on average nominal wages and salaries, economy-wide, for each country starting in 1977 and finishing in 2001.[4] That data is converted to annual growth rates by computing,

[4] Data limitations forced us to start in 1984 for France, 1983 for Austria, and in 1981 for Finland. This maintains compatibility in wage data used. However the sample can be extended to 2005 in five cases.

$$y_t = \Delta \log(Y_t) = \log(Y_t / Y_{t-1}) \qquad (7.1)$$

where Y_t = total wages and salaries paid in a given economy in period t. The data is differenced and therefore stationary.[5]

Our data are taken from the OECD's *STAN Data Base*; and our sample of countries includes the US (a benchmark, representing the popular view of an economy with flexible wages and labour market institutions); then Germany, France, Italy, Austria, Belgium and the Netherlands to represent the core of the Euro Area; Spain, Ireland and Finland representing the more successful countries in the periphery; and finally the UK, Denmark and Norway. as countries that have chosen to remain outside the Euro Area.

7.4 Statistical results

As Table 7.1 below shows, the estimation results led to an AR(2) model at the first stage of calculating national spectra for wages and salaries in each country.[6] The fact that the same order of AR model was found in each case was coincidental, but not unexpected given that we are working with annual data and that wage contracting means that the bulk of wages and salaries are renegotiated and agreed on a 1-2 year schedule in most countries. However, to be sure of this specification, we started with a higher order AR(p) scheme with p=8 and progressively reduced the order of each national model by eliminating insignificant coefficients on a general to specific basis, until we had both white noise errors and a maximum information criterion (the Akaike criterion, AIC) using the procedures described in the appendix. Each time series model therefore satisfies a set of diagnostic tests and provides a model which is stationary with white noise residuals and lowest AIC value. It has also been validated in terms of statistical significance, parameter variation[7], specification checks and structural break

[5] ADF and Philips-Perron tests of stationarity in the resulting series for each country are available upon request.

[6] Denmark required an AR(3) model to satisfy all the specification and diagnostic checks listed below. Given the results cited in the appendix, this means Denmark can only converge on the other countries in our sample if the last lag becomes zero over time.

[7] We used the LaMotte-McWorther-Test as in LaMotte and McWorther (1978). We used the fluctuations test as suggested by Ploberger et al. (1989) to test for structural breaks.

tests noted in the Appendix.

Having thus obtained a time varying AR(2) model in each case, we calculate the short-time Fourier transform as defined in the Appendix and determine the corresponding time-varying spectrum from there. The results are displayed in Figs. 7.1-7.13; and a series of summary statistics derived from those spectra, designed to highlight the relative degrees of short and medium term wage flexibility in each country, are set out in Table 7.2.

Table 7.1. Estimation by Kalman filter.

Country	Dep. variable	Sample	R^2	Akaike Criterion	Ljung-Box	Constant	Lag1	Lag2	Time
France	dlfrw	1979 - 2001	0.99	3.6e-06	5.8	0.011 (16.8)	0.617 (3.54)	0.194 (0.72)	_
Germany	dlgerw	1971- 2001	0.80	8.4e-04	4.8	0.037 (0.90)	-0.118 (-0.31)	0.385 -2.68	_
Italy	dlitaw	1971- 2001	0.99	1.9e-05	8.7	0.146 (2867.3)	0.339 (4.08)	-0.283 (-1.47)	-0.003 (-6.67)
Austria	dlausw	1977- 2002	0.99	1.7e-06	10	0.051 (710.29)	0.200 (0.204)	-0.495 (-2.33)	-0.001 (-1.94)
Belgium	dlbelw	1971- 2005	0.99	2.0e-07	4.95	0.012 (106.56)	0.546 (47.75)	0.540 (3.44)	_
Netherlands	dlnethw	1971- 2005	0.99	4.5e-06	10.4	0.036 (2.84)	0.356 (4.93)	-1.381 (-1.94)	_
Spain	dlspw	1971- 2005	0.99	4.7e-06	12.3	0.097 (406.68)	0.307 (1.99)	-0.285 (-1.50)	-0.001 (-0.65)
Ireland	dlirew	1978- 2005	0.99	1.4e-05	12	0.028 (20.76)	0.650 (2.63)	0.376 (1.17)	_
Finland	dlfinw	1976- 2002	0.99	3.8e-08	3.3	0.073 (609986.2)	0.445 (3.03)	-0.214 (-0.69)	-0.002 (-2.11)
UK	dlukw	1971- 2005	0.99	3.8e-06	16	0.036 (1.62)	0.427 (4.78)	-0.191 (-2.04)	_
Denmark	dldenw	1971- 2005	0.99	9.6e-08	9.8	0.002 (384.51)	0.629 (23.96)	-0.518 (-1.75)	_
Norway	dlnorw	1971- 2000	0.99	2.9e-05	8.4	0.094 (215.84)	0.540 (3.43)	-0.354 (-2.56)	-0.001 (-1.13)
US	dlusw	1971- 2001	0.96	6.6e-05	13.7	0.077 (8.17)	0.194 (4.50)	0.036 (0.39)	-0.002 (-3.74)

Note: Coefficient columns contain the estimated parameters (line 1), followed by t-statistics in parentheses (line 2). Df.: degrees of freedom. SSR: sum of squared residuals.

7.5 The benchmark and indicators of wage flexibility

Conventional wisdom takes the US, and the recently reformed economies such as the UK or Ireland, to be prime examples of economies with a fair degree of short term wage flexibility – sufficient at least to enjoy higher rates of growth than the other OECD economies, at lower rates of inflation and unemployment, for the past two decades. One might surmise that this flexibility has allowed these economies to maintain a lower natural rate of unemployment without inflationary pressures than the others, and empirical estimates tend to support that conjecture (Driver, 2006; Laubach, 2001). However we are not concerned with natural rates of unemployment here, but with the short run ability of wages to adjust around it so as to maintain unemployment close to its equilibrium level, or possibly around a lower equilibrium.

We therefore take the US case, in Fig. 7.1 and Table 7.2, to be our benchmark. We then compute the other countries by group, using indicators of short run flexibility of wages growth compared to the US. The country groups are: (a) The core members of the Euro Area (the most converged); (b) "Periphery" countries, also members of the Euro Area; (c) The non-members: those who have elected not to join but remain members of the European Union or with formal trade agreements with the EU (the "outs").

We take the power of the wages spectrum at business cycle frequencies or higher to be the natural indicator of the flexibility or adjustability of wages (whether correctly applied or not), and the power of the same spectrum at low frequencies as a natural measure of the persistence in wages growth. Ideally there should be greater power at the business cycle frequencies or higher; but low power at the lower frequencies. That would imply flexible wages. Unfortunately this is not what we find, even in the US. Typically the balance of power goes the other way, with low power at high frequencies and higher power at low frequencies[8]. However, this effect is not very marked in the US. So we need to add two qualifications. Where spectral power is distributed evenly across time (at each frequency band), an economy has not been tested by shocks or regime changes. In that case we cannot say if wage flexibility exists, only that it has not been used. But this does not happen in our data. Conversely, if the spectral density is distributed evenly across all frequency bands for a certain period, then flexibility is at least as important as persistence and may

[8] With the exception of Germany, Austria and Norway since 1993, Denmark since 2002, and the UK, Spain and Italy for a limited period in the 1990s: see Figs. 7.1-7.13.

be high or low depending on the level of wage variability indicated.[9]

Accordingly, Table 7.2 provides a set of wage flexibility indicators calculated from Figs. 7.1-7.13. The first two columns show the relative power of the wages spectrum (variability of wages) at short cycles, compared to the power of the same spectrum at low frequencies. This ratio gives a measure of the importance of high frequency, rapid adjustments to the growth of wages, compared to the importance of the persistent or slowly adjusting elements. In practice this means comparing the power of the wages spectra at high frequencies (frequency 2.7) with that for low frequency adjustments (frequency band 0.1-0.2). To that we add the power of the wages spectrum at the business cycle length (frequency band 0.9 – 1.1) relative to the variability of US wages at the same frequency; and also the ratio of the power of the domestic wages spectrum at low frequencies to that for US wages in the same band. These figures appear in column three, and allow a comparison of wage flexibility and wage persistence in the medium and longer term (relative to the US). Finally, we report the power of the wages spectrum at its peak to give an idea of the overall persistence or adjustability in wages (column 4).

The remaining four columns have to do with how and when the degree of wage flexibility has changed. They show how much flexibility has been lost since its peak by 2001, or the since start of the Euro. They also show when the peak flexibility and period of least flexibility occurred (in the interval since 1977). Note that, for several countries, peak flexibility was in the 1980s but there have been secondary (and often temporary) peaks in the late 1990s while countries qualified for the Euro. See the notes to Table 7.2.

[9] The US, Netherlands and Finland show this in the later 1990s.

Table 7.2. Comparing wage flexibility, summary statistics

Country	Power SR/LR mid 1980s	Power SR/LR mid 1990s	Flexibility, persistence rel. to US[a]	Flexibility: power at bus. cyclepeak	Power lost by 2001[e]	Peak flexibility[c]	Least flexibility	Structural Breaks
France	0.07	0.1	0.45 (1.2)	0.04	130%	1996	1989-90	1994-1996
Germany	0.56	1	3.0 (1.4)	0.19	58%	1993	1990-91	1990-1994
Italy	0.38	0.57	1.1 (1.2)	0.075	88%	1997	1998-2001	none
Austria	0.75	0.75	0.8 (1.0)	0.025	310%	1994, 1997	1999,2000	none
Belgium	0.33	0.33	0.43 (2.3)	0.085	300%	1998	1992,2001	1987-1989,1995, 1998, 2002
Netherlands	0.7	0.75	5.7 (0.5)	0.28	140%	1998, 2004	1999-2001	1989-1990,1997, 1999-2001
Spain	0.35	0.6	2.3 (2.0)	0.12	52%	1994, 1996	2000,2004	none
Ireland	0.23	0.4	1.4 (2.8)	0.12	120%	1987-1991	1997,2004	none
Finland	0.6	0.3	1.0 (2.0)	0.6	500%	1993	1995,2000	1993,1994-1998
UK	0.3	0.43	1.5 (1.5)	0.075	33%	1996, 2001	1980,1997	1986-1989,2000
Denmark	0.25	1	0.9 (1.7)	0.061	100%	1994	1997-01	1993-1997
Norway	0.17	0.35	1.2 (1.0)	0.07	25%	1979, 1988	1981-87	none
US	0.63	0.7	1.0 (1.0)	0.043	30%	1990	1977	none

a) Ratio of flexibility of domestic wages to US wages at business cycle frequency in 1997 (ratio of the persistence in domestic wages to the persistence of US wages at long cycle frequencies, 0.1, in 1997). The latter rises significantly after 1997, the former falls.

b) Norway, Denmark, the UK, Finland, Spain, Austria, Germany and perhaps the Netherlands have the greater wage flexibility at business cycle frequencies, than persistence at long cycles or flexibility at short cycles. These are the countries known to have undertaken reforms in the labour markets since 1992 or earlier, and does not include those economies in transition or in a catch-up phase.

c) Additional periods of high flexibility: France 1991, 1993; Germany 1999; Austria 1987,1995; Belgium 1984; Netherlands 1983,1986; Spain 2001-04; Finland 1991-92; UK 1990-95; Denmark 2002-05.

d) Other periods of special wage rigidity: Germany 1977-80; Italy 1980-85; Belgium 1988-93;Spain 1989-91,2005; Ireland 1992-96; Finland 1994-95; UK 1977-80, 1997-02; Denmark 1977-92.

e) Power (flexibility) lost since the peak at the business cycle frequency. Flexibility lost since joining EMU: France 130%, Italy 88%, Austria 310%, Belgium 300%, Netherlands 140%, Spain 12%, Ireland, Finland, and Germany 0%.

7.6 The US wages spectrum

At first sight it appears that the US, contrary to expectation, is actually *less* flexible (in wages) than many of her European counterparts. And in some respects this is true. But on closer inspection, it appears that the US does have more flexible wages growth in certain important respects. The persistence in US wages is uniformly lower; and the apparent flexibility in Europe is a result of efforts made to prepare those economies for entry into the Euro was a temporary phenomenon which didn't last. In fact, the increased flexibility of the mid to late 1990s had vanished, almost entirely, by 2000-04.

In fact the US shows a general level of flexibility which is as high as the main players in the Euro Area at business cycle lengths (the Netherlands excepted), even if it is less than that in the periphery or non-members. The difference is that flexibility in the US is fairly uniform across time and frequencies, whereas in the core Euro Area countries it is very variable – increasing at certain times, but then rapidly diminishing again (compare Fig. 7.1 with Figs. 7.2-7.7). As a result the persistence indicators are lower in the US, and the flexibility to persistence ratios higher than in most of the Euro Area economies, although the peak periods in Europe have provided greater wage flexibility for a time.

But that extra flexibility in Europe does not last very long, and the short to long run ratios soon revert to levels similar to or lower than those in the US – and particularly in the period after qualifying for the Euro in 1997-98. It is as if the Euro Area members had got reform and wage flexibility fatigue once they were safely inside the Euro and could relax under the protection of the relatively closed and disciplined Euro-economy. One can see this by comparing the dates of peak flexibility, the losses in flexibility since then, and the dates of the least flexibility over the entire sample. In the Euro Area, peak flexibility appears in the run up to joining the Euro (except in the reform economies, Spain and Ireland). And the losses in flexibility since that time are twice as large as those in the US or non-members. Moreover, the period of least flexibility always appears after the Euro regime had started (2000-4). This "reform fatigue" phenomenon should appear familiar. Exactly the same thing happened to the fiscal reforms, and the debt and deficit consolidations, after entry into the Euro was secure (Hughes Hallett and Lewis, 2006). Once the sanction of not qualifying for the Euro was lifted, market discipline appears to have been abandoned – at least relative to that in the US.

There is another way in which the results are different in the US. Underlying wage flexibility may now be greater in the US because, apart from the temporary increases in Europe, it has been increasing in the US but decreasing in much of Europe. As a result, the ratio of short run flexibility to long run persistence in wages has risen between the 80s and 90s in the US (along with Spain, Germany and Ireland). But is has fallen, and often significantly, in the other European economies. As a result, the US now shows less wage persistence than the European economies and as much wage adjustment at the business cycle frequencies as the core Euro Area economies. This, after all, is the frequency at which wage flexibility is most needed to stabilise the economy around its equilibrium and to help markets adjust to changing demand and supply conditions.

7.7 Country by country results

a) The US. The US economy is distinguished by having, relative to Europe, rather little difference between short run and long run wage variability. It is therefore characterised by a combination of wage flexibility in the traditional sense, and a lesser amount of wage contracting (long run persistence). On average, and certain peaks apart, this leaves the US economy with as much or more wage flexibility as her principle European counterparts – particularly at the crucial business cycle frequencies. Moreover, that flexibility appears to have been slowly increasing over time, in contrast to Europe, and to have suffered no decline in the late 1990s. There is also a period of marked flexibility in 1986-91 which lays the groundwork for that economy's success in the subsequent decade. Nevertheless, the structural break tests indicate that these changes are statistically insignificant. Indeed, we could not find any change of the dynamic behaviour of the growth rate of wages over the sample period.

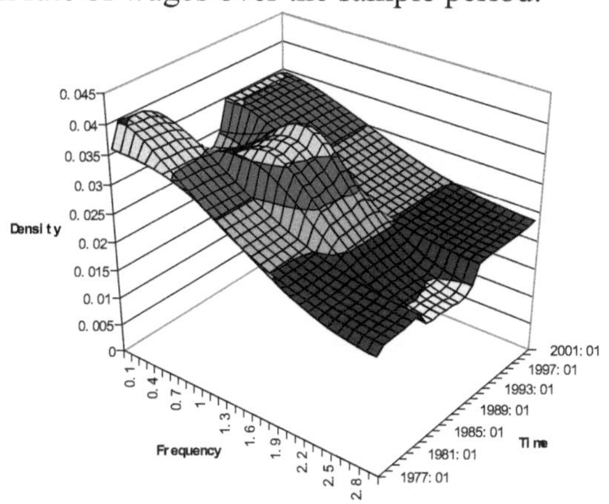

Fig. 7.1. The US spectrum

b) The Euro Area's core economies. The core EU economies appear to divide into two camps, those who have attempted to reform (Germany and the Netherlands) and those who have not (the inner core: or France, Italy, Belgium and Austria).

The inner core countries, particularly France, Austria and Belgium show both low flexibility overall and declining relative flexibility (Table 7.2). Peak flexibility for these economies appears to have been in the mid-1990s, at the point of qualifying for the Euro. Germany, by contrast, has gone through a period of remarkable transformation and structural change from 1990 to 1994 when the relentless persistence in her wages growth was shifted to create some flexibility at the business cycle frequency (a frequency of 1.3 (=2.4 years) at the beginning of the sample, and a frequency of 2 (=1.5 years) at the end of the sample). That flexibility has declined by more than half since then, but it remains larger than in other core economies. This shift reflects the impact of her reunification, and stands in contrast to the inner core economies where the increased flexibility has been concentrated around preparations for joining EMU and was a temporary state of affairs (most clearly seen in Italy and Austria). After 1998-9, the gains were almost totally wiped out again in a return to the status quo ante. These economies seem to have felt no need for reform once safely in the Euro.

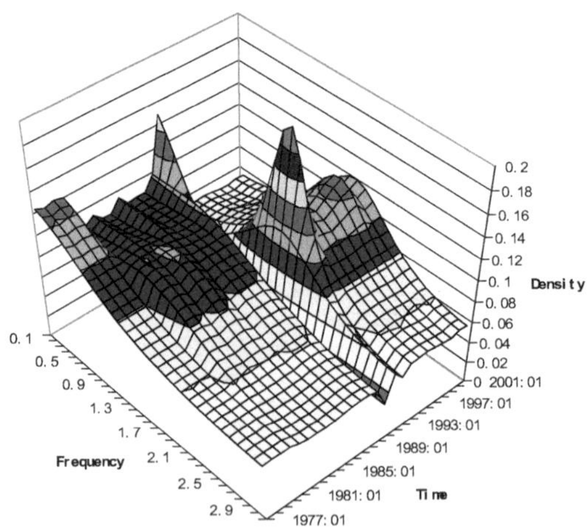

Fig. 7.2. The German spectrum

France has followed this pattern, but with some reductions in long run persistence, lower average flexibility and only token increases in flexibility before joining the Euro. For her, the period of structural changes starts *after* that in Germany (from 1994 – 1996).

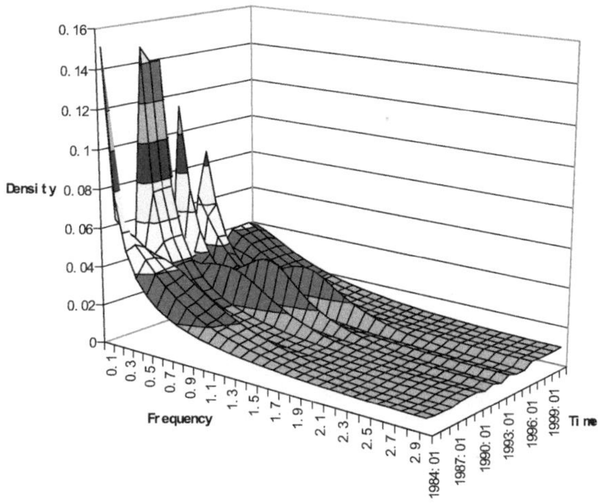

Fig. 7.3. The French spectrum

The Italian spectrum appears to be similar to the German wages spectrum. However, one big difference is that the dynamic behaviour of Italian wages growth reverted to its pre-EMU pattern in 1998. In that sense, Italy has proved to be the most inflexible country.

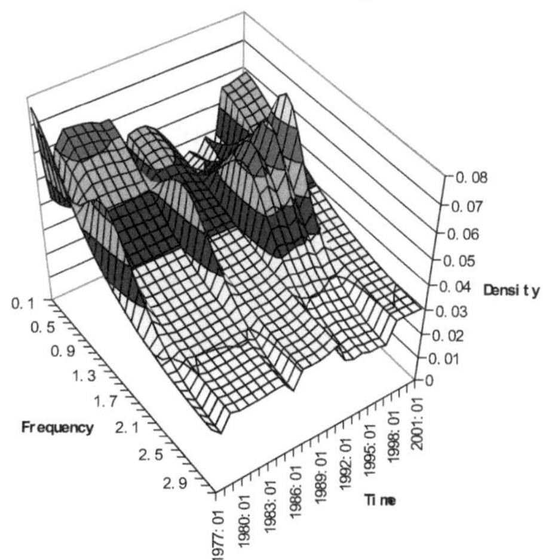

Fig. 7.4. The Italian spectrum

At times the Austrian spectrum has shown a lot of power at business cycle frequencies, but this power is always short lived and has largely vanished since the start of the Euro. However the fluctuations test reveals these changes to be too brief to be statistically significant, and at other times there is little variability in wages at all.

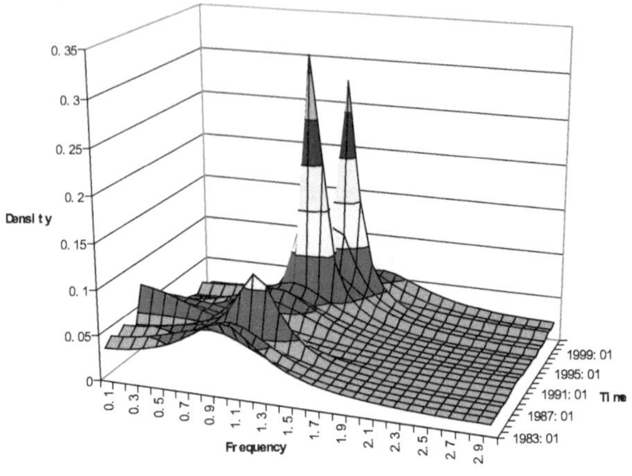

Fig. 7.5. The Austrian spectrum

In terms of the smaller economies, the Belgian spectrum is the most volatile. It is also different in shape in that, like France, all the power is at long cycles (at frequencies of 0.1 to 0.5). But unlike France, the wage persistence that this implies is not decreasing over time. And, again like France, there is little evidence of any serious attempt to create more medium term flexibility in wages.

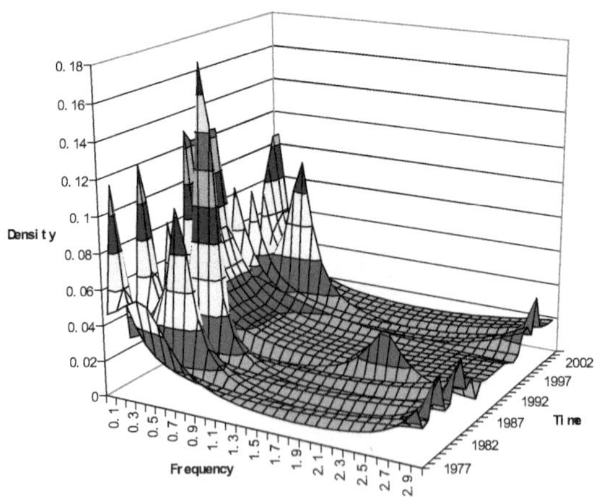

Fig. 7.6. The Belgian spectrum

The Netherlands, rather like Austria, displays rather little flexibility on average but has the ability to create extra flexibility when it is needed. The labour and social reforms, and change in strategy of the Lubbers government in 1983-86 is very clear to see. Likewise, the changes on entering the Euro and in response to the 2003-4 recession also stand out. But the economy appears to have had difficulty in sustaining these changes for any length of time ("old habits die hard"). Nevertheless Dutch wages show a lack of persistence, and the scale change shows that the Netherlands had more flexibility in wage setting than the inner core countries, Austria, or Germany, in the same way that the US does.

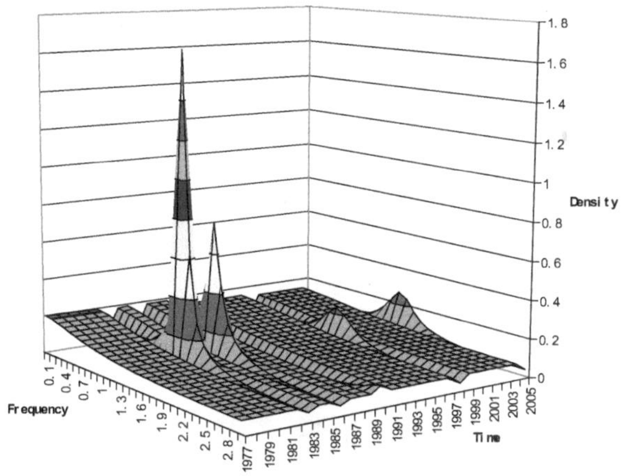

Fig. 7.7. The Dutch spectrum

c) Periphery countries. There are clear differences from the core countries here. The periphery countries have greater flexibility on average, and at the business cycle length, *and* significantly less long run persistence in wages growth. They also have short run to long run flexibility ratios that increase rather than decrease. Nevertheless the fluctuations tests do not detect any structural changes. So overall the spectra remain stable and flat, apart from periods of reform in the 1980s. Spain is the exception, with flexibility appearing at the business cycle frequency in the 1990s in preparation for the Euro. The Spanish spectrum therefore looks like the German wages spectrum, except that the extra flexibility of the 1990s appears to have been lost again by 2003.

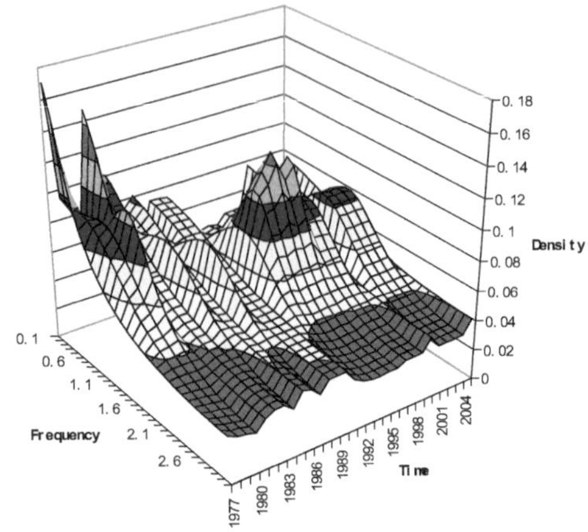

Fig. 7.8. The Spanish spectrum

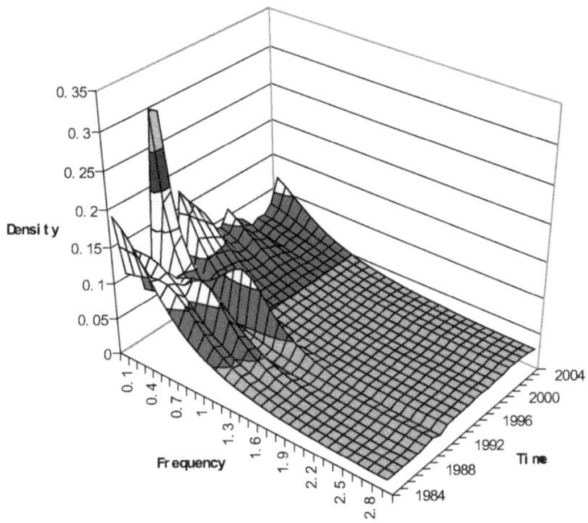

Fig. 7.9. The Irish spectrum

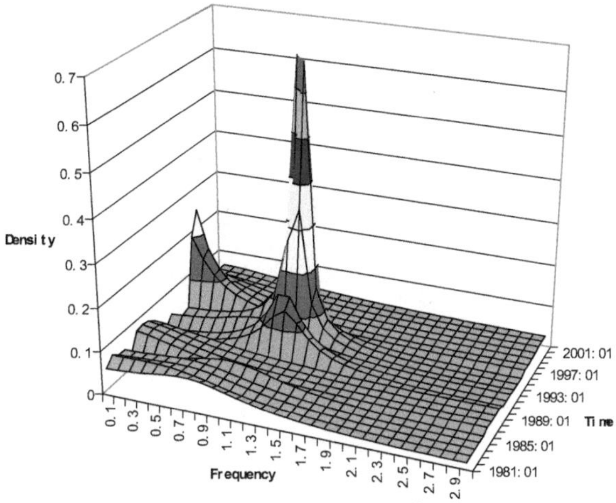

Fig. 7.10. The Finnish spectrum

Hence, like the core economies, these economies have suffered "reform fatigue" and a similar loss of wage flexibility: less so in Spain, but more clearly in Finland and Ireland where the effects of the Soviet collapse and the transition to a catch-up regime (respectively) are especially clear to see. All three have also profited from the single market, having had their period of greatest flexibility in the 1980s or early 1990s.

d) Non-members ("outs"). In terms of wage flexibility, these three economies, the UK, Denmark and Norway, occupy a position somewhere between the US and the more successful Euro Area economies. But they are probably more similar to the US. All three have higher short run flexibility on average, and at the business cycle frequency.

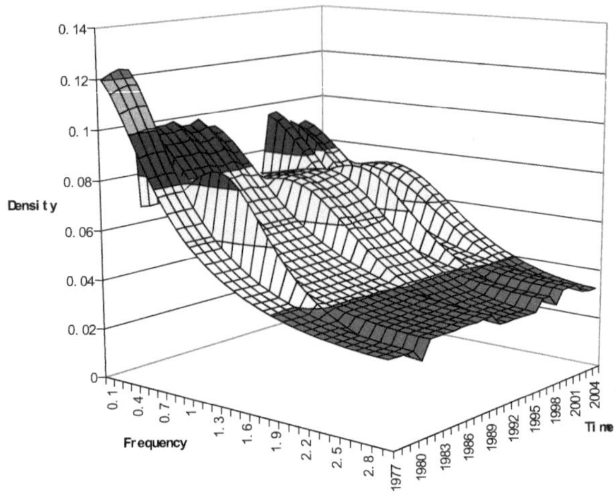

Fig. 7.11. The UK spectrum

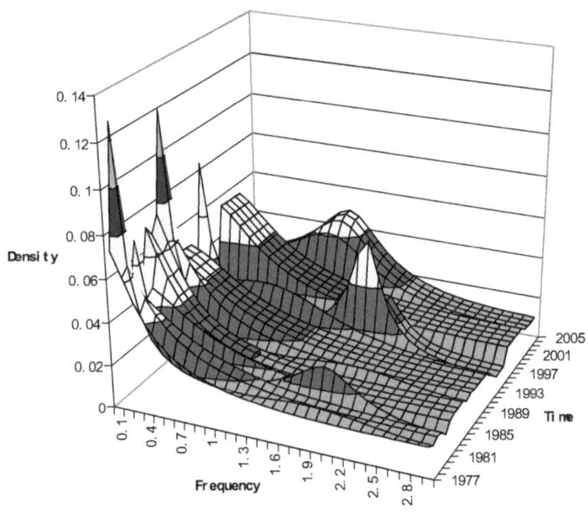

Fig. 7.12. The Danish spectrum

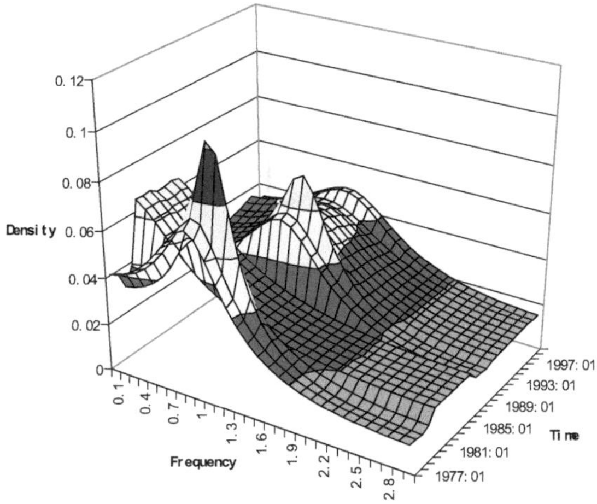

Fig. 7.13. The Norwegian spectrum

All three also show rising ratios of short run flexibility to wage persistence, as in the US, although they have more wage persistence. And all three, like the US, show no decline in wage flexibility at the end of the 1990s after the Euro was introduced – the apparent loss in business cycle flexibility in Denmark and the UK in 2000-01 having been recovered almost entirely by 2003. The UK, Denmark and Norway therefore still show the effects of the market liberalisation achieved after the days of inflexibility in the 1980s.

7.8 Conclusion

In this paper we have introduced a new technique for measuring the degree of wage flexibility in an economy. It is a remarkable thing that we have spent a great deal of time stressing the importance of wage flexibility (and the market reforms needed to create it), particularly in the European context where rigidities are considered high and a common monetary policy has reduced the options for non-market adjustments; when we have so few measures of wage flexibility in practice, or of how it compares to countries outside the Euro Area. A good part of the Lisbon Agenda is devoted to the problem of flexibility and reform, yet our supporting evidence remains anecdotal. This paper is intended to go some way to closing that gap.

Having made some preliminary estimates of wage flexibility in the European economies, it is obvious that the degree of flexibility is a more subtle concept than traditional analyses would lead us to believe. Blanket statements, such as "the US is a more flexible economy", and "the Euro Area should reform to achieve similar degrees of market flexibility" mean very little. The US is not obviously more flexible in many respects. But it is more flexible in a number of particular ways; and it has held on to its greater flexibility better. Indeed our results suggest the US may have now increased her flexibility advantage over the EU, due to "reform fatigue" in Europe.

From the empirical results, it is clear that wage flexibility is also an elusive concept. It is far from constant over time or groups of countries; and it may vary a great deal at different cyclical frequencies. The Euro Area economies have shown rather little flexibility in the core, but rather more in the periphery and smaller economies. They now probably have less flexibility than the US at the crucial business cycle frequency. More important, they have shown greater wage persistence; and some have a downward trend in relative flexibility (as measured by short run variability relative to long run persistence). Finally, they have all shown an ability to create greater flexibility when times are bad, but they have been equally unable to hold on to that flexibility thereafter. As a result, the degree of short run wage flexibility has fallen by as much 100%-150% since qualifying for the Euro, and wage flexibility is now lower than during the 1990s. That suggests "reform fatigue" has set in, similar to the consolidation fatigue that appeared in fiscal policies once inside the Euro Area.

In contrast to this, the non-member countries have shown similar degrees of flexibility to the US, and a smaller tendency to lose that degree of flexibility with the passage of time. Perhaps being small, open and exposed to world competition creates a greater sense of the need for market discipline.

Appendix: Time frequency techniques and the estimation of time-varying spectra or cross-spectra

Spectral analysis decomposes the variance of a sample of data across different frequencies. The power spectrum itself then shows the relative importance of the different cycles in creating movements in that data, and hence describes the cyclical properties of a particular time series. It is assumed that the fluctuations of the underlying data are produced by a large number of elementary cycles of different frequencies. Furthermore, it is usually assumed that the contribution of each cycle is constant throughout the sample. However, as Chauvet and Potter (2001) show in the US economy, business cycles cannot always be assumed to be constant. In such cases, the spectrum would not be constant over time due to the changing weights associated with each of the elementary cycles. A "traditional" frequency analysis framework cannot handle that case. But in recent years time-frequency techniques have been developed which can do so. They depend on using a Wigner-Ville distribution for the weights (see for example: Matz and Hlawatsch, 2003).

In this paper we make use of a special case of the Wigner-Ville distribution, known as the "short time Fourier transform" (STFT) in the engineering literature. The STFT catches structural changes (here interpreted as changes of the underlying lag structure in accordance with Wells, 1996), but assumes local stationarity. We employ the STFT for two reasons: first, the time series we analyse are already in log-differenced form (see eq. (1) above) so stationarity may safely be assumed. Moreover, standard unit root tests performed on our data (specifically the ADF and Phillips-Perron tests, results available on request) confirm that assumption. Finally, the available results on macroeconomic output data (Campbell and Mankiw, 1987; Clark, 1987) also confirm that conclusion. Secondly, if the time series is stationary, then the STFT and the Wigner-Ville distribution actually coincide (Boashash, 2003). Hence, employing the Wigner-Ville distribution directly would not have changed our results at all.

a) The initial time series model: As indicated in the text, all the data collected are for nominal wages and salaries from the OECD's *STAN Data Base*. It is annual data from 1977 to 2004. Annual growth rates in wages and salaries are then defined as:

$$y_t = \Delta\left(\log\left(Y_t\right)\right) = \log\left(\frac{Y_t}{Y_{t-1}}\right) \tag{A.1}$$

Next we employ a two step procedure. As Evans and Karras (1996) point out, if two cycles are to converge, implying similar degrees of wage flexibility at each frequency, they have to follow the same AR(p) process. We therefore estimate an AR(p) process for each growth rate individually. But, to allow for possible changes in the parameters, we employ a time-varying Kalman filter model to estimate the chosen AR(p) model:

$$y_t = \alpha_{0,t} + \sum_{i=1}^{9} \alpha_{i,t} y_{t-i} + \varepsilon_t \tag{A.2}$$

with

$$\alpha_{i,t} = \alpha_{i,t-1} + \eta_{i,t}, \text{ for } i = 0 \ldots 9 \tag{A.3}$$

and $\varepsilon_t, \eta_t \sim \text{i.i.d.}\left(0, \sigma^2_{\varepsilon,\eta}\right)$, for $i = 0...9$

In order to run the Kalman filter we need initial parameter values. These initial parameter values can be obtained estimating them by OLS across the entire sample (see also Wells, 1996)[10]. Given those starting values, we can now estimate the parameters of (A.2) using a Kalman filter estimator. To do this, we employed a general to specific approach, eliminating insignificant lags using the strategy specified below. The maximum number of lags was determined by the Akaike Criterion (AIC), and was found to be two in each case (Denmark excepted). Each time we ran a new regression we used a new set of initial parameter values. Then, for each regression we applied the set of diagnostic tests reported in Table 7.1 above, in order to confirm the specification found. The final parameter values are filtered estimates, independent of their start values.

b) Specification tests and parameter significance: The specification search above implies that we will get parameter values for each point in time. A particular parameter could therefore be significant for all points in time; or at some time periods but not others; or it might never be significant. The parameter changes are at the heart of this paper as they imply a change of the lag structure and a change in the spectral results. We therefore employed the following selection strategy. If a particular lag was never significant, then this lag was dropped from the equation and the model was estimated again. If the AIC criterion was less than before, then that lag was completely excluded. If a parameter was significant for some periods but not others, it was kept in the equation with a parameter value of zero for those periods in which it was insignificant. This strategy allowed us to minimise the AIC criterion, and leads to a parsimonious specification of the time series model. Finally, we tested the residuals in each regression for auto-correlation and heteroscedasticity.

The specification (A.2)-(A.3) was then *validated* using two different stability tests. Both tests check for the same null hypothesis, in our case a stable AR(2) specification, against alternative temporal instabilities. The first is the fluctuations test of Ploberger et al. (1989), which detects *discrete* breaks at any point in time in the coefficients of a possibly dynamic

[10] Obviously, using the entire sample implies that we neglect possible structural breaks at this stage. The initial estimates may be biased therefore. However, the Kalman filter will then correct for this since, as Wells (1996) points out, the Kalman filter will converge to the true parameter value independently of the initial values. But initial values which are already "close" to the true value accelerate convergence. Hence we employ an OLS estimate to start. In fact, we find those start values to have no effect on the parameter estimates by the time we get to 1990. Hence our results are robust.

regression. The second test is due to LaMotte and McWorther (1978), and is designed specifically to detect *random* parameter variation of a specific unit root form (our specification). We found that the random walk hypothesis for the parameters was justified for each country (results available on request). Finally, we chose the fluctuations test for detecting structural breaks because the Kalman filter allows structural breaks at any point and the fluctuations test we use is able to accommodate this.[11] Thus, and in contrast to other structural stability tests, the fluctuations test is not restricted to any pre-specified number of breaks.[12]

Once this regression is done, it gives us a time-varying AR(p) model. From this AR(p) we are able to calculate the short–time Fourier transform, as originally proposed by Gabor (1946), to determine the corresponding time-varying spectrum. We briefly introduce the STFT here: for details, the reader is referred to Boashash (2003). The basic idea is to find the spectrum of a signal $x(t)$, at time t, by analysing a small portion of the signal around that time.

c) Spectral estimation: Consider a signal $s(\tau)$ and a real, even window $w(\tau)$, whose Fourier transforms are $S(f)$ and $W(f)$ respectively. To obtain a localised spectrum $s(\tau)$ at time $\tau = t$, we multiply the signal by the window $w(\tau)$ centred at time $\tau = t$. We obtain

$$s_w(t,\tau) = s(\tau)\,w(\tau - t) \tag{A.4}$$

We then calculate the Fourier transform w.r.t. τ which yields,

$$F_s^w(t,f) = \underset{\tau \to f}{\mathcal{F}}\{s(\tau)\,w(\tau - t)\} \tag{A.5}$$

$F_s^w(t,f)$ is the STFT. It transforms the signal into the frequency domain

---

[11] Note that all our tests of significance, and for significant differences in parameters, are being conducted in the time domain *before* transferring the results into the frequency domain, because no statistical tests exist for calculated spectra (the transformations are nonlinear and involve complex arithmetic). Stability tests are important here because our spectra are potentially sensitive to changes in the underlying parameters.

[12] The fluctuations test works as follows: one parameter value is taken as the reference value, e.g. the last value of the sample. All other observations are now tested whether they significantly differ from that value. In order to do so, Ploberger et al. (1989) have provided critical values which we have used here. If the test value is above the critical value then we have a structural break: the parameter value differs significantly from the reference value and vice versa. Given the Kalman filter, these tests can be conducted sequentially.

across time. It is therefore a function of both. Using a bilinear kernel and a Gabor transform (the time series is stationary, but may contain parameter changes), Boashash and Reilly (1992) show that the STFT can always be expressed as a time-varying discrete fast-Fourier transform calculated for each point in time. That has the very convenient property that the "traditional" formulae for the coherence or the gain remain valid, but will have to be recalculated at each point in time. The time-varying spectrum of the wages growth series can therefore be calculated as (see also: Lin, 1997):

$$P_t(\omega) = \frac{\sigma^2}{\left|1 + \sum_{i=1}^{9} \alpha_{i,t} \exp(-j\omega i)\right|_t^2} \qquad \text{(A.6)}$$

where ω is angular frequency and j is a complex number. The advantage of this method is that, at any point in time, a power spectrum can be calculated instantaneously from the updated parameters of the model (Lin, 1997). Similarly, the spectrum for a particular time interval can be calculated by averaging the filter parameters over that interval.

d) Cross-spectra: By transferring the time domain results into the frequency domain, we could also show how the relationship between the wages growth in two economies has developed at different cycle lengths. That would allow us to investigate whether any convergence in degrees of wage had taken place over time and, if so, at which cycle lengths. As a measure of that relationship, we might use the coherence. However, we do not go to that far in this paper. Instead we restrict ourselves to examining the flexibility of wages, as revealed by the relative power of the associated spectrum at each frequency for each country in our sample; and whether that flexibility measure has been increasing or decreasing over time – in particular whether it has been increasing as the competitive pressures and need for market flexibility have come into play with the single market and single currency in Europe. That amounts to a search for changes in the underlying data generating process (i.e. in the AR(p) model) itself. That cannot be done with standard time-invariant econometric techniques.

e) Structural breaks: Last, a note on the figures in this paper. We first present the time-varying spectra and then discuss the structural break tests. One can see from these figures that the spectra change. However, one cannot infer directly from those figures alone that the changes in the spectra are all statistically significant. The figures for the time-varying spectra have to be accompanied by the fluctuation test results. Once a significant structural break has been identified by the fluctuations test, the results of that will show up as significant break in the wages behaviour in the associated spectrum. We have picked out all the relevant break points in Table 7.2 of the main text.

References

Andersen, T. M., Haldrup, N., and Soerensen, J. R. (2000), Labour market implications of EU product market integration, Economic Policy, vol.30, p.107-133.

Artis, M., Marcellino, M., and Priorietti, T. (2004), Dating the Euro Area business cycle, in L. Reichlin (Ed.), The Euro Area business cycle: Stylised facts and measurement issues, Centre for Economic Policy Research, London.

Barro, R. J., and Sala-I-Martin, X. (1992), Convergence, Journal of Political Economy, vol.100, p.223-251.

Baxter, M., and Kouparitsas, M. A. (2005), Determinants of business cycle comovement: A robust analysis, Journal of Monetary Economics, vol.52, p.113-158.

Boashash, B., (2003), Time-frequency signal analysis and processing, Elsevier, Oxford.

Boashash, B., and Reilly, A., (1992), Algorithms for time-frequency signal analysis, in B. Boashash (Ed.), Time-frequency signal analysis - Methods and applications, Longman-Cheshire, Melbourne, p. 163-181.

Bruno, M., (1986), Aggregate supply and demand factors in OECD unemployment: An update, Economica, vol.53, p.35-52.

Calmfors, L., (1998), Macroeconomic policy, wage setting and employment: What difference does the EMU make?, Oxford Review of Economic Policy, vol.14, p.125-151.

Calmfors, L., (2001), Unemployment, labour market reform and monetary union, Journal of Labor Economics, vol.19, p.265-289.

Campbell, J. Y., and Mankiw, N. G. (1987), Permanent and transitory components in macroeconomic fluctuations, American Economic Review, vol.77, p.111-117.

Canova, F., (1998), Detrending and business cycle facts, Journal of Monetary Economics, vol.41, p.475-512.

Chauvet, M., and Potter, S., (2001), Recent changes in the US business cycle, mimeo, University of California.

Clark, P. K., (1987), The cyclical component of the U.S. economic activity, Quarterly Journal of Economics, vol.102, p.797-814.

Delors, C., (1989), Report on Economic and Monetary Union in the European Community, Office of the Publications of the European Communities, Luxembourg.

Dowrick, S., and Nguyen, D.-T., (1989), OECD comparative economic growth 1950-85. American Economic Review, vol.79, p.1010-1030.

Doyle, B., and Faust, J., (2003), Breaks in the variability and comovement of G7 economic growth, International Finance Discussion Paper, no 786, Board of Governors, Federal Reserve System, Washington, DC.

Driver, R., (2006), Whatever happened to the Goldilocks? The role of expectations of the NAIRU in the US and the UK, Oxford Bulletin of Economics and Statistics, vol.68, p.45-80.

Evans, P., and Karras, G., (1996), Convergence revisited, Journal of Monetary Economics, vol.37, p.249-265.

Frankel, J., and Rose, A. K., (1998), The endogeneity of the Optimum Currency Area criterion, The Economic Journal, vol.108, p.1009-1025.

Gabor, D., (1946), Theory of communication, Journal of the Institute of Electrical Engineering, vol.93, p.429 - 457.

Grant, A. P., (2002), Time-varying estimates of the natural rate of unemployment: A revisitation of Okun's Law, Quarterly Review of Economics and Finance, vol.42, p.95-113.

Harding, D., and Pagan, A., (2001), Extracting, analysing and using cyclical information: mimeo, Australian National University.

Hughes Hallett, A., (2003), Modelling shocks and adjustment mechanisms in EMU, in H. M. Treasury (Ed.), UK membership of the Single Currency: An assessment of the five economic tests, HMSO, London.

Hughes Hallett, A., Hougaard Jensen, S. E., and Richter, C., (2005), The European economy at the cross roads: Structural reforms, fiscal constraints, and the Lisbon Agenda, Research in International Business and Finance, vol.19, p.229-250.

Hughes Hallett, A., and Jensen, S. E. H., (2003), On the role of labour market reform for the enlargement of a monetary union, CESifo Economic Studies, vol.49, p.355-379.

Hughes Hallett, A., and Piscitelli, L., (2002), Does trade cause convergence? Economics Letters, vol.75, p.165-170.

Hughes Hallett, A., and Lewis, J. (2006), European fiscal discipline before and After EMU: Permanent weight loss or crash diet?, Macroeconomic Dynamics, forthcoming.

Hughes Hallett, A and Richter, C. (2006), Is the convergence of business cycles a global or regional issue? The US, UK and Euroland, International Journal of Finance and Economics, forthcoming.

Inklaar, R., and de Haan, J. (2000), Is there really a European business cycle?, CESifo Working Paper No 268.

Kalemli-Ozcan, S., Sorenson, B., and Yosha, O. (2001), Economic integration, industrial specialisation, and the asymmetry of macroeconomic fluctuations, Journal of International Economics, vol.55, p.107-137.

Kalemli-Ozcan, S., Sorensen, B., and Yosha, O. (2003), Risk sharing and industrial specialisation: Regional and international evidence, American Economic Review, vol.93, p.903-18.

Kaminski, B., Wang, Z. K., and Winters, L. A. (1996), Export performance in transition economies, Economic Policy, vol.23, p.423-444.

Koedijk, K. and Kremers, J. (1996), Market opening, regulation and growth in Europe. Economic Policy, vol.23, p.423-444.

LaMotte, L. R., and McWorther, A. J. (1978), An exact test for the presence of random walk coefficients in a linear regression, Journal of the American Statistical Association, vol.73, p.816-820.

Laubach, T. (2001): Measuring the NAIRU: Evidence from 7 economies, The Review of Economics and Statistics, vol.83, p.218-231.

Lin, Z. (1997), An introduction to time-frequency signal analysis, Sensor Review, vol.17, p.46-53.

Mankiw, N. G., Romer, D., and Weil, D. (1992), A contribution to the empirics of economic Growth, Quarterly Journal of Economics, vol.107, p.407-437.

Matz, G., and F. Hlawatsch (2003), Time-varying power spectra of nonstationary random processes, in B. Boashash (Ed.): Time-frequency signal analysis and processing, Elsevier, Amsterdam.

Peersman, G., and Smets, F. (2005), Industry effects of monetary policy in the Euro Area, The Economic Journal, vol.115, p.319-342.

Ploberger, W., Krämer, W., and Kontrus, K. (1989), A new test for structural stability in the linear regression model, Journal of Econometrics, vol.40, p.307-318.

Prasad, E. S. (1999), International trade and the business cycle, The Economic Journal, vol.109, p.588-606.

Quah, D. T. (1993), Galton's Fallacy and tests of the convergence hypothesis, Scandinavian Journal of Economics, vol.95, p.427-443.

Saint-Paul, G (2004a), Did European labour markets become more competitive in the 1990s? Evidence from estimated worker rents, Discussion Paper 4327, Centre for Economic Policy Research, London.

Saint-Paul, G. (2004b), Why are European countries diverging in their unemployment experiences?, Discussion Paper 4328, Centre for Economic Policy Research, London.

Sibert, A. (1999), Monetary integration and economic reform, The Economic Journal, vol.109, p.78-92.

Sibert, A., and Sutherland, A. (2000), Monetary regimes and labour market reform, Journal of International Economics, vol.51, p.421-435.

Stock, J. H., and Watson, M. W. (2002), Has the business cycle changed and why?, NBER Working paper 9127, NBER, Cambridge, MA.

Stock, J. H., and Watson, M. W. (2003), Understanding changes in the international business cycles, Journal of the European Economic Association, vol.3, p.966-1006.

Wells, C. (1996), The Kalman Filter in finance. Kluwer Academic Publishers, Dordrecht.

Index

A

automatic stabilisers, 64

B

bailout, 67
benefit duration, 146
benefit replacement rate, 146
Broad Economic Policy Guidelines, 1
budgetary consolidation, 155
budgetary deficit, 57
budgetary policies, 155
budgetary spillovers, 30

C

consumption function, 115
contagion effects, 67
convergence, 205
coordination dividend, 2
credit constrained, 110
critical debt level, 120
crowding out, 55

D

deregulation, 156
Deregulation, 141
detrending technique, 207

E

ECB, 94
Economic and Monetary Union (EMU), 1
economic interdependence, 1
effects of fiscal policy, 107
efficiency, 11
employment, 137
EMU, 68
Euro Area, 70
Euro Area (EA), 30
European business cycle, 5
European Central Bank (ECB), 1
European Commission, 70
Excessive Deficit Procedure, 1
exchange rate pass-through, 33

F

fiscal consolidation, 116
fiscal convergence, 112
fiscal policy, 57
fiscal policy transmissions, 31
fiscal reforms, 214
Fiscal Theory of the Price Level, 9
fluctuations test, 218

G

government debt, 107

I

identification, 64
impulse response functions (IRF), 28
inflation persistence, 33
inflation targeting, 185
institutional framework, 145
interactions of monetary and fiscal policies, 8
interest rate, 55, 57
internal market, 10

J

J-curve, 33

K

Kalman filter, 226
Keynesian macroeconomic theory, 162

L

labour market flexibility, 204
labour market reforms, 12
Labour market regulations, 146
Lerner index, 131
Lisbon Strategy, 1, 129

M

Maastricht deficit criterion, 107
mark-up, 130, 156
monetary policy, 157
monetary policy transmissions, 31
monetary targeting, 157
monetary union, 67
MSG3 Model, 155

N

New-Keynesian, 7
no bail-out clause, 3
non-Keynesian, 163
non-Keynesian effects, 115
non-linearities, 117

O

objective function, 191
open economy, 63
openness, 146

P

panel cointegration, 117
policy coordination, 2, 179
policy rules, 33
product and factor market regulation, 130
product market reforms, 12
public consumption, 162
public debt, 60
public investment, 162
public sector, 162
public-sector deficit, 162

R

Ricardian behaviour, 115
Ricardian Equivalence, 57

S

simulations, 156
Single Market Programme, 133
Solow residual, 131
Spectral analysis, 225
spillover, 67
spillovers, 2, 155
Stability and Growth Pact, 1
structural break, 206
structural policy, 155
structural policy reforms, 157
structural reforms, 10, 129
structural unemployment, 141
structural VAR, 59
Structural VAR, 29

T

taxes, 162
Taylor rule, 185
technology frontier, 11
Threshold Autoregressive (TAR) model, 113
threshold regression analysis, 112
time-frequency analysis, 207
total factor productivity, 137
total factor productivity growth, 156

V

VAR approach, 28
variance decompositions (VD), 29

W

wage bargaining, 146
wage flexibility, 215
welfare effect, 191
welfare loss, 194

Kolibri 360 GmbH
Ferdinand-Jühlke-Straße 7
99095 Erfurt, Deutschland
produktsicherheit@kolibri360.de